™

TM

References for the Rest of Us!™

BESTSELLING BOOK SERIES

Do you find that traditional reference books are overloaded with technical details and advice you'll never use? Do you postpone important life decisions because you just don't want to deal with them? Then our *For Dummies®* business and general reference book series is for you.

For Dummies business and general reference books are written for those frustrated and hard-working souls who know they aren't dumb, but find that the myriad of personal and business issues and the accompanying horror stories make them feel helpless. *For Dummies* books use a lighthearted approach, a down-to-earth style, and even cartoons and humorous icons to dispel fears and build confidence. Lighthearted but not lightweight, these books are perfect survival guides to solve your everyday personal and business problems.

> **"...Dummies books consistently live up to their brand-name promise to transform 'can't into can.' "**
> — *Ottawa Citizen*

> **"...clear, straightforward information laced with a touch of humour."**
> — *The Toronto Star*

> **"...set up in bits and bites that are easy to digest, full of no-nonsense advice."**
> — *The Calgary Herald*

Already, millions of satisfied readers agree. They have made For Dummies the #1 introductory level computer book series and a bestselling business book series. They have written asking for more. So, if you're looking for the best and easiest way to learn about business and other general reference topics, look to For Dummies to give you a helping hand.

™

CDG BOOKS
C A N A D A

Curling
FOR DUMMIES®

by Bob Weeks

CDG
BOOKS
CANADA

CDG Books Canada, Inc.

◆ Toronto, ON ◆

Curling For Dummies®

Published by:
CDG Books Canada, Inc.
99 Yorkville Avenue
Suite 400
Toronto, ON M5R 3K5
www.cdgbooks.com (CDG Books Canada Web Site)
www.idgbooks.com (IDG Books Worldwide Web Site)
www.dummies.com (Dummies Press Web Site)

National Library of Canada Cataloguing in Publication Data

Weeks, Bob
    Curling for dummies

Includes index.

ISBN 1-894413-30-X
    1. Curling. I. Title.

GV845.W387 2001   796.964   C2001-901625-5

Printed in Canada

1 2 3 4 5 TRI 04 03 02 01

Distributed in Canada by CDG Books Canada, Inc.

For general information on CDG Books, including all IDG Books Worldwide publications, please call our distribution centre: HarperCollins Canada at 1-800-387-0117. For reseller information, including discounts and premium sales, please call our sales department at 1-877-963-8830.

This book is available at special discounts for bulk purchases by your group or organization for resale, premiums, fundraising and seminars. For details, contact CDG Books Canada, Special Sales Department, 99 Yorkville Avenue, Suite 400, Toronto, ON, M5R 3K5; Tel: 416-963-8830; Email: spmarkets@cdgbooks.com.

For press review copies, author interviews, or other publicity information, please contact our marketing department at 416-963-8830, fax 416-923-4821, or e-mail publicity@cdgbooks.com.

For authorization to photocopy items for corporate, personal, or educational use, please contact Cancopy, The Canadian Copyright Licensing Agency, One Yonge Street, Suite 1900, Toronto, ON, M5E 1E5; Tel: 416-868-1620; Fax: 416-868-1621; www.cancopy.com.

 is a trademark under exclusive licence to CDG Books Canada, Inc., from **CDG BOOKS** CANADA Hungry Minds, Inc.

About the Author

Bob Weeks started curling at the age of 13 and has continued a love affair with the game ever since. As a player, he has competed in several provincial championships, winning one. He has also won a few cashspiels of note, as well as the odd turkey draw.

However, he has become more successful as a curling writer (which wasn't hard) for the past two decades.

Bob is the editor and co-publisher of the *Ontario Curling Report*, which is now in its twenty-seventh year of publishing. And for 12 years, he has written a weekly column on curling in the *Globe and Mail*, while providing coverage of curling's major events for Canada's national newspaper. He has written on curling for publications across Canada and is a regular commentator on both radio and television.

He is a two-time winner of the Scotty Harper Award for the top curling story in Canada, and in 1995 he authored *The Brier: The History of Canada's Most Celebrated Curling Championship*, the first comprehensive history of that great event.

When not writing about curling, Bob is the editor of *SCORE Golf Magazine,* Canada's leading golf publication. He is also heard talking about golf on a nationally syndicated radio program and serves as the golf analyst for TSN.

Bob still curls regularly — although not competitively — at the Weston Golf and Country Club, in Toronto, where he lives with his son, Chris.

Dedication

This book is dedicated to my mother, Deane, and to my sister, Carol — two great women who are always right on the broom and have helped me slide along in life.

Author's Acknowledgements

I had a great deal of help and inspiration while putting this book together. First, the inspirational folks: my fellow publishers at the *Ontario Curling Report*, Peter Birchard, Alf Phillips Jr., and Ken Thompson, for giving me a shot way back when and keeping me going these days; David Langford, Neil A. Campbell, and Steve McCallister, for guidance at the *Globe and Mail*; my curling rink, which includes Brian Trepanier, Mark Pierog, Mark Linton, Colin Imrie, Tim Patterson, Glenn Greenwood, and Angelo Stroumos (I know, it's a big team); to Bob Wallace and Jamie Wilson, my original front end; my buddies on the bench: Perry Lefko, Norm Cowley, Con Griwkowsky, Jim Bender, Ardith Stephenson, Bill Small, Jeff Timson, Doug Maxwell, Vic Rauter, Ray Turnbull, Linda Moore, Don Duguid, Don Wittman, Mike Harris, and Joan McCusker; a special thanks to a curling media great who has hung up his pen and slider, Tom Slater, who read every word of this book and provided his critique; and to Sandra Schmirler, for showing us all what's important in life.

A couple of extra special thank-yous: to my father, who taught me how to curl and, therefore, started me in all this nonsense; and to Roisin, for being there whenever I needed her.

Now the helpers: Warren Hansen was always quick to answer my e-mail pleas for help. He probably knows more about curling than any person alive. Thank goodness he doesn't hold grudges! Kudos to Fred Veale for his knowledge on rocks; and to three great coaches from three different parts of the world: Bill Tschirhart from Canada, Mike Hay from Scotland, and Keith Wendorf from Germany.

Lino Di Iorio is crazy about curling and provided me with some wonderful information about the delivery. Scott Taylor, who is equally nuts, did the same.

A few past greats came to the rescue when I needed a little more detail. Ed Werenich and Neil Harrison provided insight from their many years of experience. My old pal John Kawaja, who was in the middle of moving to Portland, Oregon, was also there to answer a few questions that came from left field.

Thanks to Mike Burns for his photo resources and to Doug Ball for snapping the pictures inside these pages. Also, another thanks to the folks at the High Park Curling Club for allowing me to use their facility for the photo shoot.

Melanie Rutledge didn't know an in-turn from an out-turn when she started this project, but I know she's on her way to the Scott Tournament of Hearts now.

Finally, a special thanks to Chris Weeks. You may only be eight, but you're my hero.

Publisher's Acknowledgements

We're proud of this book; please register your comments through our Online Registration Form located at www.hungryminds.com.

Some of the people who helped bring this book to market include the following:

Acquisitions and Editorial

Editorial Director: Joan Whitman

Associate Editor: Melanie Rutledge

Copy Editor: Pamela Erlichman

Cover Photo: Michael Burns

Production

Director of Production: Donna Brown

Production Editor: Rebecca Conolly

Layout and Graphics: Kim Monteforte, Darlene Eiler, Heidy Lawrance Associates

Illustrations: Allan Moon

Interior Photos: Doug Ball

Proofreader: Allyson Latta

Indexer: Belle Wong

General and Administrative

Hungry Minds, Inc.: John Kilcullen, CEO; Bill Barry, President and COO; John Ball, Executive VP, Operations & Administration; John Harris, CFO

CDG Books Canada, Inc.: Ron Besse, Chairman; Tom Best, President; Robert Harris, Vice President and Publisher

Hungry Minds Consumer Reference Group

Business: Kathleen Nebenhaus, Vice President and Publisher; Kevin Thornton, Acquisitions Manager

Cooking/Gardening: Jennifer Feldman, Associate Vice President and Publisher

Education/Reference: Diane Graves Steele, Vice President and Publisher

Lifestyles: Kathleen Nebenhaus, Vice President and Publisher; Tracy Boggier, Managing Editor

Pets: Kathleen Nebenhaus, Vice President and Publisher; Tracy Boggier, Managing Editor

Travel: Michael Spring, Vice President and Publisher; Brice Gosnell, Publishing Director; Suzanne Jannetta, Editorial Director

Hungry Minds Consumer Editorial Services: Kathleen Nebenhaus, Vice President and Publisher; Kristin A. Cocks, Editorial Director; Cindy Kitchel, Editorial Director

Hungry Minds Consumer Production: Debbie Stailey, Production Director

◆

The publisher would like to give special thanks to Patrick J. McGovern, without whom this book would not have been possible.

◆

Contents at a Glance

Cartoons at a Glance

page 7

page 29

page 237

page 311

page 185

page 107

page 285

Fax: 978-546-7747

E-mail: the5wave@tiac.net

Table of Contents

Part VII: The Part of Tens 311

Chapter 21: Ten Top-Notch Curling Skips 313

Chapter 22: Ten Memorable Curling Shots 317

Chapter 23: Ten Tremendous Curling Games 321

Foreword

Congratulations on picking up this book. You are about to start playing what I believe is the greatest game in the world. I say that because curling has been a big part of my life for a long, long time.

I have often been asked how I became involved in the sport of curling.

My introduction to the sport was born out of necessity. My family lived for a few years in Miramichi, New Brunswick. Our house was out of town, which means I was faced with a long bus ride to and from school. It was particularly agonizing, since that bus stopped at practically every corner of town before getting to my stop.

There were two alternatives to the dreaded bus ride home; one was much quicker, albeit dangerous, and the other took a while longer . . . but would ultimately change my life.

I never told my parents, but I would occasionally take advantage of the "quick" way home — a freight train! A regularly scheduled train came through town every day shortly after school finished and conveniently passed by the perimeter of the mill property where we lived. After a couple of friendly waves and smiles, the train conductor would routinely slow down, allowing us (I wouldn't have had the guts to do this alone) to hop on and enjoy the speedy ride home. Unlike kids today who "tailgate ride," we had the full cooperation of the train conductor (I am sure that in today's politically correct world, this kind of transportation is no longer a possibility!) About two minutes after we'd started, he would slow the train down near the mill and we would jump off safely.

The slower alternative was to walk over to the Newcastle Curling Club, where my mother, Mary, would be playing in the regular afternoon ladies' draw. I preferred this route on cold or wet days and on days when I missed the train. I was guaranteed to get home warm, dry, and safe, if a bit late.

In the beginning, my only reservation was that I had to suffer through an hour of curling before leaving for home.

My mother has often told me that curling influenced me before I was even born. While pregnant with me, she would watch from behind the glass while my father played club games in Chandler, Quebec. It was in the town of Newcastle, in New Brunswick, however, that I caught the bug while watching my mother finish her afternoon games. From this point forward, the game would firmly embed itself in my life.

I quickly became my mother's biggest fan and most ardent critic (and forgot completely about the freight train). From behind the glass, every shot seemed easy, every mistake in strategy, clearly evident. In short, at the tender age of 11, I had the strategy of the game completely mastered . . . or so I thought.

Curling has dominated the ensuing 29 or so years of my life. From junior mixed bonspiels as a teenager, where first loves, kisses, dances, and a few trophies were had, to, ultimately, two world championships, curling has been the axis upon which my life has revolved.

The wins and losses have come and gone, as has most of the prize money. What *has* endured from those years are the friends and the memories.

You see, curling is more of a fraternity than a sport. Played by more than a million Canadians, it is nevertheless often dismissed as a fringe sport — a game for the old or not-so-athletically inclined. Curlers know that this could not be farther from the truth. Top-level curling today is dominated by highly skilled athletes who are as technically adept as the world's best golfers, and, at the recreational level, young and old, skinny and not-so-skinny, male and female, can play in a friendly social and competitive atmosphere.

I have often said that curling is the easiest game in the world to learn, and the hardest to master. Bob Weeks has given us *Curling For Dummies* to make the learning that much easier and enjoyable. His skill with the written word and his extensive knowledge and respect for the game are evident on every page of this book. Simple, concise, and insightful, *Curling For Dummies* delivers all you need to know about the game of curling. Bob is a friend and a former teammate, and I know that he is excellent at communicating with "Dummies."

— John Kawaja

Two-time world champion

Introduction

Welcome to *Curling For Dummies*. Curling is a sport that's played around the world, yet I've always found it surprising that there aren't more instructional books to help out beginner curlers, as well as those more seasoned players who want to improve their game.

I'm not really sure why this is the case. It's downright strange, because curling, like golf, lends itself really well to the printed page. Aside from getting the physical part of the sport under your belt, there's a whole mental level you can explore, too. This is the analytical side of the game — the strategy behind why you throw a particular shot the way you do. Like chess, curling is a thinking person's game. And while the fundamentals of the sport haven't changed, other parts have. I'm talking about equipment, training, and competitions. The rules and strategic practices have also evolved. The game has grown up.

When I learned how to curl, the only instructional book available was by a guy named Ken Watson, called *Ken Watson on Curling*. That book was over 20 years old when *I* picked it up. It's out of print now. Although there have been a handful of other instructional books written over the years, as well as a couple of tribute books (one which I wrote, on the history of the Canadian men's curling championship), there is, I feel, a real need for an up-to-date book that just tells you how to play.

I mentioned this to some friends in publishing, and they thought it was a good idea. Little did I know they were going to get me to write the book, but after wearing me down with repeated requests (okay, there was one), I agreed. *Curling For Dummies* is the result.

About This Book

I want this book to appeal to a wide variety of people. If you don't know a thing about curling, this book shows you the basics. If you have played a few times, you can use this book to improve your game. If you've been a long-time curler at the club level, this book is a valuable refresher course. And if you're a world champion, then you might want to pick this book up to see if I've mentioned your name (you think I don't know all about you world-champion types?).

This book covers curling from start to finish — from stepping onto the ice for the first time to playing in major competitions. It's not just about instruction, though. I've included some background information and anecdotes about the game that will help you become not only a better player, but a true curling aficionado. Little-known facts about the origins of the sport, entertaining stories about some of the game's greatest players — on and off the ice — tips on how to get the most out of being a fan, what to do if you want to become a coach. It's all here.

Why You Need This Book

If you are reading this book, you are probably interested in curling. That interest can take many forms. Maybe you've just been nominated to organize the annual end-of-season bonspiel at your club, and you want some fresh ideas. It could be that you've undergone another kind of nomination — into the after-work curling group at the office, and you have no idea where to begin. The first game is next week. Maybe your daughter went curling at a friend's birthday party, and she hasn't stopped bugging you about it since. Or then again, you may be starting to feel like your playing days are over, and you want to move behind the glass, into coaching. No matter what brings you to this book, you will find helpful information you can take away and use.

So who am I, and what makes me the right guy to tell you what to do (when it comes to curling?). You have a right to know.

I grew up in a curling family. Both my parents were good curlers who won significant championships over the years. My father almost made it to the world championships, and my sister was the Ontario university champion.

In the town where I grew up, the hockey rink was right next to the curling rink. On Saturday mornings, I'd play hockey and then walk over to the curling club (in all my equipment, except my skates), where I'd watch my father finish his regular game.

Although I didn't play until I was 12 or 13 years old, once I was big enough to handle a curling rock, hockey was replaced. Curling was everywhere in our household. We would watch it whenever it was on television, talk about it over dinner, even play it using tennis balls on a narrow stretch of hall carpet.

I became a fairly good junior player and began to win more and more. I hooked up with some other top Juniors and we played every chance we could; weekend after weekend, practising three times a week, living, eating, breathing the game. Our goal was to make it to the Canadian championships, and we were on our way, having earned a spot in the Ontario final, along with seven other teams. Although we played well, as the round robin wore on, it became apparent that we weren't going to win it. I can remember my father coming up to me just as we were nearing the end of the competition and saying that we could finish no worse than third. He was really proud of me, but I was mad and devastated. I had worked all year to win, to be the Ontario champion. Anything less was just not going to cut it.

But in some ways, that third-place finish at the Ontario finals spurred me on. I finished my time as a junior curler, and left home for university, where I hooked up with another great group of players. We embarked on the competitive circuit. We won numerous titles in our four years of school, including a provincial championship, beating the reigning world champion in the final game. That was, without a doubt, the highlight of my career as a player.

After graduating from university, I moved back home and found myself deep into the competitive circuit, where I had some more successes, but also a number of struggles. I won a few significant cash events, teamed up with former Canadian and world champions, and basically worked hard at the game. But it soon became apparent that for me, mixing a career and playing curling at a top level was impossible. The drive to play had begun to wane, but not my love of the sport.

So rather than getting out of curling completely, I just moved off the ice, covering it for a number of different publications, two of which are the *Ontario Curling Report*, where I am editor, and the *Globe and Mail*, where I've been the curling columnist for 13 years. I still play socially at the club I started out at, 25 years ago.

I've now played in or reported on games all over the world, watched five-year-old kids curl for the first time, and seen world champions crowned. I've talked to winners past, present, and — presumably — future, about strategies and deliveries, sweeping and training, playing in big games and small. I've tried to wrap all of that up in this book to give you a sense of what this great game is all about. *Curling For Dummies* is, among other things, a compilation of the 25 years I've been involved in this game.

Although I have a lot of great memories, both from playing and covering the game, what stands out are the many friendships I've made. It's safe to say that nearly a quarter of a century after I started playing the sport, my closest friends are still curlers, many of whom started playing as kids, the way I did.

How to Use This Book

This book is easy to use. You don't have to start at the beginning and read right through until the end. You can read it in any order, since each section deals with a specific aspect of the game. If you scan the table of contents and something catches your eye, just flip to that page and get going. You can always come back to the beginning again, if you want. If you are a beginner curler, however, I *am* going to part with tradition and suggest that you start reading at Chapter 1. You'll thank me later.

I've done my best to explain all the funny terminology used in curling by including explanations right in the text. If you come across a word or phrase you aren't sure of, though, you can flip to the glossary at the back of the book.

How This Book Is Organized

Curling For Dummies is broken down into seven parts. Each chapter within these parts covers an important area of the game, in most cases carrying through to the finer points. There are lots of cross-references to other chapters, so you can continue reading about something you find especially interesting. That's another way to avoid reading the book from cover to cover.

Part I: Getting Started

This part gives you some background on the sport, its history, and how it is played. I talk about the allure of the game and why people seem to fall in love with it. There's also some history here, which is important to know if you're going to become a curling junkie. For instance, you need to know that Scotland invented the game and still lays claim to being its spiritual home, but that it's Canada that has really developed and grown the sport — to such an extent that it's truly ingrained in Canadian culture.

Part II: Curling Fundamentals

This part gives you a handle on where you play, how you play, and what you need to play properly. Do you know what kind of broom you should use or what you wear on the bottom of your shoes to help you slide down the ice? The answers are in this part. So, too, are explanations of the ice and the rocks — the two most essential parts of the sport (outside of the curlers themselves, of course). There's a chapter on the rules of the game, as well as one on the makeup of the team, which gives you tips on how to assemble four players who want the same things you do.

Part III: Hurry Hard! Playing the Game

This is the more detailed instructional part (don't worry, it's still fun), where I tell you how to do all the stuff you need to know to get out on the ice and compete. Chapter 9 is about how to throw the curling rock (called the *delivery*). Chapter 10 tells you about the different shots you can throw. And in Chapter 11, I show you how sweeping the rock affects the way it travels down the ice (I bet you've always wondered about that, haven't you?) and how to become a good sweeper. This part even has a chapter on the many different types of curling games you can play.

Part IV: Getting Better

This part kind of builds on the foundation set up in Part III. If you know how to play, here's where you come to get better. If you don't know how to play, you need to read Part III first. In this part, I give you some pointers about the strategic side of the game. That's moving your thinking up a notch to focus not only on how you're throwing your rocks, but also where on the ice you're throwing them. I break down the difference between having last rock and not, and I show you how you can score lots of points in a big end (if you have no idea what I'm talking about here, then you definitely need to read Part III). I also give you some pointers on practising your game and staying in shape, as well as some nutritional guidelines (surprise, surprise, these don't include beer!).

Part V: Behind the Glass

Curling isn't just about playing the game. It's also about coaching it and watching it. If you've ever thought about being a coach, give Chapters 16 and 17 a read. And what about being a fan? Chapter 18 tells you what to look for to increase your enjoyment of a game, whether you're watching it live, or from the comfort of your easy chair.

Part VI: The Events

This part is dedicated to curling championships in Canada and around the world. Do you know how the *Brier* (that's the Canadian men's championship) got its name? That's in Chapter 19. Chapter 20 talks about international competitions, including the Olympics, where curling has recently become a full-medal sport.

Part VII: The Part of Tens

Every ...*For Dummies* book has a Part of Tens. It's a proud tradition. Here's where I stick my neck out and give you my picks for greatest players and greatest shots. I think Al Hackner's double takeout at the 1985 Brier was the best shot in curling history. Do you agree? You can look over the lists and come up with your own to challenge me. If you're looking for more information after reading this book (I doubt you will, but just in case), Chapter 24 contains a list of curling information sources where you can go to find out even more.

Icons Used in This Book

Look for these handy icons throughout the book. They draw your attention to valuable information and interesting curling tidbits.

This icon points out some information that's a little more detailed than usual.

When I make a suggestion about improving your game or getting the most out of some other aspect of curling, this bull's-eye marks the spot.

I use this icon to highlight a point that I think you need to keep in mind.

When you see this rock and broom, I want you to note a key curling term or concept.

This icon signifies that you're about to read a great curling story or anecdote.

Part I
Getting Started

In this part . . .

I shamelessly try to whet your appetite for curling. How? By telling you why so many people around the world have a great passion for the game, by sharing with you the colourful history of the sport and its coming of age in Canada, and by giving you a short (I promise) geography lesson about who curls where in the world. You may just be surprised at the number of people who love this game.

Chapter 1

What Is Curling?

In This Chapter

▶ Getting to know the basics of the game

▶ Understanding why curlers sweep

▶ Discovering why curling is so popular

▶ Realizing the benefits of curling

Curling is the greatest game in the world. I say that without reservation, as someone who has played the sport at many different levels for more than 25 years, and covered it professionally for about 20.

Why?

Glad you asked.

Curling, first and foremost, is a game of fun and respect. For more than 500 years, the essence of curling has been based on reverence for the rules, admiration for your opposition, and a belief that playing and enjoying the game is more important than winning it. Along with these ideals, many of the traditions from the earliest days of the game have continued. For example, opponents shake hands at the start and conclusion of every game. That's not just in fun club games, but right up to the final of the world championships.

And while curling has moved from its early days of being played outdoors on frozen ponds into facilities where computers control the climate, it is still virtually the same sport, with the same rules and rituals. It's kind of nice to know that, in our fast-paced and ever-changing world.

What's This Game of Rocks and Brooms About?

In its simplest form, curling is a game where two teams of four players each slide 40-pound granite *rocks* (also called *stones* — the terms are used interchangeably) down a sheet of ice toward a target at the other end. Each team tries to get more of its stones closer to the centre of the target than the other team.

That might sound a bit complicated, but if we break it down farther, you can see that it's actually pretty easy.

Figure 1-1 is a diagram of a curling sheet, with important markings indicated.

It's about throwing rocks

In curling, the team you play on is called a *rink*. The rink is made up of four players: the *lead*, the *second*, the *third* (also called the *vice*, *vice-skip*, or *mate*), and the *skip*. Each player has specific duties, which I outline in Chapter 6.

Each player on the team throws two stones in each *end*. An end is similar to an inning in baseball, with a curling game generally consisting of eight or ten ends. Each team throws 8 stones in an end, making for a total of 16 stones sliding down the ice in one end. That's quite a bit of action. The players alternate throwing with their *opposite number,* the player on the other team who

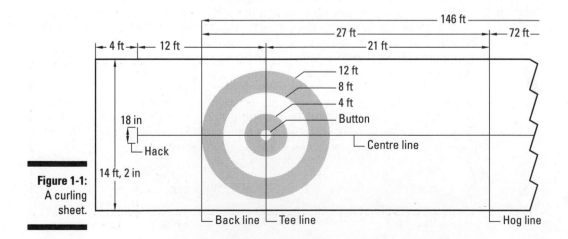

Figure 1-1: A curling sheet.

plays the same position they do. So, the lead on your team throws a stone, followed by the lead on your opposition. Then your lead throws again, again followed by the other lead. The seconds and thirds then take over, and on it goes until the skips, who throw the last stones of the end, take their turns.

It's about rocks that curl

The key to understanding curling is to know that when you throw a rock down the ice, depending on its rotation — which is applied intentionally — it will *curl*, or *bend*, one way or another. (Strangely enough, although you might say the rock curls, this is not how curling got its name. More on that in Chapter 2.)

It's sort of like when a pitcher throws a curveball in a baseball game, except that the curler doesn't have control over how much his rock bends, whereas the pitcher does. How much (or little) a rock curls depends more on the conditions of the playing surface.

Once all 16 rocks — 8 by each team — have been thrown down the narrow *sheet* of ice (the sheet is the name given to the entire playing surface), the score for that end is counted, based on the final positions of the stones in the *house*. The house is that group of concentric circles at either end of a curling sheet. It looks like a giant bull's-eye frozen in the ice. The house is made up of four circles measuring 12 feet, 8 feet, 4 feet, and 1 foot in diameter. The smallest circle is known as the *button*. These circles are usually painted different colours, such as blue, red, and white.

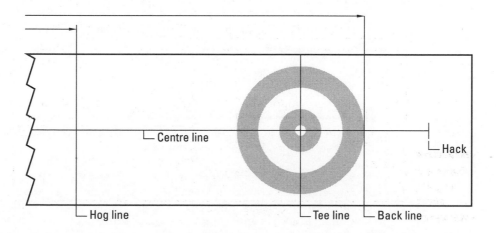

It's about shooting and scoring

Only one team can score in an end. A team scores one point for every rock that it has closer to the centre of the house than the other team. The position of the stones in the house is irrelevant — as long as they are touching the circles. In other words, a rock that ends up right in the centre of the house receives no more points than a stone just touching the far outside of the house.

It's about sweeping — more than just cleaning up around the house

"What about all that sweeping?" I can hear you asking. Yes, to those who have only watched curling and don't know much about it, sweeping is probably the most unusual aspect of the game. It's almost funny to watch grown adults furiously sweep those large stones as they slide down the sheet.

Sweeping makes a rock bend less and travel farther. The lead, second, and third all take turns sweeping the rocks. The skip, who is like the team's quarterback, is the only one who doesn't regularly sweep stones. More on getting the hang of sweeping in Chapter 11.

It's a thinking person's game

This quick and dirty rundown of the game might make curling sound easy. Just slide those big stones down the sheet of ice and see where they end up.

Not so fast. There is actually a great deal of thought that goes into deciding just where you're going to try to place those rocks when you throw them — so much so that curling has often been described as a cross between shuffleboard and chess.

Strategy is a very important part of the game. Generally speaking, it is the skip who determines a rink's strategy. During the game, the skip stands at one end of the sheet and tells her other three players where they should place their shots (that's how she gets out of sweeping!).

A team's strategy can be simple or complicated, depending on the skip and the level of competition. Of course, it doesn't always go according to plan! That's another part of what makes curling so much fun. No two games are alike; the unpredictability is always appealing. I devote an entire chapter to strategy in curling (Chapter 14), so flip ahead if you'd like some quick pointers.

Why Curl?

Why should you take up curling? There are plenty of reasons to curl, not the least of which is that it's just plain fun. Win or lose, I've rarely left a curling club without a smile on my face. People who curl seem to share a certain fun-loving attitude towards this winter pastime. Even at national and world championships, I've seen players in the middle of a high-stakes game share a few laughs. (Imagine seeing that at a hockey game!)

Great reasons to curl:

- It's a sport you can play at any age.
- It's open to both sexes.
- It's easy to learn.
- It's inexpensive to play.
- It's good for your health.

And, you can find curling clubs just about anywhere in Canada — not to mention more and more in the United States and around the world.

You can play at any age

Curling is a game that can be played by kids just out of diapers and by elderly folks as well. It's not unusual to see players in their nineties throwing stones down the ice. I even knew a man who was more than 100 years old and who still competed every week.

There are provincial and national competitions for curlers of all ages — and I mean *all ages*; from 8-year-old children, to teenagers, to young adults, to those of us over 40, 50, 60 . . . well, you get the idea.

Curling leagues tend to be based on age, but more often than not, you'll see a team composed of players of all ages, say a couple of 20-year-olds playing with a couple of 50-year-olds. I played with my father for many years in regular club games. Some of the best teams have been made up of fathers and sons, sisters and cousins.

Because the game can be played at a level that doesn't require speed or a great deal of physical strength, age really has no bearing on being able to compete.

You can play with your wife — or girlfriend, or husband, or boyfriend, or...

Curling with your significant other can be a lot of fun. There really are no gender inequalities to speak of in curling. Men and women can play at the same level, whether it's highly competitive or highly social. One of the most popular forms of curling, *mixed*, has men and women playing together. Mixed curling is one of the staples of the schedule at many curling clubs. Husbands and wives play together — or sometimes against each other — as do boyfriends and girlfriends. They battle it out on the ice and then enjoy an evening of socializing afterwards.

At a more competitive level, men's teams and women's teams often play against each other in tournaments, called *bonspiels*. And guess what, guys? The women win more often than you might think. Nowadays, some events disregard a team's makeup completely. It doesn't matter what combination of men or women is in the lineup — just get on the ice and play.

The reason women and men can play together and against each other is that the qualities that go into playing the game aren't based on size, or, to some degree, how strong you are. Although those can be benefits, they aren't vital to good play.

You can learn how to play in one day (really, you can)

Unlike many other leisure sports, you can become fairly proficient at curling in a matter of hours. You might not be ready to challenge for a national championship after your first lesson, but you can certainly step onto the ice, learn the basics, and play a game — all in one day. Many curling clubs run a morning-afternoon program, where you are taught in the morning and play in a bonspiel that afternoon.

The basics of the game are relatively simple, and the technique isn't that difficult, either. As long as you have a bit of balance, a touch of flexibility, and a little elbow grease stored up, you can become a good curler in no time. Although you can definitely refine your game to become a better player — I give you lots of tips on refinement later in the book — starting out in the sport is a cinch.

You don't have to spend an arm and a leg (you need them to play, anyway)

Another great thing about curling is that it's one of the least expensive sports to play. A heavy sweater, a pair of gloves, and some equipment that you can usually buy for less than $100 is all you need. Even if you tried really, really hard, you'd have a tough time spending more than about $500 or $600 rounding up all the best equipment available.

Just try walking out of a golf shop or hockey store with all the top-level gear you need to play without worrying about taking out a second mortgage. Suddenly, curling starts to look very attractive.

Membership fees at clubs are equally reasonable. Most curling clubs will let you play for a season (which lasts roughly from the start of October to the end of March) for about $300 to $500. You won't need to move into the poor house to join.

Some facilities rent sheets out on a per-game basis, if you just want to play a single game without necessarily taking out a membership. It's usually about $10 per person for two hours of play.

You don't have to be in rip-roaring shape

Curling is good exercise. That may come as a surprise to some who have only watched the game and not played it, but believe me, go out and play and see if you don't feel some new muscles the next morning.

Having said that, one of the other attractions of the game is that you don't have to be in outstanding physical condition to curl well. Although more and more of the top players adopt serious training regimens and are indeed true athletes, at the grass roots level, you're likely to see a few "round-bellies" out enjoying a game.

There are some obvious physical benefits to playing the sport, but you can also get by without any serious strenuous effort. Most players leave the ice with all their teeth, without any muscle pulls, and without the need for physiotherapy the next day.

People with physical disabilities can curl, as well. I have curled with people with only one leg. At one time, one of the best players in my club was a gentleman who had just one arm and one leg.

Curling is easy to play and easy to enjoy. Because of that, more than a million people around the world compete each winter, whether it be in an after-work league with office colleagues — or in the world championships.

Noted curlers and curling enthusiasts

✔ Hockey star Wayne Gretzky: Says he is on the edge of his seat when he watches curling.

✔ *Hockey Night in Canada* play-by-play announcer Bob Cole: Competed in two Canadian championships as the skip of the Newfoundland team.

✔ Singer Shania Twain: Curled in her hometown of Timmins, Ontario.

✔ Hockey player Keith Primeau (Philadelphia Flyers): Regularly attended curling matches at 1998 Winter Olympics in Nagano, Japan.

✔ Actor Paul Gross (*Due South*): Is making a movie with a curling subplot, called *Men with Brooms*.

A Game for Everyone

Curling is one of the most democratic sports. Although I golf, the chances of me playing in the Masters or Canadian Open Championship are just about nil. Yet, no matter what my skill level, I can go to my local curling club and sign up for *playdowns* (a series of competitive games) that will eventually lead to the world championship. I may not get there, but at least I have a chance.

Once on the ice, though, just about anything can happen. Going back to golf for just a moment — unless I pay thousands of dollars for a spot in a pro-am, the chances of me playing with Tiger Woods are, again, just about nil. Yet, over the years, I've played with and against world curling champions — even beaten two of them in meaningful contests. A number of other "average" curlers can say the same. That's because even the best curlers in the world are usually just regular folks, many of whom play a weekly club game or friendly tournament like the rest of us.

In Canada, where the majority of curlers are found, curling is the antithesis of an elitist sport. Head out to a local club and you're likely to see lawyers playing alongside plumbers, accountants lining up against firefighters, mail carriers taking on Members of Parliament. Once they're on the ice, no one really cares what they do — they're just curlers, plain and simple.

It's also not hard to find somewhere to curl in this sprawling country of ours. There is an old saying among curlers that you can travel just about anywhere in Canada and find three things: a post office, a bank, and a curling club. These days, your chances of finding a bank or a post office might not be so hot, but turn a corner, or stop and ask someone, and you'll likely find a curling club, filled to the brim with people playing the game and enjoying themselves.

A Community's Heart and Soul

Curling clubs are often the heart and soul of a community, especially if it happens to be a smaller centre in Western Canada. On cold winter evenings, the local curling club can be not just the sporting hub, but the social hub, as well. Romances that led to marriages have begun in curling clubs. In fact, some curlers have even been married right on the ice. But, perhaps more than anything, curling is just a fun sport to play. It's fairly easy to understand and play (although it might not look like it at first — that's why you're reading this book!), and it's one of the best ways to get through our cold Canadian winters.

Chapter 2

Kilts and Cannonballs: Where Curling Comes From

· ·

In This Chapter

▶ Uncovering curling's roots

▶ Appreciating Canada's love affair with curling

▶ Discovering that curling isn't just for cold climates

· ·

No one is really sure where the first curling stone was thrown. That knowledge is undoubtedly lost in the melted ice of some long-ago pond or *loch* (lake). But it's quite certain that even if they didn't throw that first stone, the Scots are the people who gave the game its roots, formalized its rules, and imbued it with many of the traditions curlers around the world celebrate today. Scotland's cruel winter climate was softened somewhat by curling matches played all over the country. As the temperature dropped, the participants put away their golf clubs and picked up their heavy stones. Contests became friendly grudge matches: neighbours took on neighbours, and whole villages took on other villages, playing against each other in healthy competition. There was even a Grand Match, where thousands of players competed at once. Though curling is now played in many other countries, and by a greater number of people, Scotland will always remain its spiritual home.

It is also safe to say that Canada provided the fertilizer necessary to enhance the growth of the game. Canadians have made curling an important part of their sporting culture in the past hundred years. Today, more than one million Canadians take to the ice each winter to participate in the old game — that's more than in the rest of the world combined! Some also play at a competitive level, travelling across the country to curl for cash prizes on a semi-professional basis. The highlight of the year, the national men's championship known as the *Brier,* draws more than a quarter of a million spectators and a television audience in excess of four million.

But Scotland and Canada aren't the only countries that curl. In fact, thanks in part to its recognition at the Olympic Games, curling is played all over Europe (including most of the former Eastern bloc countries), as well as in Asia, Australia, New Zealand, and Africa. Although it is in its infancy in many of these countries, it's official: Curling is truly a world game, and it's here to stay.

Origins of the Game

The truth is, no one's really sure where curling started. The waters of the game's beginnings have become quite muddied over time (it's that frozen loch thing — I'm sure the key to it is at the bottom of one, somewhere). I do know that the game can be traced as far back as the 1500s, to frozen ponds or lochs somewhere in Europe. Both European and Scottish historians lay claim to the sport's beginnings — and there is evidence for both sides. It's unlikely that the truth will ever be known. But in reality, it doesn't matter so much where curling started as where it put down roots.

Continental Europe

Those who contend that the first stone was thrown somewhere on the other side of the English Channel turn to art, of all things, to bolster their argument. (Well, they use lots of other evidence, too, but the whole art angle is pretty interesting.)

Famous European paintings that depict a game suspiciously resembling curling:

- *Hunters in the Snow,* by Dutch painter Pieter Bruegel the Elder, painted in 1565

- *Winter Landscape with a Bird Trap,* also by Bruegel the Elder, painted in 1565

- *Winter,* by Dutch painter Jacob Grimmer, painted in 1575

- *Hyems,* an engraving by R. de Baudous after a painting by N. van Wieringen, from the late 1500s

What do these four pieces of art share in common? Beyond the fact that they all depict people sliding around on the ice with curling-type stones? In all cases, in fact, the sport depicted is likely *Eisschiessen* (ice-shooting), not curling. It's been played for centuries in the Austrian Alps, where Bruegel was known to have spent some time. Eisschiessen is likely a forerunner of curling; certainly the games have a great deal in common.

The curling Terminator

Eisschiessen has been a popular game in Austria for centuries and is still played avidly to this day. It has so much in common with curling that it's probably the game's European ancestor.

In a fashion similar to curling, you fire "stones" — known as *eisstocks* — down a sheet, without the aid of sweepers. These eisstocks, which look like bathroom plungers sitting on a small wheel, are made of wood and have a rubber edge. They're quite a bit lighter than curling stones and don't react the same on the ice.

While it doesn't take a great deal of muscle to get the eisstocks down the ice, one of Austria's past national champions in the sport is none other than Arnold Schwarzenegger's father.

Scotland the brave

Most people regard Scotland as the birthplace of curling because there are so many Scottish traditions associated with the game. But early evidence is a bit inconclusive. Scottish records have references to curling as early as 1540, while other documents suggest it may have had its start in other parts of Europe.

There was a lot of debate in the early 1800s, by men of the cloth on both sides, about whether curling originated in the land of the kilt or in Continental Europe. In his book *An Account of the Game of Curling,* published in 1811, Reverend John Ramsay argued in favour of the latter, saying many of the words associated with the game had Dutch or German origins.

But Reverend John Kerr, who led the first visit by Scottish curlers to Canada in 1804, stated that more indications — such as early written accounts and the existence of early curling stones — pointed to curling being of Scottish origin.

Although the game's birthplace may not be clear, it is a fact that the Scots were the ones who took a shine to it, playing it all over the country — sometimes in their kilts — and forming clubs as early as the 1700s. A large number of Scots took up the game in these early days, and, as you might guess, there were a lot of differences in the rules, depending where you played. In some places, playing with teams of eight was common. In others, sweeping was limited to a small portion of the sheet of ice. And unlike today, when curling stones are all of a fairly similar shape and size, back then there were what can only be called wild and interesting variations. Gradually, however, the curlers agreed on a set of rules — and the game has never looked back.

The Stirling Stone

What is believed to be one of the oldest existing curling stones, the Stirling Stone, was found at the bottom of a pond in Dunblane, Scotland. (No human skeletons were alongside, indicating that the curlers apparently got off the thin ice just in time.) The Stone weighs in at 26 pounds, about half of what one of today's stones weighs, and it is somewhat square in shape. It has a groove on one side, presumably to make it easier to handle.

The stone is engraved with the date 1511 — seeming to indicate beyond a doubt that the first stone was thrown by a Scot, as it was found on Scottish land. This date would make it the earliest reference to curling on record. But after examining the stone further, scientists think it actually dates from much later than 1511. It's clear that, even centuries ago, the rivalry between the Scots and the Europeans over who started the game was alive and well!

Though you don't need to know exactly where curling started, you should be aware that it has a long and distinguished past, with many traditions that continue to this day. Just remember: When you find yourself discussing the history of the game over a couple of cold ones — and you will — don't ever try to tell a Scot that curling started anywhere else but Scotland!

Canada Rocks

Curling in Canada isn't as old as it is in Scotland, but its roots are deep and strong just the same. From its earliest beginnings, and through its many growth periods, it has become a vital part of much of Canadian sporting culture. There's an old joke about the three buildings you can find in just about every community — big or small — a post office, a bank, and a curling club.

Scots who immigrated to the New Land brought their love of the game with them and began playing wherever they settled. With many winters to pass, curling flourished, and gradually, the new curlers in the new country began to organize themselves into clubs.

In fact, the oldest sporting club in North America is the Royal Montreal Curling Club, founded in 1807. Little did the 20 prominent businessmen who organized it know that it would still be going strong close to two centuries later.

Prairie roots

As Scottish immigrants moved westward, so, too, did the game. By the mid-1800s, curling clubs began popping up all over the West and the game took hold. Curling boomed across Manitoba, Saskatchewan, and Alberta as in no other place.

Curling in the West was most popular in farming communities. And why not? With the prairie winters howling, curling was the perfect way to await the arrival of spring. Once the crops were harvested, farming families took to the ice.

Curling clubs of all shapes and sizes sprung up. Most were housed in barn-like structures with natural ice, with room for one, maybe two, sheets. Despite their rough settings, they were popular spots from the time the harvest left until it was time to plant again in the spring.

The iron crowd in Quebec

Curling was more of an elitist sport in Quebec and Ontario, played by the wealthier folks of the country club set. And in the late 1800s in Quebec, they didn't even use rocks. There, the popular utensil was a *curling iron,* in effect a curling stone made of steel. (Maybe they were leftover cannonballs! See the sidebar, "Curling with cannonballs on the Plains of Abraham.") These beauties weighed in at about 60 pounds — 20 pounds heavier than the granites in use in the rest of the country at that time. The Quebec "iron curlers" used to say that playing with mere granites was beneath them, and that playing with curling irons was the only way to go.

Curling with cannonballs on the Plains of Abraham

On September 13, 1759, in the battle of the Plains of Abraham, the British captured Quebec from the French in what would be an important contributing factor to the birth of Canada over a century later.

What does this have to do with curling, you ask? The story goes, that after the battle had been decided, the soldiers of one of the platoons involved — the 78th Highlanders — gained permission to melt down cannonballs for use as curling rocks. With nothing much to do and a long, cold winter ahead, these Scottish soldiers spent many an hour curling on the St. Charles River. They may have been the first rock-throwers in what was to eventually become Canada.

But the Quebec players' use of the irons was a major stumbling block in forming a national organization and championship. It was impossible to mix irons and granites — like trying to listen to an eight-track in a cassette player. However, in 1925, two events occurred that signalled the end of the iron era:

✔ A large, season-ending tournament was held at the fabled Montreal Forum, using granites. For many of the iron players there, it was nothing short of a revelation. They were playing on artificial ice (a rarity back then), and the conditions of the playing surface could be better controlled. The granites performed beautifully on this surface. It was enough to sway many of the staunchest iron players. It also didn't hurt that they were playing in one of the greatest ice palaces in the land.

✔ Wealthy Montreal businessman and curling supporter Howard Stewart offered to buy up any remaining iron stones and replace them — free of charge — with granite ones. (He ended up buying more than 200.) Part of his motivation for this was that his family's company, Macdonald Tobacco, was using curling as a way to build nationhood. A pro-granite curler, he felt that the irons were a stumbling block to establishing a national championship.

In 1933, the *Dominion Curling Association* was formed. Known today as the *Canadian Curling Association,* it was Canadian curling's first national governing body. Curling was firmly (and officially) established as one of Canada's great winter pastimes.

In Canada today, there are more than one million regular curlers coast to coast. It's estimated that many more play once or twice a year at company outings or other social functions. This easily makes Canada the largest curling nation in the world. There are more curlers within its borders than in the rest of the world combined.

Around the Globe

Curling is popular in many countries around the world and continues to invade new nations each winter. Once reserved for countries with cold climates, it has spread to locations you might not expect. Much of curling's growth is thanks to its introduction into the Olympic movement, first as a demonstration sport in 1988, 1992, and 1996, and then as an official medal sport at the 1998 Winter Olympics, in Nagano, Japan.

Oh, say, can you curl

The United States boasts the largest curling population after Canada. As had happened in Canada, transplanted Scots brought curling with them, forming clubs in the United States as early as the 1830s. Curling was extremely popular across what would later become the northern border with Canada. Clubs sprang up and flourished in large cities such as Boston, Buffalo, New York, Detroit, and Chicago, and smaller centres such as Rochester, Green Bay, and Duluth.

Curling in the United States reached its height in the 1950s and 1960s when the nation boasted a club in every state across the northern border. A good many players took to the ice regularly, and local and national associations took root. The first U.S. men's championship was held in 1957 in Chicago and televised to a significant American audience. It seemed that curling had taken hold. But all that changed just a quarter of a century later. Attracting new players was proving difficult. The sport just didn't appeal to a nation that was increasingly on the economic and social fast track. Instead, the United States looked to sexier professional sports, such as baseball, basketball, football, and hockey, to get its fix. Another problem was the lack of programs to develop young players. A whole generation of both social and competitive curlers was never introduced to the game.

But it's not all doom and gloom for curling in the United States. A solid base of curlers has developed in recent years, despite the numbers dropping from their 1950s and 1960s highs. As well, clubs have sprung up in unusual locations, like Florida, California, and Texas. There was even a major international bonspiel held in Las Vegas! Many of these new clubs are populated by ex-patriot Canadians and Scots who have gone to great lengths (such as curling in hockey arenas in the middle of the night) to continue playing their favourite sport.

Curling in the United States has also benefited from its recognition as a medal sport in the Olympics. The huge sporting industry in the United States is now putting significant financial resources behind curling development, which may lead to the game becoming strong once again.

Europe and the rest of the world

Curling traces its roots back to the mid- to late-1800s in Continental Europe. The sport has a long history in Sweden, Switzerland, and Norway, while it began shortly after the turn of the 20th century in Germany, Italy, Denmark, and Austria.

Other countries that have caught the curling bug:

- **Bulgaria, the Czech Republic, and Russia:** Curling joined the list of other winter sports in many former Eastern bloc countries after the fall of the iron curtain in 1989.

- **Japan and Korea:** Curling was introduced to Japan and other Asian countries around 1970. Japan took to the game especially: In only a short time, it developed a small but solid grass roots program and it trained several world-class *rinks* (teams) that competed at the World Curling Championships and Olympic Games. Korea participates in the Pacific Curling Championships, a regional qualifying event for the world championships.

- **Australia and New Zealand:** What these countries lack in facilities, they more than make up for in enthusiasm. Both Australia and New Zealand have sent teams to the world championships and had respectable showings. The formal alliance with the rest of the curling world came as a result of Canadian Hugh Milliken, a national mixed winner in Canada, whose determined efforts have spawned a curling community Down Under. Hugh spent thousands of dollars to get the game going and almost single-handedly negotiated its membership in the World Curling Federation.

- **South Africa and the Ivory Coast:** Although it may be hard to believe, there are even curlers in South Africa. Records show that some events were played in these countries in the 1970s, although neither has participated in any significant playdowns.

Some of these nations only looked at curling seriously when it entered the 1988 Winter Olympic Games as a demonstration sport. In 1991, curling's global governing body, called the *World Curling Federation (WCF),* persuaded many of these countries to join — even though lots of them lacked both clubs and curlers. It's fair to say that the WCF had an ulterior motive here: It needed a minimum number of member nations (25) for curling to be recognized as a

Curling, Mexican-style

Josele Garza may have thought driving in the Indianapolis 500 was tough, but it's nothing compared to another task he took on. Garza, a former Indy car driver, is one of Mexico's first curlers, and he's trying to gain a foothold for the sport there. After watching curling on television during the 1998 Winter Olympics, Garza organized a group intent on setting up the sport in Mexico. They travelled all the way to Winnipeg for some instruction and a crash course on the sport. Garza and his group then set up Mexico's first curling club. It's pretty tough getting ice time in Mexico City with just five arenas — not to mention the almost unplayable conditions — but if enthusiasm counts, Garza may well be the father of Mexican curling.

full medal sport at the Olympics. It finally got there in 1998. Guess the new members decided to sign them up first and worry about training later.

Since 1998, some WCF countries have followed the same trail blazed by the Jamaican bobsled team on their way to the 1988 Winter Olympics. They've begun forming legitimate teams in the hopes of taking a run at playing in the large international competitions. A few, such as Australia, New Zealand, and Japan, have been successful, and are now regular competitors at the world championships. Others, such as Russia and Bulgaria, are still learning the intricacies of the sport, but appear determined to become serious competitors. Table 2-1 lists the 34 member nations in the World Curling Federation, the year they joined.

While it may have come from humble beginnings, curling is now a world game. In terms of number of players and international status, however, Canada still dominates the sport.

Table 2-1	World Curling Federation (WCF) Member Nations		
Country	*Joined the WCF In*	*Country*	*Joined the WCF In*
Andorra	1991	Japan	1985
Australia	1988	Korea	1994
Austria	1982	Latvia	2001
Belarus	1997	Liechtenstein	1991
Belgium	1998	Luxembourg	1976
Bulgaria	1990	Mexico	1991
Canada	1966	Netherlands	1975
Czech Republic	1990	New Zealand	1991
Denmark	1971	Norway	1966
England	1971	Romania	1991
Finland	1979	Russia	1992
France	1966	Scotland	1966
Germany	1967	Switzerland	1966
Hungary	1989	Chinese Taipei	1998
Iceland	1991	United States	1966
Israel	1999	U.S. Virgin Islands	1991
Italy	1972	Wales	1982

Part II
Curling Fundamentals

In this part . . .

You see how curling is played, where you play it, what equipment you need to compete, and how to find some friends to play it with. Consult Chapter 3 if you're unsure about which type of brush to use, or if you've always wanted to know what that guy who looks like he's watering the ice is really up to. Chapter 6 has helpful tips about assembling a team. And if you're interested in the nuts-and-bolts aspects of how the game is played, flip to Chapters 7 and 8. This part explains the basics of the game.

Chapter 3

The Equipment

*F*or a lot of sports, this chapter might be the biggest in the book. Take golf, for instance. Equipment from clubs to balls and everything in between could fill an encyclopedia. And hockey would be much the same, with plenty of descriptions of pads and helmets.

Curling is different. At most facilities, you can get by with a pair of clean running shoes and a heavy sweater. While you can certainly buy the Rolls-Royce of curling equipment, you can also play with just the bare minimum. But if you are going to get serious about the game, then it pays to invest in some gear that's designed exclusively for curling.

Shoes and Sliders

In curling, one shoe makes you go and the other makes you stop. It's sort of like having a snow tire on one foot and a skate on the other. The secret to how this works is on the bottom of the shoes (see Figure 3-1). The sole of one shoe is a slippery surface (the shoe on the left in Figure 3-1), while the other has traction (the shoe on the right). You can either buy shoes that have the soles prepared this way, or you can add the surfaces to regular shoes.

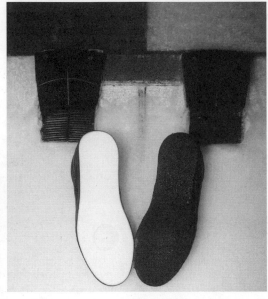

Figure 3-1:
The shoe on the right has the gripper on it, while the shoe on the left has the slider.

If you're a right-handed player, then the bottom of your right shoe has what's called a *gripper* on it. There are a number of different styles of gripper, but essentially, it is designed to help you keep your footing on the ice. One of the most common types of gripper has a rubber sole with tiny bumps on it.

This gripper is used for pushing out of the hack (the foothold) and, more importantly, for propelling you down the ice when you're sweeping or just trying to get to the other end.

Your other shoe has the *slider* on it. The slider acts similarly to a skate, except that it doesn't have any sharp edges to dig into the ice. It is a surface that has little friction against the ice and will glide along, carrying you with it. If you're a right-handed player, your slider goes on your left foot. More on why this is so in Chapter 9.

When you slide down the ice, it's almost like skateboarding. Your *gripper foot* (the foot with the gripper on the sole) pushes off every few feet while your *slider foot* (the foot with the slider on the sole) remains still and just skims across the ice surface. When you deliver the rock, the gripper foot pushes off from the hack and you travel out on your slider.

Types of slider

Over the years, a number of different materials have been used to allow curlers to slide down the ice. One of the first sliders was made of solder, while others were fashioned out of the waxed cardboard of milk cartons. Although all sliders are made to help you slide down the sheet, there are a number of different styles you need to know about before you choose one: If you're a beginner, I suggest a couple of modified sliders to get yourself used to the feel of whipping along the ice:

- **The tape slider:** The first time you step onto the ice, you'll probably do it in running shoes (make certain to clean the bottoms of them before you go out). It's not a bad idea to attach some electrical tape to the bottom of your sliding foot, right over the sole. This is sort of a slider with training wheels and it's good for beginners because it's somewhat slippery — therefore gives a feel for the ice — but not so slick that you might fall and break your keister.

    Take a wide roll of tape and cover the front half of the bottom of your shoe. (A lot of curling clubs will have a big roll on hand.) By taping only the front half of your shoe, you get more stability as you learn how to use a slider. When you're out on the ice with your taped shoe, you can put your heel down and get a little extra stability. When you want to slide, you just have to raise your heel up slightly to eliminate the resistance.

- **The slip-on slider:** Although most sliders are permanently affixed to the bottom of your shoe, there is an alternative. The *slip-on slider*, as its name suggests, is a unit that slips over your shoe and is held in place by a strong elastic wrap. This is one of the best sliders for beginners, as you can use it just for delivering the rock and then remove it when you go to sweep. As well, it's fairly inexpensive and will work with any style of shoe.

    The slip-on slider is available in a number of different materials. You can get a *full slider* (covering the entire bottom of your shoe) or just a *half slider* (from the midpoint of your foot up to your toes).

For those players who have taken their fair share of spills (and good-natured jibes from their fellow players) and are now used to their slider, you can choose from three types — all dependable and popular:

- **The Teflon slider:** Today, the majority of sliders are made of Teflon, the same stuff used in frying pans. It provides a comfortable, smooth surface and is soft enough to allow it to be cut to size for the bottom of your shoe.

✔ **The Asham slider:** This slider is named after Winnipeg entrepreneur Arnold Asham, who invented it. It's made of a hard plastic material that's usually quicker than Teflon and more durable. Applied in horizontal bars across the sole, it has become one of the more popular choices among competitive players.

✔ **The steel slider:** This slider gives you an extremely quick surface — too quick for some players. Definitely not recommended for beginners.

Check out Figure 3-2 for a closer look at the Teflon and Asham sliders.

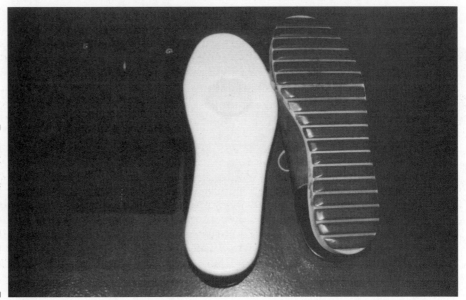

Figure 3-2:
The most common types of slider are the Teflon (on the left) and the Asham (on the right).

The speed of your slider

Different types of sliders give you different speeds on the ice. Speed is an important consideration for a number of reasons, but one of the chief reasons when it comes to picking your slider has to do with *your* comfort level on the ice. You want to feel comfortable with your slide. If you're going too quickly in your delivery, you'll have to make adjustments to let go of the stone in time. The same goes for sweeping. If you have a slider that's too quick, you won't be able to stay with the rock and sweep it properly.

Getting the right speed has become an important part of many curlers' choice of sliders. (In the past, you just took whatever slider came with your shoe.)

Try out as many types of slider as you need until you find one you like. The less friction, obviously, the faster you'll slide. Steel, for example, is extremely fast, while a thin piece of Teflon is much slower.

The general rule with Teflon is, the thicker it is, the faster you'll go.

Choose a slider with a speed that gives you enough momentum that you don't have to push yourself along at every step, and one that's slow enough that you won't lose your balance and wipe out.

Caring for your slider

You need to take care of your slider just as you would any other piece of sporting equipment. Ideally, the ice is the only surface your slider should come into contact with. However, as an experienced curler, I can tell you that this only happens in a perfect world. During the game, you'll be standing on the *backboards* (the off-ice area behind the sheet) and you might walk off the ice and into the club with your slider exposed — like when you need an emergency bathroom break!

Cover your slider at the end of a game and anytime you're not on the ice. You can buy a ready-made cover made of thick rubber that fits over the bottom of your shoe. You can also use a toe rubber — the kind you might use to cover your regular street shoes. Knit covers are available for use in some clubs.

Whatever style you decide on, I suggest you cover your slider anytime you're off the ice. If you step on a small stone or some other hard piece of debris, you'll likely scratch or pit your slider. Every mark that's left on it will affect the way it performs on the ice — and the way you curl.

The perfect balance

Lino Di Iorio is a self-confessed curling nut. Although he never curled until into his forties, he has nonetheless had a significant effect on the game. An engineer by trade, he noticed that many curlers slid on the outside edge of their sliders. He also noticed that the sliders seemed to buckle after a period of time, curling up at the sides. Di Iorio built a recessed area into his slider, just where the ball of the foot is in the shoe. This spread the player's weight more evenly across the slider. The idea worked, and Di Iorio's Balance Plus Slider became the most popular model around. Since then, Di Iorio has gone on to create a rock-throwing machine, as well as other technical devices to improve the game.

The best shoes for the game

Your gripper and slider are important parts of your equipment, but both of them have to go on the bottoms of shoes, and those are the next components to consider. With shoes, you have two choices:

✔ **Curling-specific shoes:** These shoes are built for the game and have a number of features tailored especially for the curler. In most cases, these types of shoe come with a durable *topside*, usually made of leather or another strong material, that doesn't wear down too quickly, and some form of inside lining, which gives a bit of warmth to your foot. Although these shoes look like any other sporting shoe — with laces and the regular stitching — they are specially designed to handle the specific movements of the feet in a curling game. For instance, the upper toe part of the gripper shoe is usually very robust because it gets dragged along the ice during the delivery. More on making a perfect delivery in Chapter 9.

These types of shoe usually come with the gripper and slider already affixed to the bottom.

✔ **Regular athletic shoes:** You buy these shoes and then have the slider and gripper put on. You might do this for value (they're cheaper than special curling shoes), fit, or even fashion.

If you decide to go this route, look for flat-soled shoes instead of ones that are curvy or wavy. Your gripper and slider will stay better attached to a flat-soled shoe. It's also easier to attach the gripper and slider to shoes with a flat, even sole. Tennis shoes are a good bet.

I've had both types of shoe over the years, and eventually stuck with ones made for the game. I did this primarily because my feet got too cold in regular athletic shoes and I found my game suffered because of it. If you like your feet to stay cozy, buy a pair of curling-specific shoes.

Brooms

For someone watching curling for the first time, there is nothing more unusual than seeing grown adults furiously sweeping in front of the rock travelling down the ice. What's also bizarre is that someone is usually yelling at them to sweep harder.

When and how you sweep is a vital part of curling, but what you use to do the job is even more important. Sweeping makes the rock travel farther and curl less — increasing your chances of getting your rocks where you want them to end up. More on the technique of sweeping in Chapter 11.

Choosing a broom is no different from choosing the right pair of shoes. There's some personal preference that always comes into play (as it should), but there's also scientific evidence that shows just what types of broom work best. And brooms aren't only for sweeping — you use your broom when you deliver your stone, as well.

Figure 3-3 shows the two main types of curling brooms: the corn broom (on the left) and the push broom (on the right).

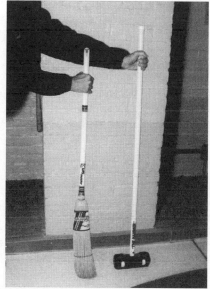

Figure 3-3: Push brooms (on the right) are much easier to use than corn brooms.

Corn brooms

From the earliest days of curling in Canada up until the late 1970s, no matter where you went, the familiar sound of corn brooms whacking the ice in rhythmic strokes echoed through the club. *Corn brooms* are actually made of long strands of straw attached to a wooden handle. The straw is put on in two or three layers (depending on the model) and cut to an even length. The handles are available in different thicknesses for different-sized hands. An average corn broom weighs 5 or 6 pounds, though the size of the handle affects the weight, too.

Although they are still in use today, corn brooms are definitely in the minority. They've been replaced with the synthetic push broom, which I tell you about a little later in this chapter. Why the replacement? The main reason is that corn brooms are downright demanding to sweep with. The straw on the broom is stiff and bunched quite thick. In order to get the full use of it, you have to move the broom back and forth quite vigorously. Your top hand moves it back and forth in a sweeping motion, while your bottom hand acts as a *fulcrum* (the point of support). It's an extremely aerobic task. Slinging a corn broom for eight or ten ends and playing three games a day leaves even the best-conditioned curler aching all over. Even with a good set of gloves, it's likely that you'll leave the club with plenty of blisters on your hands.

There are other reasons, too. Corn brooms wear out quickly. Back in the early 1980s, it was nothing for top players competing in a Brier to go through a dozen brooms in a week. At $25 to $45 apiece, this became an expensive proposition.

And corn brooms are, well . . . messy. No other word for it. Not only do they leave *chaf* (small bits of straw) all over the ice, but larger straws can also break off, wreaking havoc when they get underneath rocks.

Still, some curlers continue to play with corn brooms. The physical effort involved makes them feel as if they are accomplishing something. And there certainly isn't anything like the sound of two good sweepers "pounding the corn" on a last-shot draw to win the game.

Push brooms

Push brooms, also called *brushes*, were first used in Europe, particularly in Scotland. They became the standard there by the 1940s, and gradually North Americans were won over. Unlike corn brooms, push brooms aren't as physically taxing to sweep with, don't wear out as easily, and, according to some, are more effective. They can be made out of horse or hog hair, or synthetic. Over time, the various types of synthetic models have gained popularity. I outline the different types you can choose from later in the chapter.

Canadians scoffed at push brooms for some time. Most felt that push brooms weren't effective because they looked too easy to use. Curlers just didn't exert themselves the way they did with the corn brooms. How could there be any benefit to something that didn't cause you to grunt, groan, and throw your back out? (Of course, most of these naysayers had never tried a push broom.) As well, all of the top competitive teams were still using corn brooms, and if they were winning with corn, then that must be the key! Corn brooms were a tradition in Canada — one that took some time to overturn.

It wasn't until a young curler from Calgary, named Paul Gowsell, adopted the push broom in the late 1970s, that the transition began.

Gowsell is a two-time world junior champion, and also made it to the 1980 *Brier*, the Canadian men's championship. He's one of the most successful competitive curlers in Canada, and he and his team accomplished it all with push brooms.

> # A different sort of delivery
>
> In addition to being the man who introduced push brooms, or brushes, as they're often called, to Canada, Paul Gowsell was one of the most outrageous curlers ever to take to the ice. Young, brash, and rebellious, Gowsell even looked the part with long hair and a straggly beard. During one event, he was playing a par- ticularly slow opponent, something that drove the Calgary curler nuts. Exasperated, Gowsell left the ice and made a phone call. About 20 minutes later, with the opposition still debating a shot, a pizza was delivered to sheet 3, where Gowsell and his team were playing. Pepperoni, anyone?

Gowsell's team discovered — as did countless other curlers who watched them — that the push broom has a lot of benefits:

- ✔ **Push brooms are easy to sweep with.** This allows the sweepers to remain effective without feeling as though their arms are going to fall off.

- ✔ **Push brooms are always in contact with the ice.** This makes them better sweeping tools.

- ✔ **Push brooms are clean!** They don't leave bits of straw all over the ice. (As the switch to push brooms took hold in Canada, ice conditions improved considerably, which led to better shot-making.)

Today, fewer and fewer corn brooms are made. They've simply been outswept by the push broom.

Most beginning curlers should start with a push broom. It's easy to use, fairly inexpensive (at least you won't be replacing it every 10 or 12 games) and provides good support when you're learning to throw the rock.

Types of push broom

If you've decided to go with a push broom, there are a number of different styles to consider.

Horse or hog hair

The earliest push brooms were made of horse or hog hair. These coarse strands provided great friction on the ice and were effective. As more and more people began to use them, however, a fault became apparent. Much as with the corn broom, the hair would fall out of the broom and end up on the ice. If curlers thought it was bad when a rock travelled over a piece of straw, it was nothing compared to seeing a rock hit a hair.

The stone would skitter sharply off in strange directions, seemingly oblivious to the forces of physics. Once a rock hit a hair, there was little the sweepers could do except watch helplessly.

As these types of incident became common in clubs, more and more curlers switched to the synthetic brush.

Synthetic

Even here, there are different styles. Some are synthetic wrapped over foam, making the head of the broom look somewhat like the upholstered arm of a chair. Others have a synthetic surface — usually made of a nylon–fabric mix — placed over a hard surface. The foam models have a bit of give to them, which some curlers like. The harder ones let you feel like you're in better contact with the surface of the ice. It's best to test out different models and pick the one you feel comfortable with.

Most of the synthetic models have another great advantage: replaceable heads. When the fabric wears out (you can tell when it gets very smooth and takes on a sort of sheen), you simply buy a new head, instead of an entire broom.

Some push brooms come with a swivel head, which allows even more contact between the broom and the ice.

Gloves

A good pair of gloves keeps your hands warm and protects them when you sweep.

The best curling gloves are made of deerskin or other leather and have elastic around the opening that lets you pull them tight. Most come with a Velcro fastener that closes across the back of the wrist.

It's important to ensure your gloves fit well. If there's too much rubbing against your hands, you're a prime candidate for some nasty blisters. To see whether you've found that perfect fit, put one of your gloves on and hold out your hand, palm up, with your fingers outstretched. You shouldn't be able to pinch any excess leather in the palm area.

Some curlers prefer to wear mitts, which keep their hands warmer. But, if you play any position other than skip, I suggest you wear gloves, since you'll be sweeping at least four rocks every end. See Chapter 6 for more on how the team is made up.

Sweaters

Outside of a place to display all your championship crests, a curling sweater really only has one purpose: to keep you warm. Depending on the temperature of the rink where you play, choose a sweater that is loose enough to allow you some movement for sweeping and for throwing stones, and warm enough to keep you comfortable.

Many clubs have their own sweaters, which show the club's colours. By all means, buy one if you're enthused and want to show your club colours and spirit, but any regular type of sweater or fleece top also does the trick.

Pants

Curling pants are specially designed for the game. When you deliver the stones, you need to stretch in the leg area, and therefore you need to get pants that will allow you to do just that.

Curling pants are much like cotton or polyester sweatpants; they have some give to them. You want a pair that won't restrict your movement and will still keep you somewhat warm.

You're best to look at a curling pro shop, located in most larger clubs, for such pants. Although there are a number of different manufacturers, most are pretty standard. The fit should be just like a normal pair of pants, with a bit more room in the waist for the times you bend over.

One thing about curling pants: They won't win you any fashion awards. Most are black and made of polyester that doesn't look all that great. But as my grandfather used to say, "Only a fool is uncomfortable." Go with comfort over style.

Another thing about curling pants. When you deliver, your trailing knee tends to spend a lot of time on the ice. For this reason, the pants wear out in the right knee (if you're right-handed) before anywhere else. If this happens to you, don't worry. It means you're throwing the stone well and probably a lot, too.

Chapter 4

The Ice

To state the obvious, curling is played on ice. The same frozen surface that hosts sports such as hockey, figure skating, speedskating, and broomball. But unlike the ice in any of these sports, the ice in curling has some pretty specific requirements that need to be met if the game is to be played properly. And as someone entertaining the idea of playing a few ends (which I assume you are if you're reading this book), it's good to know what these requirements are. Knowing how the ice should look and feel will really help improve your game.

Bad ice is a curler's worst nightmare. All the skill you've built up can be wasted on ice that isn't quick enough or doesn't have enough curl. Good ice is a curler's dream.

Hockey uses the fabled Zamboni machine to maintain ice conditions (yes, it's named after Mr. Zamboni). In curling, however, the task of looking after the ice — of preparing it before games, cleaning it up afterwards, and taking care of it in between — falls to a single (and very important) person: the *ice technician* or *icemaker*. And while the ice on a curling sheet may just look like an unwieldy frozen surface to you, it takes a lot of skill, experience, and yes, a bit of luck, to get it just right. Because so many factors affect the condition of the ice, the battle for good ice is one that never ends.

This Isn't Hockey Ice, You Know

Ice is ice, right? Just frozen water. Well, yes and no. The surface of the ice in curling needs to be as consistent and as well kept as possible. It takes a lot of tender loving care to do that.

Curling ice is kept at a colder temperature than hockey ice — usually about three or four degrees colder. This has to do with the level of *firmness*, or *hardness*. A hockey player needs to be able to dig the blades of her skates into the ice, so the ice needs to have a little give in it. A curler wants nothing of the sort. His ice needs to be so firm that nothing breaks its surface — especially the rock.

Another difference between hockey ice and curling ice is in the number of imperfections. Except for the very best arena ice, hockey ice is full of bumps and cracks, rough spots, bits of dirt here and there, and some uneven parts. But this can't happen in curling. Even the regular clubs have very high maintenance standards to keep the ice playable.

The ice on a curling sheet is usually between one and two inches thick and is applied in layers. Before the floor — which at some clubs is cement and at others, just sand — is flooded, though, it has to be cold enough for the ice to stick. Running underneath the floor is a set of pipes filled with a temperature-controlled coolant. These pipes are connected to a machine that lowers the temperature of the floor to a point where ice can form on top of it. Once the floor is cold enough, it's *flooded* with water from a large hose.

After a few initial floods, the *circles* are carefully inscribed into the ice surface, and then painted, and the *lines* (usually a sort of tape) are put down. (Some clubs now have the circles and lines painted on the floor of the facility first, and just flood right over them.) See Chapter 7 for more about the markings on the ice. The flooding continues until the ice reaches the desired thickness.

Pebbling the Ice

If you manage to slide into your seat at the local club before the start of the game, you'll see what looks like the ice technician "watering" the ice, just as she might do a garden. This happens before the start of every game. It's curling's way of preparing the playing surface for the coming action.

The ice technician is *pebbling* the ice, as shown in Figure 4-1. This is quite an unusual sight to see. The ice technician straps on or carries a tank of water that's connected to a hose with a small brass head at the end. The head is punctured with tiny holes. The hose attachment is called a *pebbling spout*; the entire tank and hose contraption is called a *pebbling machine*. The ice technician walks backwards down the ice, swinging the hose back and forth, sprinkling droplets of hot water over the entire ice surface. Hot water is used because it freezes quicker than cold water.

Figure 4-1:
The ice is pebbled before the start of every game.

After about 30 seconds, these droplets freeze into tiny bumps, similar to pebbles on a road. Hence, the name.

The pattern of laying down the pebble is also important, as — through trial and error — the ice technicians have learned where and how much needs to be applied. High-traffic areas — usually in the centre of the sheet — tend to need the most pebble, while the sides of the sheet don't need as much.

Now that you know *what* the icemaker is doing with that hose, the next question is, *"Why?"*

The *pebble* creates a bumpy, porous surface on which the rocks travel. You don't actually see the rock bumping along the pebble; it appears to travel quite smoothly.

This is because of the way a curling rock is constructed. If you turn the stone over, you see a small concave cup in the middle of it, as shown in Figure 4-2. The outer edge of this cup is a small band about a quarter-inch wide, called the *running surface*. This small ring is the only part of the stone that touches the ice.

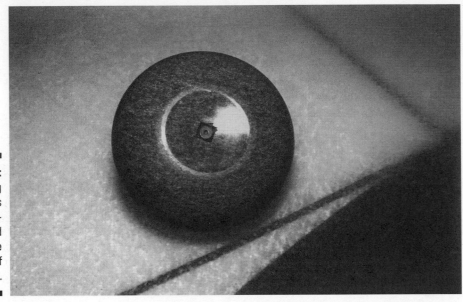

Figure 4-2:
The running
surface is
the light-
coloured
circle on the
bottom of
the rock.

If there weren't pebble on the ice, this cup and ring would act much like a suction cup and grab the ice as the stone travelled along it. Think back to your childhood days and a bow-and-arrow set. The arrows with the small suction cup tips could be tough to pull off a smooth surface such as a window, but if the outside edge of the suction cup wasn't entirely stuck to the window, air could get in and break the seal. The same is true for a curling rock. The pebble breaks the seal and allows the rock to glide down the sheet. You can test this by trying to throw a rock on ice that isn't pebbled. It takes a Herculean effort to get the stone down the sheet on un-pebbled ice. See Chapter 5 for more on how the rock is made.

The pebble on the ice wears down considerably during the course of a game. This is caused by rocks travelling repeatedly over the same part of the sheet, as well as curlers themselves walking up and down it. High humidity and increased temperatures can also cause the pebble to wear down. You might even encounter *flat spots*, areas of the ice where the pebble disappears completely. This causes the rock to grab the ice, slow down, and bend more than usual. There's that suction cup in action.

Fortunately, over the years, top ice technicians came to understand the wear and tear on the pebble and developed patterns for pebbling the ice based on where the rocks travel most. They apply more pebble to these "well-travelled" parts of the sheet, and less to others.

Bringing pebble to Germany

Up until 1969, curling in Germany was played mainly outdoors on artificial ice, with no pebble. German curlers maintained that it would only be possible to make pebbled ice indoors, where the temperature and humidity could be controlled. There had been a few attempts to produce pebbled ice — without success.

My father, William Weeks, was working — and curling — in Munich, Germany, in 1969. He returned there from a visit to Canada with a proper *pebbling spout*, and, with the assistance of his friend, Günther Hummelt, constructed a crude tank and hose assembly. They filled this thing with hot water and carted it out to a rink.

Low and behold, they produced pebbled ice.

Good news travels fast, and demand for use of the only pebbling machine in Germany increased. One club arranged to have the machine transported to and from the club just so they could have pebbled ice. It was 40 kilometres away!

My father left Germany in 1970, with a fond send-off from the curlers to whom he'd introduced the pebble. They rented out the Olympic ice stadium, installed two curling sheets, and had a farewell mini-*bonspiel* (a curling tournament) to thank him. Oh yes, and Günther Hummelt? He went on to become president of the World Curling Federation.

Maintaining the Ice

While perfectly level ice that curls is every ice technician's goal, it's not always that easy to get. Every one of these tireless workers faces a constant battle to keep the sheet clean. Although many players take it for granted, an ice technician has a tough and seemingly endless job.

These are some of the many problems that plague the ice technician in his endless quest for the perfect sheet:

- Irregular floors
- Fluctuating temperature in the pipes under the floors used to keep the ice frozen
- Fluctuating temperature and humidity of the rink
- Dirt from shoes
- Dirt from brooms
- Foot traffic up and down the ice
- Ultraviolet rays that come from artificial light sources in some arenas

Any or all of these factors can affect the ice surface. Because of this, just as with many other sporting surfaces, curling ice requires careful, consistent attention to keep it playable. And while a lot of this burden falls to the ice technician, curlers themselves also have a part to play.

Cleaning the ice

The ice is cleaned before and after every game. The ice technician uses a long, wide brush with a lamb's wool or other surface to clean it. Any bits of debris and dirt are swept up and removed. The cleaning is usually followed by the pebble application.

Breaking in the ice

Some (though not all) ice technicians go through a process where they *break in* the ice prior to the start of a game — after it's been cleaned and the pebble has been applied

Why break in the ice at all? Well, it has to do with the pebble. The pebble forms with a small peak on each water droplet. These peaks are broken off when the rocks first run over them, which causes the rocks to slow down. Consequently, you have to throw the rocks that much harder to get them down the sheet. Not good, since the harder you have to throw, the less precise your aim is. When this occurs, we say that the ice is *slow*. Breaking in the ice before the game helps avoid this, and ice technicians have developed a couple of different ways to do it.

✔ The ice technician may drag the rocks up and down the sheet using a special harness not unlike a large version of the triangular rack used to line up balls in pool. This breaks off the peaks on the droplets and gets the ice up to the proper speed right away. The process is called "boating."

✔ The ice technician may use a machine called an Ice King (see Figure 4-3). The Ice King has a long blade that, when set to a certain height, removes just the heads of the pebble. Much less labour-intensive!

Figure 4-3:
The Ice King
has a long
blade that
lops off the
top of the
pebble, so
the rocks
can travel
down the
sheet at the
right speed.

Both methods of breaking in the ice prevent the slow start that sometimes occurs at the beginning of the game. But not all clubs do this because it's time- and labour-intensive. It's more of a luxury treatment than a necessity. Because of this, it's a good idea to keep an eye on how the ice technician prepares the sheet you're going to play on. If you see that he doesn't break the ice in, expect it to be a little slower at the start of the game. It will speed up after about two ends of play.

Scraping the ice

The ice technician does most of the heavy work in ice care, and one of the heaviest jobs is *scraping* the ice.

Why does the ice need to be scraped? Because of the build-up caused by applying the pebble. If you figure that pebble is applied before every game is played, and most clubs hold as many as seven games a day on the same sheet, well, that's a lot of extra ice to deal with.

To scrape the ice, the ice technician uses the Ice King, a machine with a motorized blade, to basically shave off portions of the ice that have too much build-up and aren't level. (The Ice King is shown in Figure 4-3.) Before the advent of the Ice King, scraping was a laborious task done by hand. The new machine has saved not only time, but a few backs.

Although only a small fraction of the ice is actually removed by scraping, it still requires lots of experience to get the job done right. By watching play and seeing how rocks react, the ice technician knows the high spots on the sheet and knows what to do to bring them down. The ice is scraped on a regular basis — usually once a day.

Ice technicians may also scrape the ice to enhance the amount a rock curls. Through trial and testing, ice technicians know the proper patterns — where to scrape and in which direction — to achieve ice that allows rocks to curl a great deal. It's not a perfect science by any means, and it can easily be overdone or underdone. But a quick overnight flood can correct any mistakes.

Burning the ice

Dirt is an ice technician's worst enemy. Whether it comes off players' shoes, brooms, or even drifts down from the ceiling, it needs to be removed from the ice as soon as possible so it doesn't affect a rock travelling down it.

Bits of dirt often freeze into the ice. They can either be scraped out with the Ice King or a hand scraper, or removed by a process called *burning*. To burn the ice, a large, wheeled machine, called a *burner*, is brought out. It runs the width of the sheet and has a heated coil near ice level. As it travels down the ice at a snail's pace, it melts a thin portion of it, exposing the dirt that used to be frozen beneath. The dirt is then vacuumed up, never to plague the sheet again. At least, not that particular piece of dirt!

Many clubs have stopped burning their ice — for a number of reasons. It's very labour-intensive, often requiring two people to do it properly (one to move the burner, one to vacuum). Many ice technicians also believe that the constant melting and freezing just isn't good for the long-term condition of the ice. Some say that burning leaves small ridges in the sheet. Many top ice technicians believe that scraping achieves much more, although a number of clubs still use the burner method.

What players can do

The ice technician may know the most about maintaining the ice, and she may do the heavier tasks associated with it, but don't despair, there's plenty you, the curler, can do to keep your playing surface shipshape. In fact, it's your duty to help ensure that the ice doesn't get hacked up. Because you're on the ice constantly for long periods at a time, *you* actually make the biggest difference in the curling surface.

Clean your shoes and broom

Make sure your shoes are clean before you go on the ice. Some clubs have motorized shoe cleaners that brush off the bottom of your shoes. If your club doesn't have one, you should at the very least wipe off the bottoms with a brush or rag, especially if you've worn them outside.

The same thing goes for brooms. A small nail brush or vegetable brush can be used on the synthetic models to remove any loose particles that may be hanging on. Some clubs provide these, as well.

You may be wondering why all this apparent fuss is needed. It's necessary because dirt on the ice can get trapped under rocks and cause them to react in a strange manner. You might see a stone gliding down the sheet perfectly, only to watch in horror as it hits a piece of dirt and careens off into the side of the sheet. And I can assure you that it's especially heartbreaking when it happens on the last shot of the game.

Stay off the ice

No, I don't mean when you're playing the game. I just mean that you should exercise some caution to make sure that certain body parts (all warm, all capable of melting the ice) stay off it.

Take delivering your rock, for example. A lot of players actually slide out of the hack as they deliver a shot and then stay in their delivery position to watch the rock as it slides down the ice. Some let a hand or knee rest on the ice while they're doing this. The resulting hand or knee print in the ice can cause problems for a rock travelling over it in later ends. (Turn to Chapter 9 for more on delivering the rock.)

Try to avoid touching the ice with your hand or knee. If you do, make it brief! Hand and knee prints are common and often undetected problems for many curling clubs — but ones that are easily prevented.

Chapter 5

Rock and Roll

In all of sport, there's probably no heavier nor more awkward-looking game piece than the curling *rock* or *stone* (the terms are used interchangeably). It's tough to think of other games where many of the players can't even lift the implement that decides the score.

Once again, curling is unique. The special attributes of the curling stone are among the many things that set curling apart from other sports. Stones certainly aren't balls, and they're ten times the size of a puck. They're subtly curved and handcrafted — and you sure don't want to drop one on your toe. What's surprising is how smoothly and easily these big, cumbersome stones slide down the ice.

The stones in use today have come a long way from the first crude attempts in curling's early days. Back then, the rocks were often just chunks of stone with grips carved into them. Those gradually evolved into stones fashioned into a more or less rounded shape. Even as late as the 1870s, there still wasn't a consistent method of producing curling stones. That came much later.

Crafting a Rock

Making a curling rock is a little like carving a statue. You start with a big block of rock and chip away everything that doesn't look like a curling stone. That's an old joke, but curling is an old game, and some stones are almost ancient. Many Canadian curling clubs still use stones that are as much as 40 or 50 years old. (Depending on the amount of use, a stone can last 50 years, but the average lifespan is closer to 30 years.)

Although curling stones do wear out, when you consider the punishment they take, end after end, game after game, year after year, you have to admit that they are pretty robust. A lot of that is thanks to the way they are made.

Ailsa Craig: Another Scottish connection

When standardized stones became the norm in the late 1920s, most clubs ordered sets of them — 16 stones per sheet. All of these orders were sent to Scotland, where most curling stones were made (a Canadian company became the first non-Scottish stone maker in 1999). Up until about 1950, most of the curling stones in the world started their life as part of Ailsa Craig, a volcanic island that sits in the Firth of Clyde, off the Scottish coast. But the island was made a bird sanctuary and ruled off-limits for mining granite. So, other sources of granite were sought out. While many different types were tried — including granite from India and Canada — most of the granite used to fashion today's stones comes from Wales. The stones are still crafted in Scotland, however, and more recently, in Canada.

Types of granite used in curling stones:

- Blue Trefor: Bluish-grey in colour with white and black flecks
- Red/Brown Trefor: Reddish-brown in colour with white and black flecks
- Gray Trefor: Greyish-brown in colour with white and black flecks
- Blue Hone: Light grey in colour with white specks
- Keanie Granie: Pinkish in colour with large white and black flecks
- Ailsa Craig: Greenish in colour with large black flecks

How rocks are made

Wherever they begin their lives, all curling stones follow the same path from granite block to final product. Great chunks of granite are blasted off and shipped to Scottish or Canadian factories. These big blocks are cut down to a size closer to that of a curling stone. A hole is then drilled in the centre of the stone. Then, it is put onto a *lathe*, a grinding apparatus that spins the stone around, cutting off parts of it. More shaping takes place, and the *cup*, a small depression on the stone's top and bottom, is cut out. Next, the *striking band* is added (this is the outside middle edge of the stone, and the only part of it that isn't polished). The final trimming, shaping, and sizing — along with some polishing — is the next-to-last step. Aluminum bronze bolts are then inserted into the hole in the centre of the stone, so that the handle can be attached.

All this work is done by skilled craftsmen and can take a great deal of time. Not surprisingly, the price for a pair of stones can be in excess of $1,000.

Sizing Up Your Stone

The standardization of curling stones resulted in features that are common to all stones today. But bear in mind, no two rocks are identical! More on that later in this chapter. The stones at your local club look a lot like the ones shown in Figures 5-1 and 5-2. They weigh approximately 40 pounds, measure 5.5 inches in height and are 11.5 inches in diameter. Amazingly, a rock actually shrinks over the course of its life, going from 11.5 inches in diameter down to about 10.5 inches.

How does this happen?

The striking band

Each stone has a section called a *striking band* at its outermost point. This is the part of the stone that makes contact with other stones, as well as the boards. It's also the only part of the stone's surface that doesn't have a polished finish to it. If it were polished, bits of it would chip off, resulting in a damaged stone and lots of little polished granite bits all over the ice.

When a rock is new, the striking band is actually convex, curving away from the rounded surface of the rock. You shouldn't be able to stand a new rock on its end — the convex striking band should make it fall over. This doesn't last forever, though. Over time, the constant pounding of rock against rock and rock against board wears out the striking band to the point where it loses its convex nature and becomes flat.

When two new stones make contact, the area that actually touches is about ¼ to ½ of an inch, but as the rocks are bashed around and the convex area flattens out, the contact area can increase to 1½ inches.

"It's probably the most overlooked area of curling rock performance," says Fred Veale, of the Canada Curling Stone Company, an expert in curling rocks. "When [the striking band] goes flat, the rocks simply won't perform as they should."

When the striking band does flatten out, it causes the rocks to react differently when they meet. Two flat stones making contact won't roll very far. Two stones that still have their convex striking bands seem to have springs in them, which makes them roll farther. Think of Newton's Law: For every action, there is an equal and opposite reaction.

Figure 5-1:
The striking band is lighter than the rest of the stone.

Figure 5-2:
The running surface is the light circle in the middle of the rock (seen on the rock on the left).

The running surface

Despite the fact that the stone is large, very little of it actually touches the ice surface. The part that does is called the *running surface* (or *running edge*). It's the outside edge of a small concave cup located on either side of the stone. (The lowest point of the cup is in the middle, which is the point of insertion for the handle.) The running surface is usually about three to seven millimetres wide. Why do both sides of the rock have this cup? It's all about longevity. When one side wears out, you can flip it over and play

You can do more than just curl with your rock

Curling rocks are pretty cumbersome, but if you put your mind to it, you can find other uses for them. Here are a few less-than-usual ideas for unused curling stones.

✔ A paperweight: But you'd need an awfully big desk.

✔ A doorstop: Even a hurricane wouldn't be able to move a door held by this jam.

✔ A hammer: Don't hit your thumb with this one.

✔ An anchor: Be careful hauling this one back in.

✔ A nutcracker: The toughest walnut doesn't stand a chance.

✔ An iron: Keep your shirts nicely pressed with this iron made of granite.

✔ A wildflower press: Preserve that corsage from your high school prom.

✔ A sun hat: Just think how strong your neck muscles will be.

✔ A barbell: You can get all pumped up.

✔ A game piece: For the biggest Monopoly board ever.

using the other side. Rocks are pretty handy that way. (Since the handle is removable, it can be attached to whichever side is up.)

In days gone by, the cup's diameter was slightly different on either side, with one cup being wider than the other. The reason for this stems back many years, to when much curling took place out-of-doors. When games were held outside, the small cup was used. When play moved inside, the larger cup took over. Some of these stones are still in play in different parts of the world, but today's stones generally have two similar sides.

If you look closely at your stone, you'll find that it carries a *scribe line* etched thinly into it, usually just over the striking band (or below it, depending on which side is up). The scribe line is an important indicator for the ice technician; it lets him track the amount of time each side of the stone is used.

How a Rock Curls

The game of curling has been made popular by something that has baffled some of the greatest minds in the world. Namely, that the stone *curls*, or *bends*, on the ice as it travels down the sheet.

Exactly how a rock curls has been the subject of much debate over the years — and even the topic of several papers published in credible scientific journals. The fact is, curling stones do strange things when they're on an icy rink — things that no object does on any other surface.

A stone curls because friction between the stone and the ice — as well as a small, microthin layer of water that melts underneath the stone — causes one side of the rock to turn faster than the other (the outside is turning faster than the inside). The maximum amount of curl occurs when the speed at which the stone travels down the ice equals the speed of the turn of the handle.

From your point of view, when you throw the stone, you purposely turn the handle either clockwise or counterclockwise, depending on which way you want your rock to bend. The rotation shouldn't be too fast; your rock should only turn about two-and-a-half to three revolutions the entire trip down the ice. When you first release it, your rock won't curl too much. In fact, on most ice surfaces, it won't begin to curl until it gets about one-third to halfway down the sheet. It usually curls the greatest amount as it slows down.

So much of how your stone curls depends on the ice conditions in the club you're playing in. Sometimes your stone will curl a total of six feet or more. Other days, the same shot might only move a foot or so. There's nothing you can do to make the stone curl more or, with the exception of sweeping, less. To play well, you have to keep a sharp eye on how the ice is reacting and play your shots accordingly.

Thankfully, you don't have to be a scientist to curl or understand why stones bend. You just have to accept that they *do* bend. Besides, it would be an awfully boring game if the stones just travelled straight.

Having said that, you *do* have to be aware of the fact that stones won't always curl the same amount. The amount of curl will vary, depending on the conditions of the ice and the particular stone you're throwing.

There is even something called *negative ice*. Negative ice causes a rock to curl in the direction opposite what you intended. This has more to do with the ice than the stones, but it is something to keep an eye out for. Negative ice happens when the ice has a tilt to it. If you are throwing a stone that should move from right to left, but the ice is slanted from left to right, your stone has quite an uphill battle to complete the shot as you intended. In fact, it won't complete it; gravity will pull it in the direction of the tilt, from left to right.

As Unique as a Snowflake (Just Heavier)

When you arrive at a curling club, the stones are lined up behind the sheets. There are 16 stones on each sheet divided into two groups of 8, each group a different colour.

HEART & SOUL

No stone unturned

Being familiar with my opponent's stones once allowed me to win an important game. My team had advanced to the quarter-finals of the Canada Life Bonspiel in Toronto. This tournament was one of the largest in the world. Making it to the quarter-finals was quite an achievement.

Early in the game, we recognized that the skip on the other team had one stone that was much slower than his other one. At that time (I'm not telling how long ago it was), individual stones weren't numbered. You just had to hope you picked the same two each time you came to throw. But my teammates quickly identified the "bad" rock. At the finish of each end, they jumped up to clean off the stones that were in play and made sure that this heavy stone was pushed way back into the corner so that when the next end was played, it would be the last stone thrown. Since the skip throws last in an end, that stone was his. (More on which team members throw when in Chapter 6.)

Sure enough, time after time, the opposing skip came up embarrassingly short with his second stone. He wasn't able to figure out what was going wrong until later on, and by that time, it was too late.

Most clubs now use a molded plastic top — it's usually yellow, red, or blue — that covers most of the top of the stone, and also forms the handle. These types of handle also have the sheet number and the stone number — from one to eight — engraved on them so that each stone can be identified.

Although most curling stones look the same, each one is different. Each stone is individually made, and is therefore subject to all the natural flaws of that process. As well, stones are subject to bumps and drops of every description over the course of many games. They will be hit with great force, they will run over dirt and straw on the ice, and they will be hammered into the backboards or the hack. Ouch!

You need to realize that every rock is unique. Some will curl more than others, and some will need to be thrown harder than others. Since you throw the same two stones throughout the game, you should get to know their tendencies and quirks. This also gives you an advantage over your opponent.

I keep track in a small book of the different rocks at my home club. For instance, I know that the yellow No. 5 stone on sheet three curls more than the other stones on that sheet. Over time, I've paired the stones up as best I can so that when I step onto the ice, I know exactly which two stones each player on my team should throw. This can give your team a real advantage. Trust me, my notebook is well used. Don't just get to know your own team's stones. Get to know your opposition's, as well. If my opponent is throwing that yellow No. 5 stone, I know that my next shot won't curl quite as much. I can adjust my shot accordingly.

How Rocks Get Fixed

Although they are made of granite, curling stones *do* wear out. The parts of the stone that wear out the most are the striking band and the running surface. It's pretty obvious why the running surface wears out; years of sliding over the ice like that would wear anything (or anyone) out. But a lot of curlers — even experts — forget about the "abuse" the striking band takes.

Fixing the striking band

When new, the striking band is convex in shape, but it becomes flat over years of use, absorbing more of the force when the rocks collide. The rocks don't react properly when this happens. They may not roll as much after they hit.

To correct a flattened striking band, the rock is *re-profiled* by shaping the striking band back into a convex.

But it's not always that easy. Some granite is just too dense to allow for the grinding that's necessary to restore that convex shape to the striking band. Ailsa Craig, also known as *common green*, is one type of granite that doesn't yield to re-profiling. When the striking bands on these rocks go flat, they've unfortunately reached the end of their lifespan.

Fixing the running surface

Year after year of use, not to mention misuse, can cause the running surface, or running edge (that's that 3- to 7-millimetre-wide edge on which the stone travels) to get pitted, flattened out, and otherwise damaged, which prevents the rock from curling properly.

Pitting occurs when moisture gets into the granite, which is a porous material. When this happens, tiny holes form in the running surface. The edges of these holes are sharp — so sharp that they might even leave scratch marks on the ice.

Pitting can happen in many ways. One of the most common is when rocks are brought out of storage at the beginning of the season and placed on the ice. Their temperature is often quite high compared to that of the ice. When warm rock meets cold ice, it can sometimes freeze and become sort of stuck. When you try to move the rock, a few tiny pieces of it might even come off. On very badly pitted stones, you can actually see the snow that builds up in the tiny holes.

Championship rocks

Great care is taken to provide the best curling conditions at championship events. The rocks used in these games are very carefully selected. In the simplest sense, the stones used for events such as the world championships are no different from the ones you use in your club. They are the same weight and size, for example. But there's a difference between the ice in arenas, where most of these big tournaments are played, and the ice in a club. Rocks tend to react differently on arena ice — with the most common complaint being that they don't curl enough.

For this reason, a careful search for just the right stones always takes place. Unfortunately, without actually testing them, there's no way to determine how a stone will curl on arena ice. So, rocks are taken from local clubs and tried out on the arena surface to see how they react. When ones that curl are found, they are dutifully noted.

One set of championship rocks belongs to the Manitoba Curling Association and is considered the best set when it comes to arena ice. These rocks have actually been fitted with a certain type of insert, which allows them to curl more on arena ice. These stones are often carefully boxed up in wooden crates and shipped to the site of the national or world championship, just so that good curling conditions can be guaranteed. Talk about star treatment.

For a long time, experts tried to find the perfect way to recondition the running surface of stones. It was thought that sharpening would work — and on some stones, it did. But the sharpening came close to ruining other stones. The results weren't consistent. Another attempt at reconditioning involved polishing the running surface. That, too, had mixed results.

The most successful method of repairing the running surface to date is to actually cut out a portion of the middle of the stone and replace it. A skilled craftsman takes an existing rock and cuts out a section on the bottom of it (and perhaps the top) measuring about 6.5 inches in diameter and ¾ of an inch deep, and replaces it with a new piece of granite, carefully fashioned to fit the hole.

The process is definitely labour-intensive, but less expensive than buying new stones. It can add another 30 or so years to a rock's life.

Chapter 6

The Rink

*L*et me save you the effort of flipping back to Chapter 4, where I talk about the special characteristics of curling ice. This is not another chapter on curling ice — you haven't lost your marbles, and neither, as far as I can tell, have I. This is a chapter about the curling team — who's on it and what each team member does. I also give you some tips on forming your own team, and remind you (again and again, because it's so important) that while the individual players have to be good and have to carry their weight, it's really the team as a whole — the unit — that has to gel if you want to play well and win. It's kind of an elusive thing to catch, but trust me, there's nothing quite like it. I've played on enough rinks that *have* caught it — and haven't — to know.

In curling, a team is called *a rink*, and is made up of four players. That can be confusing, because the building the rink plays in can also be called a rink. And just to mix things up even more, when the rink steps onto the ice at the rink, the game begins with an *end*.

An *end* is similar to an inning in baseball, with an entire curling game consisting of eight or ten ends. An end consists of 16 rocks played between two teams. Each team throws 8 rocks; each player throws 2. When each rink has played its 8 rocks, the end is complete and the score can be tallied.

Despite some of these baffling terms, one thing is clear: Curling is a team game. That may sound like a simplistic statement, but every shot of every game requires the skills of the rink as a whole. Every stone that travels down the ice has had some input from each member of the rink. While one player throws the rock, two more sweep. At the other end of the ice, the fourth player decides where the rock is to be thrown and tells the sweepers when to put their brushes to the ice.

In fact, curling may be the most cooperative team sport ever. There are a lot of times in other "team sports" when the action focuses on a single player:

- In baseball, only the pitcher throws the ball and only the batter hits it. Several innings can pass before a player, say an outfielder, has anything to do that affects the game.

- In hockey, goals are scored one player at a time. Players often sit on the bench for long stretches with no input into the final score.

But curling is different. (I know, I've been saying this a lot, driving the point home. Guess what? I'm going to keep saying it.) In curling, all four team members contribute to the outcome of every stone that's delivered. Each player has a job to do in order for the rink to have a chance to win. And the score isn't determined until all the rocks of an end have been played.

The Team as a Whole

A curling rink is made up of four players:

- The *skip*
- The *third* (also called the *vice-skip*, the *vice*, or the *mate*)
- The *second*
- The *lead*

The lead and second together are called the *front end* while the third and skip are the *back end*. Each position requires certain skills and therefore a certain type of player.

All four team members throw stones alternating with the other team. The order of play is the lead, second, third, and skip. The skip is the only player on the team who doesn't take a turn sweeping. The other three players sweep whenever they aren't shooting. Table 6-1 lays out which team member throws which stones in an end, and which corresponding team members sweep those stones.

Table 6-1 Who Shoots and Who Sweeps the Shots Thrown in an End		
Shot #	*Who Throws*	*Who Sweeps*
1 and 2	lead	second and third
3 and 4	second	lead and third
5 and 6	third	lead and second
7 and 8	skip	lead and second

The Lead

When you first start to curl, you'll often find yourself in the position of lead. That's because most curlers assume that if your team messes up with the first two shots of an end, you can still recover with the next six. While there is some truth to this — which is why players new to the game usually start out playing lead — it's still a challenging position that can have a huge effect on the outcome of an end, and indeed, a game.

The two most important rocks in an end of curling are the eighth rock, thrown by the skip, and the first rock, delivered by the lead. The first stone sets up the entire end. It determines how the end will be played, whether defensively or offensively, and often plays a part in the final score.

When you play your next game, take note of how many times a lead stone remains in play at the conclusion of the end. You might be surprised to see how vital those first two rocks can be — even after the other six have been thrown.

For that reason (and others that I get to later in this section), the lead is a very important part of any curling team.

Throwing stones

The person playing lead must have great *touch*. This means you can quickly and accurately judge the weight of the shot you are throwing, and can increase it or decrease it in small amounts with ease. As lead, you must have great aim — delivering the rock exactly where you're asked. If the lead rock ends up even a couple of feet farther down the sheet than called for, it can change the entire outlook of the end.

As well as placing stones, if you're the lead, you have to be pretty good at getting rid of them, too — the opposition's, not yours. Taking out opposition stones is sometimes as important as keeping your own. If the lead fails to remove a shot, the complexion of the end can change drastically. See Chapter 10 for more on taking out opposition stones.

Being first to throw each end means the lead is the first one to pick up on any changes in the ice. A good lead notes things like whether the ice is getting faster or slower, and whether a rock is curling more or less than in previous ends. The lead should relay this information to the rest of the players before they shoot.

Sweeping

After throwing your two stones, you turn into a sweeper for the rink's remaining shots in the end. You sweep shots delivered by the second, third, and the skip.

What does this require of you? You'd better be in good shape — really good shape. As lead, you must be able to sweep six consecutive rocks in every end of the game. That's a lot of sweeping, with only a break to shoot your own rocks in between. And the game has no timeouts or breaks, either. You just finish one end and then start right into the next, adding to the physical demands of sweeping.

Physically sweeping a rock is just one part of the job of brushing (the terms *sweeping* and *brushing* are used interchangeably). You must also be a good judge of how fast the rock is travelling to reach its intended target. If the rock doesn't seem to have enough momentum to get to the proper place, you must know enough to sweep it. If it seems to be moving too fast, then you must know enough not to sweep. In both cases, this is information that can be immediately passed on to the skip at the other end of the sheet to help him make quick decisions on what to do with a shot.

Sweeping instructions are relayed from the skip most of the time, but a good lead knows how to recognize the speed of the stone in relation to its destination and take the necessary action.

The lead is often the spark plug on a rink — the player who encourages the others and keeps the team's spirits up. The lead is also the player who takes the most ribbing.

Lots of teams jokingly maintain the myth of the lead as the least important player. Some rinks make the lead carry all the brooms on and off the ice. This is purely team fun, however, and has nothing to do with the actual importance of the position.

The Second

There can be up to four rocks in play by the time the second comes to shoot — two from your team and two from the opposition. Your team's strategy for the end should be pretty clear at this point.

Throwing stones

The second is usually the best hitter on the team. That's because the second is often called upon to *play hits* — a defensive shot to remove opposition rocks. If you're second, you need to be able to throw both accurately and hard.

But playing hits isn't the second's only job. On the flip side, you also need to throw delicate offensive draw shots, placing the stones exactly where the skip calls for them. This has become especially true since the introduction of the *free guard zone rule*. The free guard zone rule is an offense-stimulating rule brought into curling in 1994. It means that stones placed in front of the house can't be removed until after the lead's stones have been thrown. This rule means that the best defense is often a good offense. I explain the free guard zone rule in more detail in Chapter 8. Chapter 10 explores the different types of shot and when to use them.

Sweeping

As second, you sweep the shots delivered by the third, the skip, and then by the lead at the beginning of the next end. I have always found playing second more physically demanding than playing lead. Even though you both sweep six rocks in a row, the lead gets a break after the skip rock to deliver his shots in the next end, while you have to keep right on sweeping. You tend to sweep the third and skip rocks pretty hard, which makes it extra tiring.

If you're the second, you need to be a good sweeper and a good judge of weight. You usually confer constantly with the lead about the speed of the ice and how it changes through the course of the game. Both of you might use a stopwatch to time the rocks and compare the results.

The second also has to work with the lead on a system for sweeping. Since the two of you sweep the last four stones together, you have to decide things like who sweeps closer to the rock, and, if you're able to switch sides, who sweeps on which side of the stone. More on sweeping in Chapter 11.

The Front End: Working Together

Because they do a lot together, the front end (the lead and second) almost works as a team within a team. Not only are their duties quite similar, they're also responsible for getting a lot of pertinent information and passing it on to

Don't just stand there — make sure you're in the right place

It's hard to think that you might get penalized for just standing around, but in competitive curling, that's exactly the case. And while it's not a penalty in fun games, you should know where to position yourself when waiting your turn to play. (This is especially important if you are lead or second, because you spend the most time on the sidelines.)

In general, if you're not the skip and you're not throwing, you should stand between the two *Hog lines* off to the side of the sheet. (The Hog lines are located 21 feet from the *Tee lines*. In order to be in play, a rock must cross the Hog line at the target end of the ice.) For more on the Hog lines, Tee lines, and other markings on the ice, turn to Chapter 7.

Try to stand still so you don't distract the player on the other team while he delivers his stone.

If it's your turn to throw, you can stand behind the sheet of ice — again, keeping very still — while your opposition throws her stones.

Not standing in the proper place is one of the most common violations in curling. And while there's no hard penalty, like losing a point or having to remove a rock, it is frowned upon just the same.

the third and skip. They might report on the speed and condition of the ice, or on the degree of its curl. The back end (the third and skip) depends on the front end to keep them informed about this stuff. They're worrying about other things, as I explain later in this chapter.

It's important for the front end to keep quiet during decision-making, unless the skip asks for help. Leave the strategy up to the skip and the third. If they ask what you think, then, by all means, let them know. But if you butt in, it can cause a lot of problems, sort of like having too many cooks in the kitchen.

Another time you should avoid giving an unsolicited opinion is when the skip comes down to throw a shot. If I'm playing skip, and am in the hack getting ready, and my second or lead comes along and suggests an alternative shot, 99 percent of the time, all it does is throw off my concentration. By the time the skip comes down to shoot, he's sure of the shot he wants to throw. Let him throw it.

You're probably thinking, "Okay, I'm playing either lead or second, minding my own business and not bugging the skip, but when do I know how to sweep?" It's up to the skip (or when the skip is throwing, the third) to tell you when the rock is curling too much or if it's not on the *line* (the line on which the stone travels so that it ends up where it's wanted). On experienced teams, however, the lead and second are responsible for sweeping if the

The call to sweep

Your skip or third will let you know — usually in no uncertain terms — when to start sweeping a rock. He'll yell down the ice at you and you'll put your brush to the ice.

There are lots of variations on the call. It could be something as simple as:

"Yes!" or "Sweep!"

Then again, your skip might go with something more original, like:

"Hard!" or "Hurry!" or "Get on it!"

If he really wants you to sweep hard, you might get a combination such as "Hurry hard!" or "Real hard!"

Generally speaking, you can determine how much sweeping is needed by the amount of panic in the skip's voice.

When the skip or third wants you to stop sweeping, the most common instruction you hear is "Whoa." Sometimes you hear "Off," and if he really doesn't want you to sweep (meaning the rock has to either slow up or curl more) you might get a "Right off."

stone is light — that is, if it appears that it will fall short of the intended target. More on sweeping in Chapter 11.

Sometimes when the skip is playing a shot, he and the third both call out instructions for the sweepers. They'll often make opposite calls — one telling you to sweep, the other to stop. What should you do? Always defer to the team member in the house — that's the skip, or the third when the skip is shooting.

Get to know your skip's voice so you aren't confused when you play. In some clubs, there can be four, six, or ten games going on at once, and it's easy to mistake voices. If in doubt, look up — you can usually tell by the skip's expression what's being asked for, even if you can't hear it.

The Third

The third is the best shotmaker on many teams, and the most well-rounded player, too. A good third has all the shots, is an able sweeper, and has a keen sense of the game's strategy. The third works with the skip in deciding the team's overall strategy for a game, and, in many cases, is the point of contact between the skip and the front end.

Throwing stones

The strong suit of any third should be his draw shot. More often than not, you're called on to play delicate draws that are crucial in deciding the outcome of the end.

Thirds also play a lot of *soft weight hits*, stones that just tap another one back or move them around in the house, positioning them for later in the end. He may also play regular *takeout shots,* stones that remove other stones with force.

A third who is a skilled shotmaker *sets the table* for the skip. That is, he plays key shots that set up the final stones of the end, which are thrown by the skip. If you have a good third on your team, the skip's shots become much easier. If you have a great third, he can really take the pressure off the skip's last rocks by throwing terrific shots himself.

Holding the broom

As the third, you have to *hold the broom* for the skip while he throws the seventh and eighth rocks. (This is something the skip does for all the other players as they play their rocks. The broom acts like a target at which players throwing the stones aim.) I discuss holding the broom in more detail when I talk about the position of skip, later in this chapter.

After you throw your two rocks, you go down to the far end of the sheet and join the skip. When it's his turn to throw, the two of you decide on the shot you want to play and on how much ice you need to make the shot. Before the skip heads up the ice to throw the shot, he'll tell you where to position the broom. You repeat the process for the skip's final shot. Note that while you hold the broom for the shot, depending on the makeup of your team, you and the skip jointly decide on the shot to be played. Sometimes the skip will just tell you the shot he wants to play. At other times, he might ask you what you think. The bottom line, though, is that the skip has final say.

When the skip is playing his stones, it's up to the third to call sweeping for the front end. If you're playing third, you need to be perfectly clear on the shot the skip wants and how he wants to achieve it.

The back end (the third and the skip) has to be completely in sync so they can *call the sweepers* to do the right thing for the shot. (If you want the players to sweep, you *call the sweepers on.* If, on the other hand, you don't want them to sweep, then you *call the sweepers off.*) It's sort of like the left hand knowing what the right hand is doing.

Keeping score

Another job of the third is to mark the score. At the conclusion of the end, you and the opposition third must agree on the points scored in that end. Once you reach an agreement, the rocks are removed and the next end begins. The third on the team that scores hangs up the points on the scoreboard.

It's important that you and the opposition third verbally agree on the points scored in the end before the rocks are removed. Don't assume your opponent thinks the same way you do or you may be in for a rude surprise. Let's say there are two stones that are pretty close. If you remove them before the opposition third has confirmed, he could very well dispute it. If you don't get confirmation and two stones are fairly close, you won't get to count what might have been an extra point. In other words, if you don't confirm it, you don't get to count it.

If I'm playing third I will say, "That's two for us," to the other third and wait for a confirmation. If I don't get it, then I invite the other third to have a look. If there's any question, we usually measure the rocks. See Chapter 8 for descriptions of the different types of device used to measure rocks.

The coin toss

The third takes the coin toss at the start of the game that determines which rink gets to play last rock in the first end. Almost without exception, the winning team *does* take last stone. Having last rock is a big advantage. Because your team shoots last, you get final say in the score for that opening end. It means you can get off to a fast start. For the rest of the game, the last rock is awarded to the team that doesn't score in the previous end. So if you score two points in the first end, your opposition gets last rock in the second end. In most club games, the losing team gets to choose which set of rocks they want to use. At important championships, the loser of the toss gets nothing because the tournament organizers usually assign the colour of the stones.

The Skip

The skip is much like the quarterback on a football team. He is the team leader. The skip tells the other team members how and where to play their shots. The skip dictates the strategy of the game. The skip delivers the final two stones of every end.

The skip also gives the team its name. Curling rinks are referred to as the "Smith team" or the "Jones team," after the skip's last name.

Throwing stones

The skip is also usually the best all-around player on the rink (with the exception of sweeping, because the skip doesn't sweep any stones). As skip, you must be able not only to throw *all* the shots, but to do so under pressure, oftentimes with the game on the line. It takes a cool customer to *skip a team* — when you win, it's great, when you lose, that loss can rest squarely on your shoulders.

Understanding strategy

Besides being a great shotmaker, the skip must excel at the strategy of the game. As many games are lost because of poor strategic decisions as of poor shooting. Making all the shots in a game means nothing if you aren't putting them in the right spots.

And it's not only about the shots your team plays. You must also keep a constant eye on your opposition to figure out their strengths and weaknesses. Often, I've changed the way I call my shots because I know a player on the other team has problems with one type of shot. I know one team in my club that is much better at playing draw shots rather than takeouts, for example. Against them, I get my teammates to play shots that will force the other team to play takeouts rather than draws. For instance, I might ask my lead to play the first shot of the end right into the house rather than playing a shot in the free guard zone, as is usually the case. The other team will then usually have to play a takeout (more on this type of thinking in Chapter 14 on strategy). It's even more important to know the tendencies of the other skip. Does she like to draw or hit? Does she like to throw the in-turn or the out-turn? Knowing this type of information can allow you to force her into playing a shot she may not be comfortable with.

You can hone your understanding of curling's more strategic aspects by reading a book on curling's strategy. But you can hone it even more by playing. Every end of every game gives you experience that is vital for any skip. (Now of course, what fool writing a book that contains a vital chapter of its own on curling strategy wouldn't promote it? I cover it in Chapter 14.)

Because of this need for experience, most players usually spend a few years at other positions — learning the game, gaining knowledge, and developing their talents — before becoming skip. It's rare for any player to jump onto the ice for the first time and immediately start skipping. It takes time to understand the situations and the strategy, and there's no better on-the-job training than playing for an experienced skip.

You can learn a great deal from players who've been around the game and skipped for a number of years. Watch where they play the stones in certain situations, such as when they have last rock and when they don't. Observing other skips is one of the first steps to becoming a good skip on your own.

Reading the ice

As skip, you need to know where to put the broom down for the target. This changes depending on the particular shot you're calling for, the end you're playing, even the entire game. So another of the skip's qualities is an ability to *read the ice*. That means you must be able to determine how the ice will react with every shot thrown, and to set up the proper target for it.

Being able to read the ice is key, because if the skip puts the target in the wrong place, it really doesn't matter whether the stone *hits the broom* (hits the target) or not. The shot is missed because the target was in the wrong place to begin with. The skip didn't read the ice well.

It takes skill and experience to read the ice properly. This comes through trial and error over the course of many games, as well as from getting to know the idiosyncrasies of the sheets in your club. I know that at my club, for example, on one sheet next to the wall, a rock curls a great deal towards that wall. On another sheet, I know that a rock going down the centre curls more with the in-turn than the out-turn. (More on in-turns and out-turns in Chapter 9). I've gotten to know these quirks over the many years I've played on those particular sheets. But that doesn't mean I rest on this knowledge.

Every time I step onto those sheets, I keep a close watch on how the stones react as they come down the ice. Every sheet changes a little bit for every game, so you just never know. The ice is never the same twice, and it's the job of the skip to understand just what's happening. You do this by watching every stone — both yours and your opponents' — come down the ice. You log these shots in your memory bank as the game goes on and try to remember them when you need to throw a stone down that part of the sheet.

Follow the play throughout the game and watch for changes in the ice. Don't assume it will stay the same all game long.

It's also important that you watch the delivery of the player throwing the stone. Don't just look where the other skip holds the broom, because the player throwing the stone may not actually release the stone at that broom. If your opposing skip puts the broom down on the ice right on the Centre line as a target and the player comes a bit wide, you must log that in the back of your mind, as well. Make note of where the stone came out and where it stopped. You'll be able to use that later in the game, should the situation arise.

I've even known a few teams to intentionally try to deceive their opponents. The skip puts the broom down but the players are really aiming at one of his legs, just to try to throw off the other skip.

Forming the Team

In many cases, it's the skip who gets the team together. Just as you might have a captain pick the team in a pickup baseball game, the skip usually asks other players to join a rink.

As you put your team together, follow these steps:

1. **Decide what type of players you want:** As skip, you need to know the qualities of a good lead, second, and third, and know how to assess talent accordingly. Choose players that complement your own playing style.

2. **Decide what the rink's objectives are:** If you want to play three times a week, for example, it's no good asking a player who can only commit to one game a week. If you want to try to play for a national championship, then your rink will likely have a different makeup from one that just wants to play in the club for fun.

3. **Contact your prospective team members:** I like to meet face-to-face with players I want on my team and ask them to play with me. I tell them which position I want them to play and the objectives of the rink.

Before you talk to any prospective player, have an idea of how often you want to play and at what level. That can be as important as the talents of the players on your team.

Once your team is formed, get to know how they throw the stones and their *tendencies* — how they slide, how they like to sweep, whether they prefer the in-turn or the out-turn. This helps you understand how to call the game for your team.

For example, I know the fellow who plays lead for me has a tendency to come wide on his out-turns. I therefore adjust the broom accordingly by moving it closer to the rock when he is shooting. I know he will hit the spot I want the rock to come out on, even though he won't actually hit the broom. Get to know your team and it will help you play better as a unit.

Putting It All Together

Curling is, first and foremost, a team game. That means the rink is greater than the sum of its individual players. Playing well together is one of the keys to a successful rink. Teamwork depends on a number of factors:

- ✔ **Communication:** All team members must know which shots are being played so they can contribute. If the sweepers don't know where a stone is supposed to end up, they can mess up the sweeping. If the player delivering the rock doesn't know what weight to throw, the shot will likely be missed. Make sure your team communicates before every shot.

- ✔ **Knowing their role:** Each team member must know the role he is playing and be willing to play it. The lead should want to play lead and understand what that position requires. The same is true for the second, third, and skip.

- ✔ **Having a plan:** All team members must agree on the goals for the game about to be played and for the season as a whole — before they step on the ice at the start of the year.

- ✔ **Getting along:** All team members must like being with each other, on and off the ice. I think this is the most important ingredient of a team that works. You will spend a lot of time together, so it's important that you enjoy each other's company. I've always found that teams that get along off the ice play better on it.

Chapter 7

Hogs and Hacks: Understanding the Playing Field

· ·

In This Chapter

▶ Sizing up the sheet

▶ Getting around the circles

▶ Understanding all the lines

▶ Getting a grip on the hack

· ·

Curling can be a strange-looking game to those who've never seen it before. And it can be extremely difficult to try to understand the playing field, with all those lines and circles.

It can look a little like shuffleboard or maybe a giant game of darts. But once you learn the purpose of all those markings, it begins to take shape. It's really a very uncomplicated sport, especially when you consider that it's been played for hundreds of years in a way that has remained largely unchanged.

Understanding the playing surface is a pretty important part of learning to curl. If you are going to figure out how to play the game, you must have a good fix on the playing field.

The Game

To better understand the playing field in curling, a quick refresher course on the basics of the game isn't a bad idea.

The objective of the game is to slide large, granite stones down an ice surface towards the *house* (that's the group of circles at either end of the *sheet*). A team scores one point for every rock it has closer to the centre of the house than the other team. (This doesn't always mean that you aim for the bull's-eye, however.)

A great deal of strategy comes into play to determine exactly where you place your rocks. Many times, you don't want your stones to end up in the house at all. Because of the role strategy plays in the game, curling is often referred to as "chess on ice." I discuss strategy in Chapter 14.

Every team has four players — the *lead*, the *second*, the *third* (or *mate,* or *vice*), and the *skip*. Each player throws two rocks in each *end*, alternating with the player on the opposition team who is playing the same position. So (assuming your team is throwing first), your lead throws a stone, followed by the lead on the other team. Both leads throw again and then it's your second's turn, and then the turn of the second on the opposition, and so on, until all players have thrown their two rocks.

An end is similar to an inning in baseball. It is one frame, or one section, of the overall contest. When all 16 rocks — 8 for each team — have been thrown, the end is over. The points are allocated after the 16th rock has been thrown. I discuss the game's scoring system in more detail in Chapter 8, but for now, you should know that only one team can score in any given end. The end can also be *blanked,* meaning there is no score. This occurs when an end finishes with no rocks in the house.

The lead, second, and third also take turns sweeping the stones as they travel down the sheet. Sweeping makes a rock travel farther and curl less. When one player is delivering the stone, two more are sweeping it. The skip doesn't sweep any stones; she instead stands at the far end of the sheet and indicates to the player throwing where she would like the stone to end up. The skip is like the quarterback, calling the plays and determining the strategy. Chapter 11 offers more on the ins and outs of sweeping.

The name of the game

Oddly enough, the fact that rocks curl as they travel down the ice isn't the reason why curling is called curling. Curlers didn't begin to purposely twist the rocks as they delivered them until 1900 or so, and as we know, curling dates back several hundred years before then. So how did curling get its name?

One theory is that the name comes from the sound that the rocks used to make as they travelled across the frozen ponds — a sound that was once described as "horse murmuring," in a poem written by James Graeme in the 1750s.

This led to curling being called "the roaring game" — because it sounded as though the rocks "roared" over the Scottish lochs.

Another idea for the name comes from the word *kuting* or *quoiting*, which was a term used for rocks in the 1600s. Perhaps, over the years, the words evolved into the term we are familiar with today: *curling*. No one is quite certain, however, and as with so many aspects of the game, the origins of its name remain shrouded in the mists of time.

As the rocks travel down the ice, they bend — either left to right or right to left. This is one of the qualities of the game that makes it so interesting. The direction of the bend is determined by which way the rock is spinning. If you turn the handle on the rock clockwise (known as an *in-turn* for right-handers), the rock bends from left to right. Conversely, if you turn it counterclockwise, the rock curls from right to left (known as an *out-turn*).

Another one of the skip's jobs is to figure out how much the rock will bend on each type of shot. (No two sheets are alike; they each have a different amount of curl, and this amount can differ from one night to another.) Once she's done that, she puts her broom down on the ice as a target for the player throwing the stone to aim at. The player delivers the stone at the broom, turns it the proper way — this is called *giving it the handle* — and hopes it has the right combination of weight and turn to end up in the spot the skip called for.

At the conclusion of the end, all the rocks that are still in play are removed and the game continues in the other direction, with rocks now being thrown at the house at the other end of the sheet. The direction of play alternates this way from end to end. A game usually consists of either eight or ten ends. Most club or fun games are eight ends, which takes about two hours to play. Games of a more serious nature last for ten ends, and take about two-and-a-half hours to play. If there is a tie, an extra end is played to determine the winner. To up the ante, some of the competitive games have time limits, with each team allotted a certain amount of time to finish the game. If one of the teams fails to complete the game in time, it forfeits, and the game automatically goes to the other team.

The Sheet

With the game basics under your belt, it's time to turn to the playing surface itself and get a better understanding of it.

At first glance, curling ice looks like a long slab of frozen water with a couple of bull's-eyes at either end. It is not a wide surface by other sports' standards, and there are a number of lines at various parts of the ice, all with meaning — some official, some not.

Each lane — known as a *sheet* — is 146 feet long. The number of sheets varies from club to club. Some have just one, while others, such as the massive Avonlea Curling Club in Toronto, have 16. There is no standard number of sheets per club, but the more common layouts are either four or six sheets.

The width of the sheet depends on where in the world you play. In Canada, the rules dictate that a sheet of ice be 14 feet 2 inches wide, while under international rules, the width is stretched by an additional 14 inches to 15 feet 4 inches. Figure 7-1 (on the next page) is a diagram that shows you what a Canadian curling sheet looks like.

Don't worry about memorizing the exact measurements of the sheet. There's no quiz before your first game. There are, however, a number of other parts of the sheet that you should be comfortable with before you step onto the ice for your first couple of games. These include

- ✔ The rings at either end of the sheet
- ✔ The different-sized circles and what they mean
- ✔ The various lines on the sheet
- ✔ The contraptions wedged into the ice at either end of the sheet

The House

The curling sheet is marked by two sets of concentric circles at either end. Each set of circles, which bear an uncanny resemblance to a bull's-eye in darts or archery, is known as the *house*. It also goes by *rings* or *circles*. Your team scores points by having rocks in the house, but that doesn't mean you throw every rock so it ends up there. As I point out in Chapter 14, it's sometimes better to have rocks in front of the house.

The house is made up of four concentric circles:

- ✔ **The 12-foot:** This is the outermost circle, so named because it has a *diameter* (the length from one side of the circle to the other passing through the middle) of 12 feet.

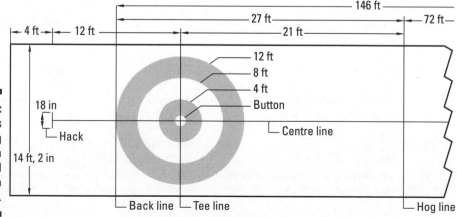

Figure 7-1: The sheet is 146 feet long and is like a shuffleboard court in appearance.

✔ **The 8-foot:** This is the next circle in, with a diameter of — you guessed it — 8 feet.

✔ **The 4-foot:** This is the next circle in from the 8-foot, with a diameter of 4 feet.

✔ **The Button:** This is the circle in the centre of the house. The size of the Button varies depending on the club you're playing at, but it's generally 1 foot in diameter, just big enough to allow a rock to cover it.

The Button is often enlarged for televised events (to about 2 feet in diameter) to accommodate a sponsor logo, shown from a camera located directly above the sheet. At the Brier (the Canadian men's championship), the event sponsor, Nokia, has its name and corporate logo right in the centre of the enlarged button. This is just a visual change, however; it has no effect on the way the game is played.

✔ **The Tee:** This is the small hole in the centre of the house. It comes into play when the distance between two opposing rocks and the centre of the house is too close to call using the naked eye alone. When this happens, a device called a *measure* is placed in the Tee to determine which rock is closer to the centre. More on measuring rocks in Chapter 8.

In curling terms, the rings of the house are referred to by their measurements. You don't need to add the word "circle" to the end. For example, you hear players talking about "drawing to the 8-foot" (which means throwing a stone so that it ends up coming to rest in the 8-foot circle) or "hitting that rock in the 12-foot" (which means removing a stone that is resting in the 12-foot circle).

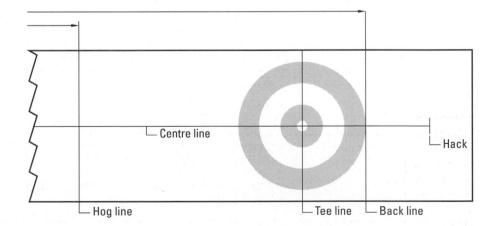

Before there were rings

In curling's early days, there were usually no markings on the ice, except for the Tee, which marked the centre of the house. This made it difficult to see the target at the other end of the sheet.

The circles (usually just lines scratched in the ice) were a later addition to make it easier to determine which rock was closer to the centre. Because it was difficult to see from the other end of the sheet, the skip would hold his broom up as a target, a practice still in use today. In later years, a small skittle or stick was knocked into the ice to better indicate the centre of the house. It wasn't until much later that the house became a regular part of the curling ice.

The circles are usually painted blue, white, and red in alternation. There is no standard when it comes to the order in which the colours occur, although more often than not, the 8-foot is white, with the 12-foot and 4-foot either blue or red, but not the same colour. Many times, the colours of the circles depend on the decor in the club. One Toronto club I used to curl at painted its house an awful brown and white to match its walls!

Contrary to most first impressions, the colour of ring does not indicate a certain point value. A rock just nibbling on the outside of the 12-foot can be worth the same as a stone sitting perfectly on the Button, in the centre. Each rock is worth one point, no matter where it sits in the house.

So, for example, if one of your rocks is perfectly in the centre of the house and another is just barely touching the 12-foot — and there are no other opposition rocks in the house — your team scores two points (each rock is worth one).

The Lines

Both ends of a curling sheet are identical in appearance. That's because you alternate the end you play at, as the game progresses. There are a number of different lines on the sheet; some run horizontally, some vertically. All these lines — no matter where they are on the ice — look pretty confusing at first. That is, until you know the purpose that each serves. These are the lines on a curling sheet:

- The Back line
- The Tee line
- The Hog line

- ✔ The Sidelines
- ✔ The Centre line

The Back line

Starting from the end of the sheet, the first line is the *Back line*. This indicates the end of the sheet of play. Measuring a half-inch in width, it runs along the back of the sheet, actually touching the outer edge of the 12-foot circle. A rock that crosses this line completely is out of play. However, if even a fraction of the rock is touching the line, the rock stays in play.

The Tee line

Moving up the sheet, the line that cuts through the middle of the house horizontally is known as the *Tee line*. This line comes into play in a number of situations, one of which is to indicate the mid-section of the house, where the Tee marks the middle of the Button (hence, the name).

The Tee line also plays a part in several rules situations. For instance, if you're having trouble with the delivery of a particular shot, you can replay the shot and try to get it right, as long as the stone does not cross the Tee line. If it does cross the line, though, it is considered played. You can't try it again — at least with that rock. Better luck next time.

The other instance where the Tee line comes into play is in the house at the *receiving end*, or *target end*, of the sheet (the end you throw the rocks towards). When a stone travelling up the sheet reaches the Tee line, your opponents can *sweep* it, usually to try to get it through the house and out of play. Before it reaches this line, only players from your team may brush it.

Sweeping, done with either a brush or a broom, makes a rock travel farther and curl less. If there is a crucial shot coming into the house and your opposition doesn't want it there, he can sweep it — but not before it touches the Tee line.

The Hog line

The next line up the sheet is the *Hog line,* which is 27 feet from the Back line. Like the Tee line, the Hog line has a dual purpose. First, at the receiving end of the sheet, your stone must get completely across this line to be in play. If your stone doesn't make it across, you're said to have "*hogged the rock,*" and it's taken off.

Hogging a rock is considered a big no-no. At some clubs, they even make you pay a price each time you hog a rock. (It's usually only a dollar or two, and it goes towards charity or junior curling.) It's all in good fun, but be prepared for some ribbing if your stone comes up short of the Hog line.

The Hog line is also the point on the sheet where you must let go of your rock, as you deliver it. This particular rule was brought into play in 1955, when it became apparent that curlers were developing longer slides that took them farther down the sheet (thanks to the technology of faster sliders and better ice). Prior to this time, no one really slid much past the first Tee line. Reaching the Hog line in your slide was simply unheard of.

Today, it's quite easy to slide the entire length of the ice. But the buck had to stop somewhere, and the Hog line was deemed to be it.

At first, the rule required you to come to a complete stop before reaching the Hog line. This was amended in later years, in recognition of the fact that curlers *were* sliding farther. The present-day rule states that the Hog line is simply the point on the ice where you have to release your rock. You can slide well past the Hog line, if you like, as long as you let go of your rock first.

The Sidelines

The *Sidelines* run vertically along both sides of the sheet. Some rinks mark the Sidelines with a physical border, such as a small piece of wood or a

The Baldwin slide

In the early 1950s, there was a major curling event held in Toronto's Maple Leaf Gardens. Known as the Tournament of Champions, its organizers had invited the top players in the land, including Matt Baldwin, the 1954 Canadian champion.

Baldwin became well known for his slide, which he developed to the point where he could travel almost the entire length of the ice. At the invitation of the organizers, Baldwin demonstrated his slide by pushing out and gliding down the sheet. As he reached the halfway point, he nonchalantly removed his hand from the stone, rubbed his nose and then replaced his hand on the rock. He only stopped when he — and the stone — came to rest on the Button.

Curling fans became aware of Baldwin's sliding technique. Later on, at the 1954 Brier (the Canadian men's championship), the crowd yelled, "Slide, slide!" every time he went to shoot. Finally, in the last game, Baldwin gave in to the crowd's demands: he slid halfway down the ice, released the stone and watched as it stopped right on the Button. "It was the flukiest shot of my life," he said, "but everyone seemed to like it." Baldwin went on to win that championship, as well as two others.

Incidents such as these led to the establishment of the Hog line rule, which states that you must let go of the rock when you reach the Hog line.

bumper. In most locations, however, they're just a couple of black lines in the ice. A rock is deemed out of play if any part of it touches one of the Sidelines.

The Centre line

Coincidentally enough, the *Centre line* runs — yup, you guessed it — down the centre of the sheet.

This line has no purpose in the rules — in fact, you won't even find a mention of if in the rule book. But for the person throwing the rock, it is a valuable visual aid with regard to aiming the rock properly. You can judge how you are doing based on where you are in relation to this line.

The Centre line is also a visual aid for the sweepers. You can judge when to sweep a rock and when to hold off by observing where the rock travels in relation to this line. For instance, if you know that the stone is supposed to end up just on the other side of the Centre line, and you see that, at about halfway down the sheet, it's nearly all the way over the line, you know that you need to sweep like crazy to limit the curl and keep it straight.

In recent years, two more lines running the length of the sheet have come into use. They extend from the edge of the 4-foot at either end, with the Centre line running between them. These lines were introduced by an ice technician named Shorty Jenkins during a televised event in the late 1980s. Jenkins coloured the ice between these two lines blue, which gave people watching at home a better view of the path the rocks took as they curled. This technique became so popular that many local clubs added these two other lines to their sheets — most of the time without colouring in between, though. These lines don't really have an official name, and they serve only as a visual aid for sweepers and spectators.

Not all clubs have these extra 4-foot lines. They aren't required, according to the rules. Nonetheless, they are a big help to players and spectators alike. If you are used to playing with these lines, and you suddenly find yourself negotiating a sheet without them, believe me, you notice the difference!

The Hacks

There are two footholds at both ends of the sheet, located four feet behind the respective Back lines. They look similar to the starting blocks a sprinter might use for the 100-metre dash. These footholds are called *hacks*. They provide resistance — or a sort of toehold — for a curler delivering a rock. Figure 7-2 shows a pair of hacks at one end of a sheet.

Figure 7-2:
Although there are two hacks, you only use one to throw the stone.

You brace your foot against one of the hacks when you deliver your stone. Which hack you use depends on whether your delivery is right-handed or left-handed. If you are right-handed, you put your right foot in the left hack — the one on the left side of the sheet. If you are left-handed, you put your left foot in the right hack. This setup aligns your throwing arm with the centre of the sheet. I delve into the finer points of delivering your rock in Chapter 9.

The hacks are usually made of solid rubber. They have some ribbing on them, which acts as a grip for your foot. Hacks can be used for a long time before they need to be replaced. Depending on the amount of use, some hacks last ten years or more.

The hacks are frozen into the ice surface, so they shouldn't slip out. When the ice technician is making the ice, she slips the hacks into place early in the flooding process. They are generally pretty secure; it's rare to see one come loose.

You can help prevent damage to the hacks by making sure fast-moving rocks (like a hard takeout shot) that come through the house are stopped before they hit the hacks. You should also try to keep them clean. The hacks tend to be little dirt receptacles, catching all the bits of straw and other debris that get loose on the ice. Use your broom or your hand to remove this dirt and prevent it from ending up on the bottom of your shoe. If it does get on your shoe, it can be tracked onto the ice and end up under a rock, ruining a shot.

A hack history

Hacks were common enough in curling's early days on Scottish lochs, but didn't provide a terribly secure foothold. (This might have had something to do with the fact that the rocks in use back then often weighed close to 100 pounds!) Instead of sitting on top of the ice, as they do today, these early hacks were cut into the ice, which increased the likelihood of a player falling through into the icy water below, while preparing to deliver the rock.

By the 1800s, players took to strapping a *crampit* onto the sole of their boot to give them the grip they needed. Cram-pits work the way spikes work for a golfer and cleats for a football player. The crampit was secure enough, but sometimes led to players scratching up the ice when they walked down the sheet.

A second type of crampit came along a bit later. This one was a small metal plate that was often melted into the ice to provide a hold. In some parts of the world, these types of crampits are still in use, although most have been replaced by the hacks we know today.

Up until about 1985, hacks were still sunk into the ice. It was an entrepreneurial curler, named Marco Ferraro, who had the idea to develop a new hack, modelled after a runner's starting block. Instead of sinking it into the ice, Ferraro mounted it on the surface.

This type of hack is now the worldwide standard.

Here's one other troubleshooting measure. Sometimes, when the ice technician pebbles the sheet, she inadvertently pebbles over the hacks, making them slippery and difficult to use as grips. You can put your hand on the hack to quickly warm it up and remove any ice that may have formed. Better yet, your ice technician should cover the hacks when she's pebbling the ice to stop any of the water from settling there in the first place.

Chapter 8

The Rules

Curling, as with all sports, is governed by a set of rules. Actually, there are a few different sets of rules, but unless you play in major competitions such as the Brier or the world championships, you really only have to worry about one set.

The tradition of curling as a sport of honesty and integrity is at the heart of this common rulebook. That means that, for the most part, you are your own curling official. If you break a rule, it's up to you to call the infraction on yourself.

There are also many "unwritten" rules in this game. It's up to you to observe the proper etiquette and to ensure that you are not in breach of it.

The Basic Rules

I suggest that you take a read through the rulebook before you play. You can pick up a copy at most curling clubs. If you don't have enough time, or if you can't get your hands on a copy, I explain the basic rules here. You should at least familiarize yourself with these, as they are the foundation of the game.

The basic rules of curling are these:

✔ Each team consists of four players.

✔ The order of play among the team members can't change once it has been set.

✔ A team scores one point for every stone that it has closer to the centre of the house than the other team.

✔ A coin toss decides which team gets last rock in the opening end (a decided advantage, which I discuss further in Chapter 14). From that point on, the team that scores in the previous end plays the first stone in the next end.

✔ You can't touch a stone that's in play or move a stone that's at rest.

With these five rules as your foundation, you could actually play a game. But many other things can happen in the course of delivering the stones up and down the sheet.

Common Infractions

Touching a stone and moving a stationary stone are two of the most common rules infractions. In this section, I include what the rulebook says about each, and follow it with a practical translation to help you handle them.

Touched stone

Touching a stone that is travelling down the ice is a more common occurrence than you might think. Eventually, every curler will touch a running stone — either with her foot or broom. Though the rulebook calls this infraction a *touched stone*, it is more commonly referred to as *burning the stone*. And that's how I refer to it here.

Here's how a burned stone is covered in the rulebook:

A delivered stone or stone in motion shall not be touched by an opposing player or that player's equipment.

Penalty: If a team declares its own violation of [the] rule, […] the non-offending team may:

(a) *Allow the play to stand;*

(b) *Remove the touched running stone from play and replace all the affected stones; or*

(c) *Place the touched running stone and all stones it would have affected where they would have come to rest had the violation not occurred.*

Prior to 1990, you immediately removed a stone from play when you burned it. It was up to you to admit if you burned the stone and stop the stone in progress.

But that rule came under fire when some players were accused of deliberately burning their own stones when they were headed for trouble. For instance, if your teammate threw a stone that looked as if it was going to knock one of your opponent's stones into the rings, you might "accidentally" hit the stone with your broom. Oops!

The rule has now changed to give an advantage to the team that doesn't burn the stone. This advantage has to do with choice.

When a curler on the other team tells you that she has burned one of your team's stones, you have three options:

 ✔ You can leave the stone — and any other stones it has affected — where it ends up. This would be a wise decision if your opponent bumped you into the rings into an advantageous position.

 ✔ You can return the stones to the positions they were in before the burned stone came into play. This would benefit you if the burned stone removed another one of your stones that was in an advantageous position.

 ✔ You can move the burned stone and any other stones to where you believe they would have ended up had the stone not been burned. You would do this, if, for example, your opponent's stone had been about to raise one of your stones into the rings, but instead got whacked with a broom and missed it. You could take the stone that would have been promoted and move it up to the position in the rings where you think it would have stopped. Similarly, you would move the burned stone to the position you think it would have finished in.

If you burn a stone, the first thing you need to do is resist the temptation to reach down and stop it. Let it finish its run. When it does finally come to rest, alert your opposition that you burned it and let them decide what to do. Although it's never a good feeling to burn a stone, it happens to the best of us. It happens at the club level as well as at the world championship level. It's just one of those things in curling.

Moved stationary stone

In addition to burning moving stones during the course of play, you might also burn a stone that's already come to rest. This often happens when the sweepers are brushing a stone around a few *guards* (a guard is a rock out in front of the house that is protecting one in the house). It can also happen when there are a lot of stones in play and the skips are trying to position themselves to sweep the stones into the house.

Where the rules come from

In curling's early days, each club had its own set of rules. While generally similar from place to place, each seemed to have its own peculiarities. For example, in some clubs, it was against the rules to sweep your own stone until it passed over the far Hog line. At others, the opposition couldn't sweep your stone at all, no matter where it was on the sheet. Gradually, though, the rules became more uniform, and some semblance of sanity came to the game.

The basic principles behind the rules haven't changed from those laid out more than 150 years ago, when the game was first formalized. I thought it would be interesting to include an early version of the rules to show you how similar they are to today's. You don't have to memorize them or anything.

These are the 12 rules that appeared in a booklet produced in 1840 for the Toronto Curling Club. I quote the original rule first, and follow it with a "translation."

1. *The Rink to be 42 yards from tee to tee, unless otherwise agreed upon by the parties. When a game is begun, the rink cannot be changed or altered unless by the consent of a majority of players and it can be shortened only when it is apparent that a majority cannot play the length.*

   Translation: This rule states the length of the sheet. Amazingly, it's only six feet shorter today. The second line was put in there because this was outdoor ice and sometimes the conditions changed drastically as the game wore on, necessitating a change in the length of ice.

2. *The hog score must be distant from the tee one-sixth part of the length of the rink. Every stone to be deemed a hog, the sole of which, when at rest, does not completely clear the length.*

   Translation: In today's English, this rule says that if you don't get your stone over the Hog line, it's not in play. What it doesn't say is that if you do end up throwing your stone this short, it's pretty embarrassing.

3. *Every player to foot so that in delivering his stone, it shall pass over the tee.*

   Translation: Stick your foot in the hack and throw the rock.

4. *The order of play adopted at the beginning must not be changed during a game.*

   Translation: You can't rotate the order of your teammates, no matter how well your second is playing.

5. *Curling stones must be of a circular shape. No stone to be changed during the game unless it happens to be broken and the largest fragment of such stone to count, without any necessity of playing it with more. If a stone roll or be upset [sic], it must be placed upon its sole where it stops. Should the handle quit a stone in delivery, the player must keep hold of it, otherwise he will not be entitled to replay the shot.*

   Translation: This rule means you can't play with square stones. Puzzle over that one for a minute. It also talks about what happens if your stone breaks, flips over, or if the handle comes off while you're throwing. These last three parts of the rule still apply.

6. *The player may sweep his own stone the whole length of the rink; his party not to sweep until it has passed the first hog score, and his adversaries not to sweep until it has passed the tee — the sweeping to be always to a side.*

   Translation: This rule spells out who can sweep where. It states that you can sweep your own stone down the entire sheet. Once it crosses the far Tee line, however, you or your opposition (or both) can sweep it. The rule still stands.

7. *None of the players, on any account, to cross or go upon the middle of the rink.*

   Translation: This is an old rule that meant no one was supposed to walk on the centre of the sheet unless they were sweeping. This was to help keep the ice clean. It was also because some players believed you could get an advantage by walking there and getting a sense of what shape the ice was in.

8. *If, in sweeping or otherwise, a running stone is marred by any of the party to which it belongs, it must be put off the rink; if by any of the adverse party, it must be placed agreeably to the direction which was given to the player; and if it be marred by any other means, the player may take his shot again. Should a stone at reset be accidentally displaced, it must be put as near as possible in its former situation.*

   Translation: This rule applies when you happen to touch a moving stone with your broom or your foot. It is slightly different today; I cover it a bit later in this chapter.

9. *Every player must be ready when his turn comes, and must take only a reasonable time to play his shot. Should he by mistake play with a wrong stone, it must be replaced where it stops, by the one which he ought to have played.*

   Translation: Two rules are actually covered here. First, you can't delay the game; you have to be ready to play (even if you haven't finished your beer). And if you mess up and throw the wrong stone, you simply replace it. Both rules are in use today.

10. *A doubtful shot must be measured by a neutral person, whose determination shall be final.*

    Translation: An objective third party (or maybe the bartender, if no one else is available) should decide which of two stones is closer to the centre, when it can't be determined by the naked eye. I tell you how to measure a stone later in this chapter.

11. *The skips alone shall direct the game. The players of the respective skips may offer them their advice, but cannot control their directions; nor is any person except the skip, to address him who is about to play. Each skip may appoint one of his party to take the charge for him when he is about to play. Every player to follow the direction given to him.*

    Translation: This means the skip is the boss and you have to listen to her. Though it's not a rule anymore, it is good common sense. Still, I've seen this one violated a few times over the years.

12. *Should any question arise, the determination of which may not be provided for by the words and spirit of these Rules, each party to choose one of their number in order to determine it. If the two so chosen differ in opinion, they are to name an umpire whose decision shall be final.*

    Translation: If the teams can't decide on a ruling, they choose one player to decide (here's a tip: pick the biggest or the loudest). If they still can't decide, then they have to call in the umpire. This is still generally in play today.

The rulebook has grown since 1840, primarily to take into account advancements in the game. But the spirit of those rules remains. Unfortunately, some amendments have been necessary due to the few players who ignored that unwritten code.

The Canadian Curling Association meets each year to review the rules and make amendments, if necessary.

Here's what the rulebook says about a moved stationary stone:

A stationary stone shall not be displaced by a player or that player's equipment, nor shall a player cause a stone to be displaced by an opposing player or that player's equipment.

Penalty Situation #1: If a team declares its own violation of the rule, the non-offending team may replace the stone to its original position. If there was any question as to which stone(s) was closer to the tee, the displaced stone shall be positioned in favour of the non-offending team.

Penalty Situation #2: If a team declares its own violation of the rule, and the displaced stationary stone would have altered the course of a delivered stone or stone in motion, the non-offending team may:

(a) Allow the play to stand;

(b) Remove the delivered stone or stone in motion and replace all affected stones to their original positions; or

(c) Place the delivered stone or stone in motion and all stones it would have affected where they would have come to rest had the violation not occurred.

There are two penalty situations involving a moved stationary stone. The first is if you're in the house and you inadvertently kick a stone that's at rest. This usually happens to skips, who often stand right in the house as they watch one of their team's stones come down the sheet. Let's say you are skip. As you move yourself into position to get a better look, you might forget about a stone in the house behind you or to your side and give it a little accidental kick. In this situation, your opponent replaces the moved stone as close to its original position as possible. The only other thing you have to worry about here would happen at the conclusion of the end. If the stone you kick and then replace is very close with an opponent's stone to counting, the opponent's stone is deemed to be closer. You can't measure the two rocks because the precise original position of the stone is really impossible to determine. The advantage goes to the non-offending team.

The other time this rule applies is when a stationary stone is moved out of or into the path of an oncoming stone. You'll see this most often when the sweepers are furiously working on a stone that is curling around another one. As it comes close to the sitting stone, a sweeper might accidentally hit the stationary stone with the broom, moving it slightly out of the way and clearing the path for the moving stone.

Again, you have three options in this situation:

✔ You can leave things as they end up, and accept the way the play finished. You would only do this if it were to your advantage.

The Labonte boot

The most famous burned stone was by Bob Labonte, a talented American curler. At the 1972 world championships, Labonte took a 9–7 lead into the final end of the championship game against Canada's Orest Meleschuk. After playing a double takeout with his last stone, Labonte believed he had limited the Canadians to just one point and won the world title. He began jumping up and down in celebration. But then the unthinkable happened: Labonte fell and kicked a Canadian stone, pushing it closer to the centre. Instead of one, it was now two for Canada, tying the game. Canada scored in an extra end, winning the world championship. Labonte became famous for this gaffe, picking up the nickname "Boots."

✔ You can remove the *shooter* (the stone that was thrown) and move the stones back to the positions they were in before the play.

✔ You can move the stones into the position you *think* they would have ended up in had the stationary stone not been burned. This would be a good decision if you think the shooter would have actually hit one of your stones and moved it into the rings.

Rules Regarding Sweeping

The rules governing sweeping have changed more than just about any others over the years. As with the other amendments, these were also adopted as a result of players abusing the rules and gaining an unfair advantage. When it came to sweeping, the introduction of the push broom, an advancement over the corn broom, had a lot to do with that. Some players realized that they could affect how a stone travelled down the sheet by sweeping it in certain ways.

Here's what the rulebook says about sweeping:

1. (a) *Between the tee lines, all members of the delivering team may sweep any of their stones that are in motion.*

   (b) *Only the skip or vice-skip of the non-delivering team may sweep their own stone when set in motion by a stone of the delivering team.*

2. *Behind the tee line, only one player from each team may sweep at one time. This may be the skip or vice-skip of either team or the lead or second of the delivering team.*

3. *Behind the tee line, each team shall have first privilege of sweeping its own stone. If the choice is not to sweep, that team shall not obstruct or prevent its opponent from sweeping the stone.*

4. *An opponent's stone shall not be swept until it reaches the farther tee line.*

5. *(a) The sweeping motion shall be from side to side.*

   (b) The sweeping motion shall not leave any debris in front of a delivered stone or stone set in motion.

   (c) The final sweeping motion must finish to either side of the delivered stone or stone set in motion.

What does all this mean? It can be boiled down to three things:

- When you can sweep
- Where you can sweep
- How you can sweep

When and where you sweep

When your team delivers a stone, any member of your team can sweep that stone between the Tee lines. That means that after, say, the lead, releases the stone, the second, third, and even the skip, can sweep it. Even the player who delivers the shot (the lead, in this case) can get up and help brush.

As that stone comes into the house and reaches the Tee line, though, only one member of your team can sweep it. What about your opponent? Once your stone passes the Tee line, the opposing skip or third can sweep it, too. They will try to sweep your stone out of the house completely, or at least far enough back that it ends up not counting. If one of the opposing team's stones hits one of your stones, and you feel it should be swept to get promoted into the house, only the skip or third on your team can do so. Say your opposition plays a shot that curls too much. It ends up hitting one of your stones in front of the house. To make sure your stone gets all the way into the house, it needs sweeping. But remember, only the third or skip can do it.

How you sweep

When push brooms first became popular in Canada, in about 1975, some players learned that they could actually make a stone slow down and even change direction by the way they swept it.

How they still abuse the rules

While there are rules in place that prohibit sweeping just one side of a stone to make it curl more or less, many of the top competitive teams still bend this rule when they sweep. The next time you're watching a top competitive game, take a careful look at the path on which the curlers sweep. Although these top players are no longer allowed to put the broom down and lean on it as they once did, you will see that very often, they only move their brush across half of the stone's path. The speed at which they sweep makes it hard to detect, but it happens frequently. It's yet another way that the world's best gain an edge over each other.

Dumping

Dumping is when you move debris underneath a stone on purpose to make it slow down. It's now against the rules, but it was in practice up until the late 1970s. If you were sweeping and saw that your teammate's stone was going too fast, you might put your broom down on a path outside the running surface of the stone, lean hard on it, and, on some ice surfaces, get some snow to come up from the ice. This snow, along with any other debris caught by the broom, would fall under the stone, causing it to slow down, and, hopefully, end up where you wanted it.

Snowplowing

Snowplowing is similar to dumping, the idea being to get your stone to slow down and stop where you want it. It, too, is now against the rules. In this method, the broom is put down width-wise across the stone's path. At the moment when the sweeper wants the stone to stop, he lifts up the broom, which causes anything that was swept up by the broom to fall underneath the stone.

A few ingenious curlers took the use of the brush to extremes in that same late 1970s time period. They discovered that if they were to furiously sweep just one side of a stone (actually, they would just put the brush down and lean on it), they could make one side of the stone move faster than the other. For a stone turning clockwise, if they swept the outside half (the 9 o'clock side), they could make the stone curl more. And if they swept just the inside half (the 3 o'clock side), they could prevent it from curling. A few of the better sweepers became so adept at this that they could actually change the way a stone was turning just by brushing one half of it.

The Canadian Curling Association, the organization that administers the rules, quickly outlawed this type of sweeping. After a few modifications, the CCA has adopted a rule, which states that sweepers must move their brooms back and forth continuously for the duration of the play. They can't just put the brush down and lean on it. It also states, simply, that it is against the rules to intentionally leave any debris in the stone's path (the dumping scenario) or to pick your broom up when it's in the stone's path (the snow-plowing scenario).

Measuring Stones

There are two occasions when you need to measure stones. (I'm not talking about the dimensions of the stones themselves. I'm talking about measuring two stones in relation to the centre of the house to determine the score in an end.) One of these occasions is when you can't tell which of two stones is closer to the centre by eyeballing them alone. The other occasion is when you can't tell — again, with the naked eye — whether a rock is in or out of the house. On both occasions, the measuring is done by the thirds. When the measuring is under way, no other players are allowed in the house. Both thirds must agree on the measure before it is finalized and the rocks are removed.

The first situation occurs when two stones end up at what appears to be the same distance from the centre of the rings. When this happens, you make use of a device known as a *measure* to determine which stone is counting. As seen in Figure 8-1, the measure is a funny-looking instrument that has one end

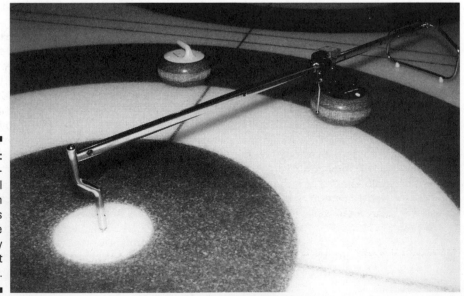

Figure 8-1:
The measure can tell you which stone is closer to the centre by the slimmest of margins.

fastened to the *Tee* (the hole in the centre of the house). It bends upward and out towards the 12-foot, where it rests on two legs. Hanging from the long, straight bar that goes across the rings is another, smaller bar that hangs vertically. This vertical bar hangs downwards and does the actual measuring. It is moved outward or inward to where the stone is resting, and placed against the inside edge of the stone. It is then screwed in place, and the entire unit is swung around to measure the other stone. If it hits the other stone, then this second stone is closer. If it doesn't reach it, then the first stone is closer.

There are a few things to know about using this particular measuring device. First, it is against the rules to try to use anything other than your eyes to measure the stones before the end is over. That means that you can't put your broom up against two stones that appear to be close, hoping to figure out which is closer.

Second, because stones are sometimes different widths, you must place the measure on the inside of the stone. This second rule can complicate things, however. Sometimes stones are so close to the centre that you don't have enough room to get the measuring device in to get a proper read. If that happens, you must rely on your eyes. If you can't agree with the other third, then you can call a nonpartisan third person in to make the call. If it still can't be decided, then neither one of them counts — it's considered a dead heat.

HEART & SOUL

Rock radio

One of the most unusual rules episodes was played out at the 1989 Brier (the Canadian men's championship), involving two-time world champion Russ Howard.

Howard is known for being very vocal on the ice, screaming out commands at the top of his lungs. By mid-week of this weeklong event, Howard had almost lost his voice and looked to other means to communicate the sweeping commands to his front end. Between games, he went out and bought two walkie-talkie headsets. He began using them in the next game to relay his sweeping instruction. The rules offi-cials from the Canadian Curling Association weren't at all pleased with Howard's use of these devices, especially when their radios began to pick up the signal from the walkie-talkies, disrupting their communication. After the game, Howard was asked not to use the headsets again. But Howard insisted that un-less there was a rule in the book that said so, he would keep right on using them. And he did, in the next match. After that, however, the offi-cials informed Howard that the rulebook had a new entry: Radio headset devices were now banned. It was the first time that the rules had been changed in the middle of a competition.

The other type of measuring is done when you're trying to determine whether a stone is in or out of the rings. For this, you use a device known as a *six-foot measure*, or a *biter measure* (see Figure 8-2). The six-foot measure consists of a six-foot-long radius bar, which is anchored to the Tee. You put the pointed end into the Tee hole. The rest of the measure reaches out to the end of the 12-foot, at the height of the middle of a stone. If it touches the stone in question, then the stone is in. If it can't reach the stone, then the stone is out.

Figure 8-2:
The six-foot measure is used to determine if a rock is in or out of the house.

The six-foot measure can also be used in the middle of an end, but only in one situation. This occurs when you need to determine if a stone is in the rings or not since it refers to the *free guard zone* (the area of the sheet extending from the Hog line to the Tee line, not including the house). Any rocks that come to rest in the free guard zone cannot be removed from play until the fourth rock of the end is thrown. Any rocks that come to rest *outside* the house, that is. If one of these rocks ends up inside the house, it *can* be taken off. If it's close, you may use the six-foot measure to determine its fate: inside the house means it can be removed from play; outside the house means it stays in play until the fourth rock of the end. This is the only time that a measure can take place before the completion of an end. (More about the free guard zone a bit later in this chapter.)

You can't always count on the rings to be perfectly symmetrical or drawn exactly to the measurement, nor can you expect the centre Tee to always be exactly in the middle of the house. For that reason, it's always a good idea to

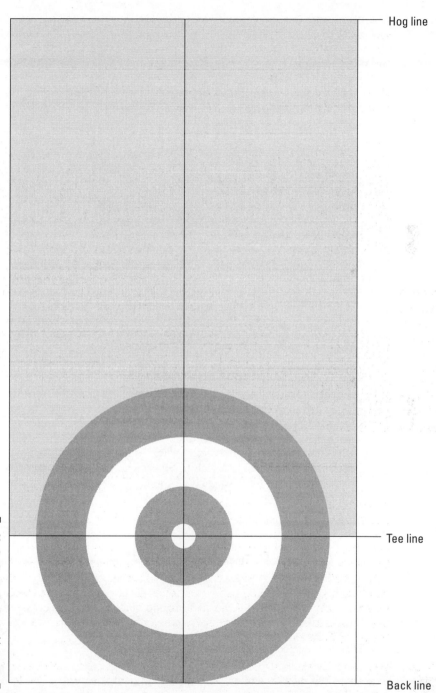

Hog line

Tee line

Back line

Figure 8-3:
The free
guard zone
is the area
from the
Hog line
to the
Tee line, not
including
the house.

measure stones whenever they are close. I can remember playing in the very early stages of the Brier playdowns at a club that I'd never been to before. At the conclusion of one end, my team had a stone that was, to the eye, clearly outside the rings. But because it was relatively close (and because the six-foot measure happened to be right beside the sheet) I decided to measure it. As it turned out, the stone was in, and it counted. Before any big game, I take the six-foot measure and just swing it around the entire house to see how it compares to the rings below it.

The Free Guard Zone

The *free guard zone* is an area that extends from the Hog line to the Tee line, not including the front of the house (see Figure 8-3). Under Canadian rules, any stone that comes to rest in this zone may not be removed until the fourth stone of the end is thrown. (The international rules push things a bit farther. In all countries outside Canada, a stone in the free guard zone may not be removed until the fifth stone of the end.) If you remove a stone in the free guard zone before that crucial fourth (or fifth) stone is played, the stone is returned to its position in the free guard zone, and your shooter is removed from play. You *are* allowed to bump a stone in the free guard zone into the rings or over to the side — you just can't remove it from play.

The *free guard zone rule,* adopted by curling in the mid-1990s, is easily the biggest change to the rules since the game was formalized more than a century ago. Much like the adoption of the designated hitter in baseball or the three-point shot in basketball, the free guard zone was added to the rulebook to create offense. That was necessary because at the highest level curling had become a defensive struggle. That translated into unappealing games for crowds and for television. Before the free guard zone, the top teams would try to get a lead early in the game and then spend the rest of the

A reason to change

Why was it necessary to add the free guard zone to the curling rulebook? In a word: technology.

In the years before the free guard zone was added, changes to equipment resulted in near-perfect ice conditions. No longer was there any straw on the ice because of corn brooms that would cause rocks to react unexpectedly. Push brooms left the surface almost pristine. And the

technology of making ice improved drastically. Along with better equipment and ice, the players themselves were technically better, thanks to several advancements in training. In short, the good players rarely missed. This made it easy for them to play precise shot after precise shot. To keep up with these changes, it became necessary to alter the rules.

game methodically removing the opposition's stones, end after end. It was like watching paint dry. One team would put a stone in play, and the other would knock it out. Stone after stone, end after end, it went on, while crowds began yelling from the stands for something to happen. Curling's governing bodies recognized the problem and altered the rules so there would be a better chance of scoring.

Sizing Up the Scoreboard

When you're new to the game, it is not only difficult to understand who has scored in an end, but to figure out what the score is when you look at the scoreboard. It's almost like teaching someone a different language. They look at the board and it's all Greek to them — until you explain it and unlock the key.

The long, rectangular scoreboard in curling is made up of three main sections, as shown in Figure 8-4. The top and the bottom represent the two different teams. They're shown by solid colours, usually the same as the rock colours. There is a series of numbers in the middle of the board, usually ranging from 1 to 18. (The high end of the number sequence might only go to 15 or 16, depending on the particular club.) Above and below each of these numbers is a nail or hook on which to hang a card with another number on it, ranging from 1 to 8 or 10, depending on the particular end. This middle section indicates the points scored, while the cards represent the ends played.

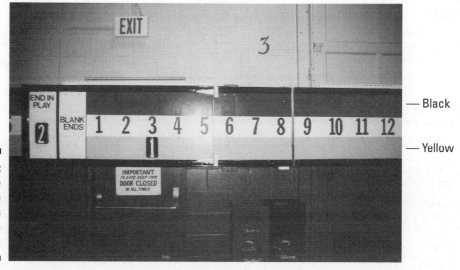

Figure 8-4:
The score after the first end is 3–0 for the yellow team.

The score after the first end

The team colours in our example are black (on top) and yellow (on the bottom). If, in the first end, the team throwing yellow rocks scores 3, the third will take the card with the 1 on it — representing the first end — and hang it on the yellow side of the number sequence, on the hook under the 3. This is shown in Figure 8-4.

The score after the second end

To take the example another step, let's say that in the second end, the rink throwing black stones scores 2. The third would take the card with the 2 on it — representing the second end — and place it on the black side of the number sequence, on the hook over the 2, as shown in Figure 8-5.

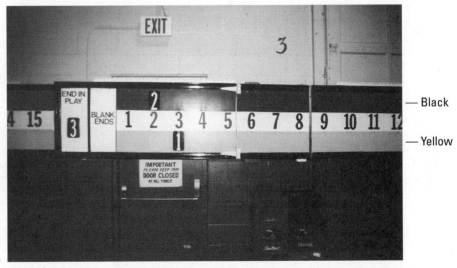

Figure 8-5: In the second end, the team throwing black rocks scored 2 points to make the score 3–2 for the yellow team.

The score after all eight ends

Figure 8-6 shows you what the scoreboard looks like after all eight ends have been played. Among other things, you can see the following: In the fifth end, the yellow stones scored two points; after the sixth end, the score was 5–4 for the yellows; the final score was 7–5 for the blacks.

Figure 8-6:
The final
score of an
eight-end
game: 7–5
for the
black team.

Etiquette

Curling is a game built on the principles of good sportsmanship. That's why the players are supposed to call rules infractions on themselves and generally aim to have fun above all else. You don't go out to try to beat up the opposition or play to win at all costs. You go out to do your best and enjoy the game.

This attitude is written in the Curler's Code of Ethics, a series of statements that, in many ways, supersedes the rulebook. This code really spells out the attitude curlers should bring with them to the rink.

The code of ethics reads this way:

- I will play the game with a spirit of good sportsmanship.

- I will conduct myself in an honourable manner both on and off the ice.

- I will never knowingly break a rule, but if I do, I will divulge the breach.

- I will take no action that could be interpreted as an attempt to intimidate or demean my opponents, teammates, or officials.

- I will interpret the rules in an impartial manner, always keeping in mind that the purpose of the rules is to ensure that the game is played in an orderly and fair manner.

- I will humbly accept any penalty that the governing body at any level of curling deems appropriate, if I am found in violation of the code of ethics or rules of the game.

These statements, and the overall mindset they encourage, are the real keys to curling. Fun, spirit, and sportsmanship are what curling is all about.

The blank end

You may play an end in a game where neither team gets any rocks in the house, so nobody scores. This is called a blank end. It's quite common to have a *blank end* in a game — sometimes it's done on purpose.

Why would a team intentionally decide not to score? It stems back to having last rock. Because having the last shot is a decided advantage, you might *blank an end* (that's the process of deliberately not scoring) to retain last shot. In curling, the team with the last rock is said to have *the hammer*. Say you're playing an eight-end game. Heading into the seventh end, the score is tied 5–5. When you come to throw your last rock of the end, there is nothing in play. You could draw your stone down to the house and score 1. While you would be ahead by 1, you would give up the all-important last shot in the final end to your opponent.

Most teams would decide to throw the stone through the house — that's generally how an end is blanked — and keep the score tied, while retaining the hammer in the final end.

Part III
Hurry Hard!
Playing the Game

In this part . . .

You add sweeping and brushing to your curling repertoire — neither of which has anything to do with personal hygiene by the way. You also learn how to actually throw a rock without your mother yelling at you. From stepping into the hack and throwing a perfect freeze (the most difficult shot to execute, in my book) to learning how to sweep with your teammates without getting completely tangled up in each other, this part of the book is all about curling with confidence.

Chapter 9

The Delivery

*I*n curling, the delivery is not about giving birth, but about throwing the stone. It's akin to the swing for golfers, the slap shot for hockey players, or the pitch for a baseball pitcher. It's how you get the stone down the ice.

The delivery is not that complicated, but there is a right way and a wrong way to do it. Actually, as I explain in this chapter, there is more than one right way to do it. There are subtle differences among the various delivery styles, but they share the same fundamentals.

Your overall objective is to deliver your stone on a line to a target (given to you by your skip) with the proper amount of force, with the handle turning in the right direction at the correct rotational speed. If you are the skip, then you pick your own line, while your third indicates the target for you.

The delivery involves a number of different qualities:

✔ **Balance:** You need to have great balance in order to slide out of the hack and maintain it without falling over.

✔ **Eye–hand coordination:** Your eye needs to know what your hand is doing. This is the relationship between what your eye sees and how your hand meets that.

✔ **Flexibility:** Your muscles must be supple enough to move your body into the correct positions required by the delivery.

✔ **Strength:** Your legs, especially, need to be strong enough to control your body weight as you thrust out of the hack and complete your delivery.

Setting Up

The *setup*, your starting position for your delivery, is one of the most vital — and often overlooked — parts of it. Although it can seem simple enough to position yourself in the hack and get ready to go, there's a lot more to it, and it's important to get it right. Your setup is the foundation of your delivery. If you get this first part right, there's a very good chance that the second part will fall into place. You'll make a good delivery.

Note: Except where specified, the upcoming descriptions are for a right-handed player (sorry lefties, you have to reverse the directions).

Feet first: Stepping into the hack

Your first task in delivering your rock is stepping into the hack. The hack is your starting block, the brace against which you'll push to move the stone down the ice. If this first crucial part of your delivery is incorrect, you have almost no chance of delivering your stone properly.

If you are right-handed, you put your right foot in the hack that is on the left side of the Centre line, with your left foot — the one with the slider on it — on the ice beside and slightly in front of the hack. The toe of the foot in the hack should point directly at your target. This helps keep your entire body aimed on line.

The ball of your foot should be resting about halfway up the hack, as shown in Figure 9-1.

Figure 9-1:
The first part of the delivery is to properly position your feet.

You might make the mistake of placing your foot too far forward in the hack, which gives you nothing to push off from (see Figure 9-2). This is quite common among newcomers. Some of the newer hacks have a mark to show where the ball of your foot should go.

Figure 9-2: Many newcomers place their foot incorrectly in the hack, which makes a proper delivery almost impossible.

The foot in the hack must also be properly braced, as you'll have almost all of your weight on this foot during the delivery.

Assuming the position

With your feet in the correct place, your next move is to squat down. You want the knee of your hack foot pointing towards your target, while your sliding foot remains flat on the ice, with your thigh and shin making a 90-degree angle (see Figure 9-3).

Your body position as a whole has you pointed at your target, which is the skip's broom, at the other end of the ice. Your hips should be level with the ice, not tilted too far up or down. They should also be square to your target line. The same can be said for your shoulders: They should also be level and square. Your head should be up and your eyes locked on the target at the other end of the ice. Don't keep your head too rigid; hold it comfortably and naturally, like a dancer does. Your spine should be straight and your upper body should be leaning slightly forward. Your weight is situated back, towards your hack foot.

Many people find it difficult to stay in the starting position for longer than 10 or 20 seconds. (I've noticed that the older I get, the shorter time I can stay in the squat.) When you're playing, by all means be ready to play the shot, but don't sit in the hack waiting until it's your turn. Your legs can cramp up or the

Figure 9-3:
In the starting position, both of your legs should be lined up with your target.

blood flow might become restricted. When you go to shoot, you won't have the necessary power to deliver your stone. Step into the hack just prior to throwing the stone.

In the starting position, notice, too, where your *throwing arm* (your right arm, in this case) falls. Hanging naturally, it should be directly between the two hacks, right down the centre of the sheet. I explain why this is so later in the chapter. Like the rest of your body, you should strive to keep your throwing arm straight, but not rigid or tight. It helps you get your stone on line.

Establishing your own routine

Many coaches emphasize the importance of stepping into the hack, because it's the foundation of your whole delivery. That may not seem revolutionary, but stepping into the hack the same way every time is. It's called a *pre-shot routine*. You should develop one right from the first time you step in to throw a shot.

I like to stand on the ice behind the hack, look down the sheet and confirm in my mind what the shot is. I then take a deep breath and slowly step into the hack. I do this the same way every time, no matter whether I'm playing the last shot of the game or the first. It keeps me in a comfort zone and comes in handy, especially in stressful situations, like when the game is on the line.

Develop your own pre-shot routine and stick to it — for every shot.

Keep your balance: Using your broom

Your broom is another vital part of your delivery. You use it for balance — much like an outrigger canoe has a balance aid built out from its side. For new players, the broom is especially key, as it helps keep them from falling over. Experienced curlers don't rely on it to stay up so much as to balance out their delivery and distribute their weight.

Holding the broom in the usual way

There are a number of different ways to hold the broom during your delivery, but one manner is generally used the most often.

In the starting position, grip the broom about two-thirds of the way down the handle, closer to the head, as shown in Figure 9-4. The long part of the handle will run up the bottom of your arm and behind your back. You want the head of your brush to be in front of your sliding foot. (This is your left foot, following my shamelessly exclusionary example of tailoring this chapter to right-handed players. Well, I could have explained everything on both sides, but then this book would be twice as long! Would you have thanked me for that?). Make sure that the sweeping side of the brush is facing up so that it's not touching the ice. If it does make contact with the ice, it tends to stick and drag, slowing you down and causing you to pull in the direction of the broom. The other side of the brush will glide beside you almost without friction, keeping you balanced, but not affecting your delivery.

Figure 9-4:
The broom is used for balance during the delivery.

Holding the broom in less usual ways

Some curlers like to rest the broom flat on the ice with their broom-side arm running straight down, more or less leaning on the handle. This method is most commonly used by players with a tuck delivery, a style of delivery in which the curler rides on the toe of his sliding foot (this is especially popular in Manitoba). A number of players use it very effectively, but most instructors and coaches agree that it can cause the shoulders to tilt and pull a player off line.

Another method is to run the broom along the top of the arm and over the shoulder. There are pros and cons to this way, too. There is no doubt that it helps promote better balance, and for this reason, a number of beginners use it — it's better than falling over, after all. But it can take too much of the weight during the delivery. I discuss the proper weight distribution later in this chapter, but for now, suffice it to say that your weight should be over your sliding foot for almost all of the delivery. Holding your broom over your shoulder can cause you to use it more as a crutch, with your weight going onto the broom rather than over your sliding foot. The result is an unbalanced delivery, with your shoulders and hips tilting too much to the left.

Although it may seem easier to use the broom-over-the-shoulder method when you first start to curl, avoid it if you can. Keep the broom under your arm and along your back. You might fall over a few more times, but in the long run, this method will lead you to a better, properly balanced delivery.

Hold onto your stones

In your setup, the starting position of your rock can have a large bearing on the rest of your delivery. If it doesn't start in the correct position, you compensate to get it back on line, which can affect other parts of your delivery and cause many types of errors. The same can be said for your grip on the handle. A good grip not only helps you put the proper rotation on the stone, it also helps keep the stone on line.

Assuming the position

The correct position for the rock at the start of the delivery is to the right of your body, on the Centre line. It should be placed just ahead of you so you don't have to reach for it. You should be able to comfortably extend your throwing arm and grasp the handle.

Getting a grip

The method of gripping the handle has gone through a change over the years. Up until about 25 years ago, instructors taught people to grip the handle using their fingertips only, with their thumb on top. The palm of the hand never touched the handle. This was supposed to limit the amount of hand action during the delivery, as too much hand action can throw a stone off line and cause missed shots. Gradually, though, this grip was modified to allow more of the hand to grip the handle. The reason for the change is as much about feel as anything else. Many players enjoy the firmer grip on the rock and feel like they are in better control. The key to being able to use this grip properly comes with the release of the rock, which I cover later in this chapter.

While some people continue to hold the handle in their fingertips, a more popular method is to grip the handle more firmly in the palm and second knuckle joint of the fingers, much as you would hold a hammer. As shown in Figure 9-5, your thumb and forefinger form a V shape when you grip the handle. Your second set of knuckles is on the bottom of the handle (don't grip it any tighter), with the part of your palm closest to your fingers resting on the side and top. Your thumb is on the other side of the handle. Notice that even with this grip, you still don't hold the stone too tightly. A tight grip leads to a tense arm, which restricts the motion in the rest of the delivery.

Figure 9-5:
Avoid using too much pressure as you grip the stone.

Positioning the handle

No matter which grip you choose, you must also have the handle in the right spot in the setup. Here again, there are two different styles, although neither is particular to any type of delivery.

✔ In the first method, the handle has two different starting points, depending on the turn you are going to use. Think of the stone as the face of a clock. When you throw an in-turn (clockwise for a right-hander), you want the end of the handle pointed at five o'clock. For the out-turn, point the end of the handle at seven o'clock. The reason for this is to allow the rotation of the stone to be applied with just a small turn of the wrist. When you release the rock with either turn, your hand will finish in a handshake

A clean start

There is one thing you need to do before your delivery, and that's clean off your stone. You want the stone you are about to deliver to be free of debris on the bottom.

To clean your stone, move it off to the side beside your sliding foot, and flip it over so the bottom is exposed. With your hand or the end of your brush, scrub the stone off, paying particular attention to the running surface. Before you turn the stone back over, sweep any debris you just removed away from the delivery area. Some curlers make the mistake of cleaning the stone off and then turning it back over on top of the debris they just removed. Turn your clean stone back over and put it back in place. You might also want to move it back and forth or spin it around to ensure that the running surface is truly debris free.

position, as if you were going to shake someone's hand After a while this occurs so naturally that you won't even think about it.

✔ The second method has the handle running straight down the target line, more or less in the six o'clock position. Because you have to turn your wrist more with this method, it is easier to move the rock off the proper line as you apply the turn. For that reason, newcomers should stick to the first method, using the five o'clock and seven o'clock method, respectively.

Delivering the Rock

Once you are comfortable with your setup, it's time to make a move — the delivery move. In general terms, keep your delivery as smooth as possible, with controlled movements (believe me, it probably won't start out smooth and controlled, but after time, you will get the hang of it).

In this part of the chapter, I refer to the *standard delivery*, the delivery style that is most widely taught. However, I suggest that you also look at the *trunk lift* style of delivery. It might suit you better. The trunk lift is a perfectly viable alternative, one that has been used by many world champions.

Pressing ahead

The first move you make in your curling delivery is to push your stone forward a little bit on the ice. This is called the *forward press*. The point of this is to establish some momentum; it is to get the rock moving so that it's easier to pull it back towards you. Imagine a car stuck in the snow. One of the best ways to remove it is by rocking it back and forth. The same principle is at work in the forward press.

The backswing

The next move you make in your delivery starts what is known as the *backswing*. You bring the rock back towards you along the target line, building the necessary momentum to allow you to release the stone and have it actually travel somewhere. It's important to keep the stone on this line so that you can maintain a straight line between you and the target (remember, that's the skip's broom at the other end of the sheet). If you veer off this line, you must compensate in order to get your rock back on line, which usually spoils your delivery. The best way to keep your rock on line is not to move it off the line in the first place! Easier said than done.

The traditional backswing

The backswing has gone through an evolution in the past six years or so. For many years, curlers used a style of backswing where the rock comes off the ice at the high point of the swing. It doesn't have an official name, but for the sake of clarity, I call it the *traditional backswing*. Here's how it works: When you bring the rock back to the hack, you actually lift it up and off the ice, all in one movement, swinging it back to about knee level, as shown in Figure 9-6. As you pull the rock back, your sliding foot moves about six inches straight back from its starting position. You lift up your body slightly, with your hack leg carrying your weight. Don't stand up completely; just rise slightly out of your squat (see Figure 9-6). Your upper body stays in the same upright position throughout. This series of movements should occur seamlessly, with no jerks or stops.

Lifting the rock off the ice in the backswing is still the most widely used style. And it's definitely an accepted way for beginners to learn.

The no-lift backswing

However, more and more curlers are adopting a style of backswing in which the rock never leaves the ice. This trend began in the early 1990s, when a number of top curlers, including two-time Canadian champion Kevin Martin, kept the rock on the ice when they delivered it. This style became known as the *no-lift backswing*. Champion and once-a-week curlers alike found that by keeping the stone on the ice, there was less chance of getting it off line (remember I said it was important to keep the rock on line — in line with the target). Today, it is the style of choice for many players. And, as an added benefit, it's easier for curlers who have back trouble, since at no time during the delivery do you have to actually lift the stone.

Figure 9-6:
At the top of the traditional backswing, the rock is a foot or so off the ice surface.

In the no-lift backswing, you slide the stone back towards you and push it forward as you thrust from the hack. This should happen in a fluid motion.

At no point should your rock come off the ice. You can even do it without a forward press: You simply start with the rock on the Centre line in front of the hack, and move it back from there.

At this point, your body — and consequently your weight — must continue to move behind the rock (if it doesn't, you fall over). Slide your foot back and behind you so your body lines up behind the rock. You are now wound up at the top of the no-lift backswing, ready to uncoil and start your forward swing.

If you're just starting out, I recommend the no-lift backswing. There are so many advantages to it, not the least of which is that it might save your back.

The forward swing

I can see you out there, practising your delivery in your living room. Right about now, you're cursing me because I've got you stuck at the top of your backswing and you want to go forward. Well, here's how that happens.

Choose your style

While the standard delivery style is the most common and widely taught today, there are a few other types that have proven effective over the years.

✔ **The trunk lift delivery:** This delivery was developed and taught by Ray Turnbull, a former Canadian champion. Because of Turnbull's extensive teaching in Europe, the trunk lift is the most popular delivery style in that part of the world. In the trunk lift, your backswing is more deliberate. You raise your body out of the hack first, keeping your hack knee bent, then pull the rock back towards you and finish as you do in the standard delivery.

✔ **The tuck delivery:** This type of delivery is most common among players from Manitoba. The slide occurs on just the toe portion of the foot as opposed to the entire foot, which is the case in other styles. Although still in use, it has lost popularity over the past few decades because it is thought to cause knee problems. I don't recommend this style to those of you just learning to curl.

Both of these delivery styles have worked for certain curlers over the years. But, just as with a golf swing, there really isn't one right or wrong way to throw the stone, as long as it ends up in the correct position.

The *forward swing* occurs when the stone begins to move towards the target. As it moves towards the target, it pulls your arm along with it. As your arm becomes fully extended, you begin to push out from the hack with the force that is necessary for the particular shot you're throwing. You use more or less force, depending on the type of shot. The different shots are discussed in Chapter 10.

Two vital parts of the delivery occur in the next couple of moves.

Use your legs, not your arms

Resist the temptation to push the stone with your arm. Your arm doesn't deliver the stone; it's just the extension from and the connection to your body. Rather, your leg that pushes out from the hack (your right leg, if you are throwing right) delivers all the power behind the stone's movement. Whether you want the stone to go just over the Hog line or remove another stone sitting in the house, the force behind your forward swing — whether it's give-it-all-you've-got or much lighter — comes from that leg in the hack. Once you become comfortable with your slide, you need to work on gauging how hard to push out from the hack. But whatever you do, avoid at all costs using your arm to add any force to the rock.

A good analogy for this was given to me by Lino Di Iorio, one of the best analysts of the curling delivery. He says to think about how you push a shopping cart when you're buying groceries. You don't push the cart with your arms; you simply put your hands on the cart with your arms extended and walk with your legs. The cart moves because of your legs, not your arms. The same is true of a curling delivery.

So, as you begin your forward swing, push out from the hack and allow your arm to fully extend, ensuring it stays relaxed. Don't allow any of your weight to shift onto the rock. Your weight should still be over your hack foot at this point, though you will move your weight forward momentarily. Some players let their arm go stiff and hold themselves up by almost leaning on the stone. This is called *riding the rock*, and it's just about the worst thing you can do. The result is an inconsistent delivery, because you have to throw the stone when you release it to get any kind of push behind it.

Shift your weight

This next crucial move occurs with your sliding foot, and can make or break your delivery. In fact, I'd say that this might be the key move in the entire delivery.

After you push out from the hack, your weight shifts feet. It travels from your hack foot (your right foot, if you're throwing right), to your sliding foot (your left foot). Your sliding foot must move into the proper position to take this weight and stay on line. *It must slide directly in behind the stone.* If you get it there successfully, it should keep your body in line as you deliver the rock, sliding up the target line towards the skip's broom. If your sliding foot is beside the stone, your body can end up sliding in one direction while your stone goes in another. The push from the hack forces your body to follow your sliding foot. Who knows which direction that may be if it's not behind your stone?

You will find it easier to support your weight on your sliding foot if it is turned outwards, with the toe pointing at about a 75-degree angle. For many curlers, this turned-out position is more comfortable than having the toe pointing straight ahead. However, it's not absolutely vital; some players keep the toe straight ahead, while still others turn it out to almost a 90-degree angle. Try out different positions until you find one that suits you.

The slide

Now that you've switched weight from hack foot to sliding foot and you've pushed off from the hack, you're into your slide. In a perfect delivery, all the work is now done. Unfortunately, I've never seen a perfect delivery. There are still a few things left to do in the slide.

The force generated when you push out of the hack propels you down the sheet. As you leave the hack, let your back leg extend out, so it can act as a rudder and balance aid, as shown in Figure 9-7. Your broom, resting on the ice now, is also helping your balance. Your upper body should be straight and upright so that you have a good visual perspective of the ice.

Again, it's important that none of your body weight is on the rock. You and the rock are actually travelling down the sheet together at the same speed (at least initially); your hand is simply connecting you to it.

Your back foot is obviously the last part of your body to get into the slide. It can assume one of three positions:

- **Turned in:** Your foot is turned over so the outside of it is on the ice. This is the most common style.

- **Turned out:** Your foot is turned so that the inside of it is on the ice.

- **Straight:** Your foot points straight back. Although this seems simple, not many curlers use this position.

The position of your back foot is a matter of personal comfort. I can't recall ever choosing among the styles — I just did what came naturally.

Figure 9-7: With your sliding foot in behind the rock, your trailing leg extends out behind you to act as a rudder.

Sliding at the broom

In a good delivery, you slide right at the target (the skip's broom) with the correct weight. If you can get this far, you're nearly home free in terms of placing your rock where you want it.

Sliding at the broom, however, is easier said than done.

One of the situations where it *is* a little easier, is when you play a shot right down the middle. You can line the rock up on the Centre line with your body just slightly to the left of it. Your knees, hips, chest, and shoulders should all be aimed slightly left of the target, for a right-hander. This is because your rock is actually right down the line, while your body, at the start, is sitting slightly to the left. Keep your body upright and your spine straight. I like to think of my spine as being perpendicular to the target line.

It's important to remember that, while your stone is lined up right along the target line, your body is actually lined up just to the left of it. This means that at the start of your delivery, there are actually two different target lines — one that your stone follows, another for your body. When you slide out of the hack, your body will move in behind the rock so that it and the rock are advancing towards the target on the same line.

Of course, not all shots are played right down the Centre line. Here comes the easier-said-than-done part. If the target is either to the left or right of the Centre line, you must move your body and the position of the rock accordingly.

One of the most common errors you can make when you do this is to actually *over-do it*, and move your body well outside the target line. This happens because the target appears to move a great deal. You feel, in turn, that you must move your body a great deal to match it. For example, if your target is the outside of the 12-foot, that represents a move of six feet from the Centre line at the target end. But in the hack, you only have to move a couple of inches to change your aim accordingly, as indicated in Figure 9-8. If you draw a line from the target back to the Centre line at the base of the hack, you see that the path your rock needs to travel isn't that far off the Centre line at all — only a few inches. This is the line where your stone should be pointed. In fact, even if you're aiming at the far outside of the sheet, your stone will still begin with a part of it touching the Centre line.

The release

The final part of a good delivery is the release, where you let go of the stone and let it travel on its way. This is another key part of the delivery, as just the slightest miscue here can put the stone off line.

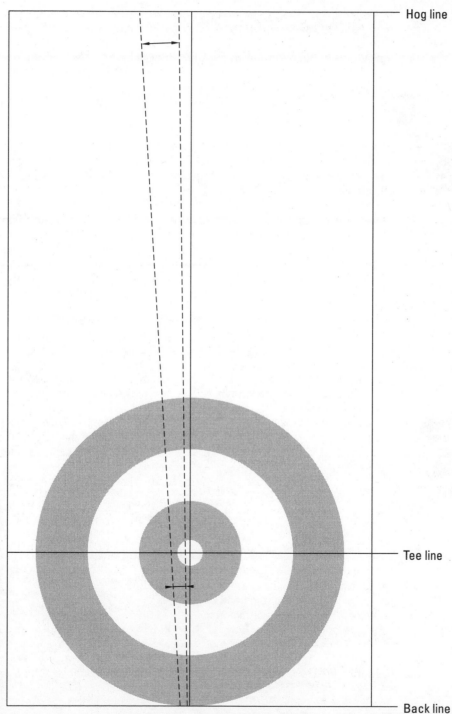

Hog line

Tee line

Back line

Figure 9-8:
You only
have to
make a
slight
adjustment
to move
your target
from the
Centre line
to the out-
side of the
12-foot.

No matter whether you are throwing an in-turn or an out-turn, your hand will end up in the same position when you release the rock. Upon the release, your hand should be extended, as if you were going to shake hands with your target. It should be at about shoulder height and pointing along the target line. It should be straight, but not tense. If you finish this way, you will have turned the rock handle enough to give it the proper amount of rotation. If you do it properly, the rotation will just occur naturally, without any real force.

Don't ever try to force the turn onto a stone. If you start with the handle in the proper position and you release as described here, you won't even have to think about *putting on the handle* (that's the curling term for giving the stone the rotation). It will just happen. If you throw a stone that doesn't turn at all, it's called a *no handle*.

The point in your slide where you release your rock is also important. It depends a great deal how far down the ice you slide, but, wherever it occurs, it should be consistent for every shot. Most of the time, your release occurs before your slide starts to slow down or just as it starts to slow down. If it happens after this, you are forced to throw with your arm to compensate.

Troubleshooting

Not every delivery you make will be spot on. Sometimes you get into bad habits, or do things subconsciously that negatively affect where your rock ends up. Here are a few common errors to look for:

- **Chicken wing:** This happens when you bend your arm during the release. If it's bent, when you go to turn your wrist to finish in the handshake position, it becomes difficult to make the movement without moving your entire arm. This is especially a problem when you throw an in-turn.

- **Drifting:** This happens when you drift out towards the side of the sheet instead of travelling directly towards the broom. You have to make a correction to get the rock back on line, which affects the path of the stone. If this happens, make sure that, in your setup, you are lined up with the target.

- **Finishing left or right:** This happens when you move your hand sideways as you release the stone, instead of straight ahead. Your rock will likely finish either to the left or right of the target line, towards whichever side you moved your hand. To correct it, make sure your hand moves up and off the rock, not left or right.

- **Hanging on:** This happens when you hang onto the rock too long. Instead of the turn occurring naturally, you have to force it, which makes the rock susceptible to being twisted off line. To correct it, practise letting go of the rock immediately after you push from the hack. This will give you the proper release feel.

- **Playing with the handle:** This happens when you try to make last-second adjustments to the position of the stone or to the rotation. Your release should be smooth and controlled.

Chapter 10

The Shots

The object of curling is quite simple: Get more of your rocks closer to the centre of the house than the other team. *How* you get your rocks there, however, can be complicated.

That's because there are many different ways to play your shots:

✔ You can play *a draw*, and deliver your shot softly;

✔ You can play *a takeout* (also called *a hit*), and deliver your shot with a great deal of force to knock another stone out of play;

✔ You can play *a guard,* a shot that comes to rest in front of the house (a defensive shot); or

✔ You can play *a raise*, a shot that promotes another of your team's stones into the house.

It's important to know as many shots as possible so you are prepared for anything in a game. Some, such as the draw or takeout, are quite common. Others, such as the *split*, are quite rare. You might play ten games and never play the split once. But it's important that you know how to play it just the same, as you never know when you might need it. I tell you about the split and other shots in more detail, later in the chapter.

You also need to understand the *intent* behind the different shots — why the skip calls them, and how they affect the situation.

What Makes a Good Shot

Every curling shot is a combination of two things: *weight* and *line*. Weight is the amount of force you use to propel the stone down the sheet. Line is the direction in which you throw the stone. Unless you have both, chances are you won't make your shot. You can have the right weight and the wrong line, which will cause your shot to end up in the wrong spot. The same can be said if you have the right line but the wrong weight. The two go hand in hand to making a good curling shot.

Watching your weight

The weight refers to how hard you push the stone. If you are asked to play a *big weight hit*, for example, that means a shot that is thrown with a great deal of force. It travels very quickly down the sheet and removes another stone from play (hopefully one belonging to the opposition). If you are asked to throw *draw weight*, on the other hand, you throw your stone with less force — just enough for it to stop on the Tee line, for example, or wherever the skip instructs you to throw it.

The weight of a shot affects the amount of curl. Stones that are thrown with big weight don't curl much. That's because they don't have time to bend as much as a stone thrown with draw weight. Generally speaking, the harder a rock is thrown, the less it bends.

Here is a list of the more common types of weight you are asked to throw, from lightest weight to the "heavyweights":

- **Draw weight:** a shot that stops on the Tee line

- **Back-line weight:** a shot that has enough weight to make it to the Back line

- **Hack weight:** a shot that has enough weight to travel all the way to the hack

- **Board weight:** a shot that has enough weight to travel to the boards at the back of the sheet, usually just a bit more than hack weight

- **Control weight:** a shot that is heavier than board weight, but less than normal takeout weight, sometimes referred to as a "quiet hit"

- **Takeout weight:** a shot thrown with the weight necessary to remove another rock from play, a pretty common weight

- **Peel weight:** a takeout shot thrown very hard and often used to remove a number of opposition stones

Clutch performers

The best players in the world are usually the most successful at consistently getting the right weight.

- **Al Hackner:** Known in curling circles as the "Iceman" because of his calm, cool demeanour when facing big shots, the two-time world champion threw what is regarded as curling's most famous shot. In 1985, while playing in the final of the Brier (the Canadian men's championship), Hackner had a last-chance shot in the tenth end in order to stay in the game. He threw a very difficult double-takeout shot that sent the crowd into a frenzy. Hackner tied the game with the shot and went on to win in the extra end.

- **Guy Hemmings:** While playing in the semifinal of the 1999 Brier, Hemmings, the skip of the team representing Québec, had to make a difficult shot to win the game and advance to the final — a draw to the exact centre of the house. Hemmings did it, but his team lost in the final the day after.

- **Russ Howard:** A two-time world champion from Midland, Ontario, Howard was always able to find the exact line and combine it with the perfect weight. He has made so many great shots that it's almost impossible to recount them all.

- **Ernie Richardson:** The only skip to win four Canadian titles, Richardson was known for his ability to focus so intently on the game that he rarely lost. Along with his family team of Arnold (his cousin), Sam (his brother), and Wes Richardson (another cousin), he is still regarded as the best ever.

You have to adjust the weight of your shots for the individual ice conditions. Your draw weight on one sheet may be entirely different than on another sheet or at another club. Because every sheet of ice is different, your weight will be different, too. A good player adjusts quickly to the different ice conditions.

Now, however, I'm going to appear to contradict myself when I tell you to try to keep your weight the same all the time. Note that I write "appear." I mean that you should keep the weight of your shots consistent in relation to the ice conditions of the sheet you're playing on. That means that if you throw your takeout weight a bit on the light side, you should do it that way all the time. It doesn't mean that you throw it with the same force — you have to take into account the ice conditions. It *does* mean that you throw it with the same weight relative to the speed of the sheet on which you're playing. If the ice is slower than you are used to, then you will have to throw it harder, but in relation to the ice, your takeout weight will still be a bit less than a normal takeout. This is necessary so the skip can give you the right ice. (If you *do* throw your takeouts lighter, then you need more ice because your rock will curl more. If you tend to throw harder takeouts, the skip knows to give you less ice.)

Staying in line

The concept of weight is only one part of throwing a shot. The other piece of the puzzle — and believe me, many days it *is* a puzzle — is *line*. The line is the direction in which you deliver the stone.

Before you deliver your stone, the skip tells you what type of shot to play. After he indicates the shot he wants, he holds the broom vertically over the spot you are going to aim for. This gives you a target of sorts, as shown in Figure 10-1. This is called *giving you the ice*. Where the broom is placed depends on the skip's understanding of how much the ice is curling. Figuring out how much or how little the ice is curling on the particular sheet, on that particular day, is the skip's responsibility. If it is curling a lot, the distance between where he places the broom and where your stone should finish is greater than if the ice is not curling too much. Ice conditions are different in every game. They can even change *during* a game.

Figure 10-1:
The skip gives you a target to shoot at by holding the broom.

Waiting for the signal

The skip indicates which shot he wants you to throw through the use of hand and broom signals. Some of these are standard signals, universally understood; others are particular to your team.

Broom signals

Here are the standard broom signals:

- ✔ **Draw:** The skip first taps the ice where the rock is expected to stop and holds the broom on the ice for you to use as the target.

- ✔ **Takeout:** The skip taps the rock that your shot is to remove and holds the broom on the desired line. About 99 percent of the time, you will remove one of your opponent's stones, but there are rare occasions when you might want to take out one of your own.

- ✔ **Raise:** The skip taps the stone that is to be promoted (one of yours, hopefully) and holds the broom up horizontally, across his chest, with both hands. The distance between his hands is the approximate distance he wants the stationary stone to move. He might also tap the stationary stone and then tap the spot behind it where he wants you to bump it.

- ✔ **Split:** The skip taps the stationary stone and then taps the ice on either side of it, indicating that he wants both that stationary rock and the *shooter* (the rock you are throwing) to roll into the house.

- ✔ **Freeze:** The skip taps the ice immediately in front of the stone he wants frozen. (A freeze is when your stone comes to rest exactly in front of another stone. This, and other types of shots, are covered later in this chapter.)

Hand signals

For beginners, there are hand signals that indicate which turn to throw, either an *in-turn* or an *out-turn*. I'll assume you are right-handed. If your skip holds out his left arm, he's telling you to throw an out-turn, so you would rotate the stone outwards in a counterclockwise direction. If he holds out his right arm, then you play an in-turn, rotating the stone inwards in a clockwise direction.

When you become more proficient, the skip no longer holds out a hand to indicate the desired turn. You are expected to know which way to rotate the handle.

Team-specific signals

There are other hand signals that are unique from team to team. Because the skip is at one end of the ice and the rest of the team is at the other, hand signals are easier to use than yelling (although there is usually a fair amount of talk between the team members, regardless, during the game).

Most of these hand signals are used to indicate the weight of the shot. Because the amount of curl is proportionate to the speed at which the stone travels down the sheet (the faster the rock, the less curl), you and the skip need to agree on how hard you are going to throw it so that he can give you

Ten excuses to use when you miss a shot

1. "Too much weight."

2. "Not enough ice."

3. "That was the skip's fault." (This one can't be used by skips.)

4. "They swept it too much."

5. "I think it hit something on the ice."

6. "I slipped coming out of the hack."

7. "My malaria is flaring up again."

8. "The third on the other team body-checked me."

9. "The sun was in my eyes."

10. "I guess I really can't make that shot blind-folded."

the right target. Many shots are missed because of miscommunication between the player throwing the rock and the skip calling the shot. If your skip is expecting you to throw a big weight takeout and you throw it with less than that, your stone will likely curl more than the skip expects and miss the target. (A word of advice here if you're not a skip: The skip never takes the blame for the miss — it's always your fault!)

On my team, I use my torso as a kind of scale. If I hold my hand horizontally across my shoulders, that means I want the player to throw the stone very hard. If I hold it across my chest, I'd like it to be normal takeout weight. If I hold it across my stomach, I want the stone to be lighter than normal.

I give these hand signals after the broom signals. This way, the player first learns which shot I want, then learns with what weight I want that shot to be played.

Make sure you sit down with your team and discuss your particular signal system. If, during a game, you find that you're not sure what the skip wants, stand up out of the hack and ask the skip to repeat the signal. If you still aren't sure, then you need to talk. Go down the ice and chat, have a conference at mid-sheet, do whatever it takes, but don't deliver the stone until you are certain of the shot.

The Draw

The *draw* is probably the most common shot in curling. When you throw a draw, you throw your stone into the rings. If you can't learn to draw, you can't curl.

Throwing it

The draw may be one of the most important shots to get under your belt, but luckily, it's pretty simple to throw. The skip taps the spot in the house where your rock is supposed to finish and then holds up the broom for you to take aim at. You take aim at the broom, deliver the stone with the right weight and turn, and it should stop on the spot indicated.

Throwing a draw is easy in theory, but it never goes quite that smoothly in practice! With a bit of work, however, you can get good at the draw.

When you throw a draw, you need to be exact with your weight. This is the tough part about the shot. You need to push out from the hack with just the correct amount of thrust so your stone travels the right distance. And the ice won't be your friend with this, either. Depending on where you throw your shot, it might need a different amount of weight. Often, when you throw a draw that starts way out near the side of the sheet, it needs more weight than one that's delivered right down the centre. Trial and error — as well as experience — helps you get a feel for draw weight.

Getting good at it

How do you become good at the draw? Practice is about the only way. (Sorry, I know you were waiting for me to divulge some long-held curling secret. The game's just not like that.)

You need to develop great touch in order to get good at draw weight. The only real way to develop touch is to practise. You also need to trust your instincts enough when you push out of the hack that you do so at the right speed, and with a fluid, continuous motion. Many great draws are ruined because a player slides out and then tries to adjust the weight by pulling it back or pushing it out with her hand. That's no way to throw a draw — you need to get all the momentum with the push from the hack. Another key is to rely on your sweepers, who can help make a rock go farther. That's why good drawers usually throw light, not heavy. Sweepers can't help a heavy stone, but they can do a lot for a light one. Chapter 15 is all about practising to make your game better.

There's another aid, as well: a stopwatch. Every draw shot — every shot, actually — takes a certain amount of time to travel down the sheet. If, on a particular sheet of ice on a particular day, your draw shot takes 23 seconds to travel from the Hog line at the delivery end to the Tee line at the other end, then you can put a measure on your shot, which can be a big help to your game.

In the early 1980s, a number of top players began timing shots as they travelled down the sheet. They figured out that they could tell if the ice was fast or slow by measuring the length of time it took. If the ice is fast or "quick," you throw softer shots, which take longer to travel down the sheet. Conversely, with slow or "heavier" ice, you throw harder shots, which take less time to travel the sheet. As the curlers became more scientific, they began timing a player from the moment he set his stone on the ice — or began the forward press of his no-lift delivery — until it reached the first Hog line. They knew immediately if the stone was going to be short or long, and could either sweep or not sweep, accordingly. However the rocks were timed, so the speed of the ice was now quantifiable. You can make use of this, too. It's easy, and can be an asset to your game, especially if you play at a number of different clubs.

The easiest way to time stones is to do it to your opposition's stones. Stand at the Hog line at the delivery end as they are throwing. As the stone reaches the first Hog line, start your timer. When the stone comes to rest, stop your watch and look at the time. The time tells you how fast or slow the ice is. If you use this tool often, you should get a fairly consistent time from your home club. When you go to other clubs, you should be able to adjust to the speed of the ice, whether it's faster or slower than at your home club.

Using a stopwatch on draw shots can also tell you whether the speed of the ice is changing. Not only does it change from club to club and sheet to sheet, but it can change *during* the course of a game, too. Regular use of the stopwatch helps you see this.

Some players do timed takeouts, as well, but for the most part the stopwatch is a tool solely for draws.

Here a draw, there a draw

There are a few types of draw shots that indicate a little more precisely where the shot is supposed to end up. They're still simple draw shots, but where and how they travel is specified in the name of the shot.

- **Draw around the guard (Figure 10-2, on the opposite page):** This is a draw shot that curls around a stone in front of the house and ends up behind it.

- **Draw through the port (Figure 10-3):** This is a draw shot that travels between two other stones. The space between the two stones is called the *port*.

- **Draw to the button (Figure 10-4):** This is a draw shot that stops right at the centre of the house. This shot is sometimes called *drawing the lid*. (Figure 10-3 and Figure 10-4 are shown a few pages ahead.)

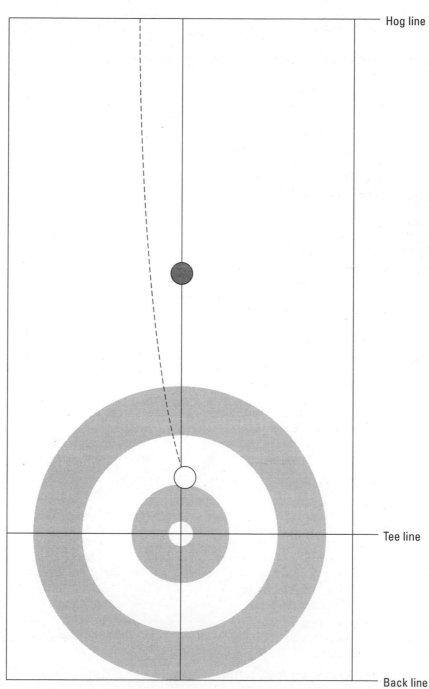

Figure 10-2:
The draw
around the
guard is
one of curl-
ing's most
common
shots.

Hog line

Tee line

Back line

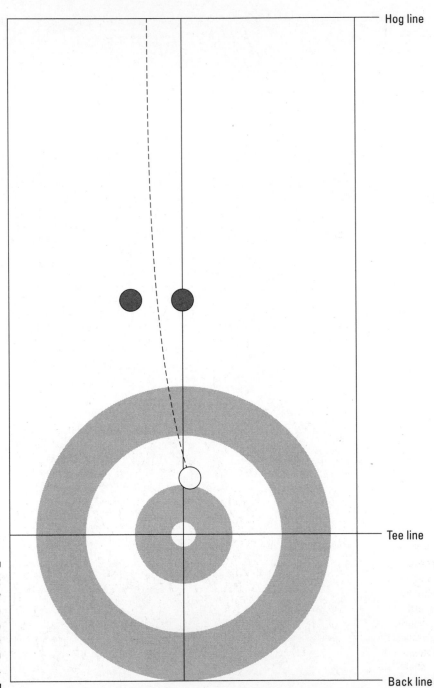

Hog line

Tee line

Back line

Figure 10-3:
A draw through the port has to navigate between two rocks.

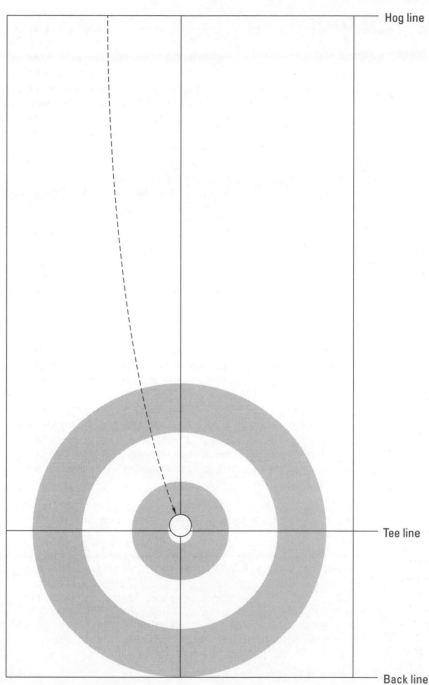

Hog line

Tee line

Back line

Figure 10-4:
A draw to
the Button
is often
the game-
winning
shot.

The Takeout

Unlike the draw, the *takeout* is a shot that can be played with a variety of different weights. In essence, a takeout is a shot that removes another stone from play. There are different ways to do this. A takeout can be thrown with just enough weight to push the stationary stone to the back or side, or it can be thrown so hard that your molars rattle when the two stones collide, and the stationary stone is removed from play.

When you throw a takeout, you sometimes want your rock — called *the shooter* — to stay in play, other times you want it to roll to another spot, or even right out of play. The skip has all of this in mind when he signals for you to make the shot.

Throwing it

For most players, the takeout is the easiest shot to play. In most situations, you don't have to be exact with your weight; it's more a matter of line. And because a takeout doesn't curl as much as a draw, it is less susceptible to the intricacies of the ice.

But being able to play takeouts with precise weight can nevertheless be a big help to your team. Here are some of the more common types of takeout shots played and how your skip calls them:

- **Hack-weight takeout:** This is a gentle takeout, often used when there are a lot of other rocks in play. It's played often when you need the shooter to curl a little bit, say to get past a *guard* (a stone that protects another stone). Another time you play hack weight is if you want to make sure your shooter stays in play.

  To call for the shot, the skip taps the hack, taps the rock to be removed, and then puts the broom down on the proper line.

- **Hit and roll:** This is used when you want to play a takeout and have your shooter roll to another part of the ice. The object here is to hit only a part of the stationary stone so you get the desired roll. The more of the rock you make contact with, the less roll there will be.

  To call for the shot, the skip touches the rock to be removed and then taps the ice where the shooter is supposed to roll to. Hit and rolls require the skip to know exactly how much of the stationary stone needs to be hit to get the required roll.

- **Nose hit:** This takeout can be played with any type of weight. The goal is to hit the stationary rock head-on (or "on the nose," hence the name of the shot). If your shooter makes the hit, it should come to a complete stop, exactly in front of where the stationary stone was.

> To call for the shot, the skip taps the stationary stone and then taps the ice in front of that stone. Or he might tap the stationary stone and then touch his nose.
>
> ✔ **Peel:** This takeout not only removes an opposition stone, but one of your own stones, as well. This strategy — removing *all* the stones from play — is often used late in the game, if your team has the lead. To peel a rock, you only want to hit a very small part of it, a quarter or less.
>
> To call for the shot, the skip taps the rock to be removed and then moves the broom quickly off to the side. He follows this with a weight indication to show that he wants big weight.
>
> ✔ **Double takeout:** This takeout removes two opposition stones. You can also throw a *triple* or *quadruple takeout* — depending on how many opposition stones you remove.
>
> To call for the shot, the skip taps both rocks, one after the other, with the same motion used for a regular takeout. The first stone tapped is the one the shooter should make contact with first.

Getting good at it

A common mistake when you first start curling is to play takeouts with too much weight. The best type of takeout is one you can control. That means your sweepers can have an effect on it and you can control what happens to the stone after it hits the stationary one.

Choose a standard takeout weight that suits your style of playing and try to keep it consistent (there's that word again). There's nothing worse for a skip who expects you to throw a certain type of weight than to sorrowfully watch

---

Saying all the right things

When your opposition makes a great shot, you shouldn't hesitate to recognize it. Try these out the next time your opponent throws a good one.

"Nice shot!"

"I wish I could have done that."

"That makes it tough."

"You lucky stiff."

"What a fluke!"

"You couldn't do that again if you tried."

"I saw you cheating on that."

"I'm pretty sure you slid over the Hog line."

"Were you trying to do that?"

"Double fault!"

Seriously, a nice word after a great shot is a sign of respect for your opponent's talents.

you deliver something heavier or lighter. Be consistent with your normal takeout weight and your skip will be better able to give you the right ice.

The Guard

A *guard* is just as its name suggests — a stone that guards another stone. In almost all cases, a guard is a stone that rests between the Hog line and the house. It either totally or partially rests in the path between a stone in the rings and the line to that stone from the hack. A perfect guard covers the path entirely. But one that hides most of the stone(s) in the house is usually pretty good.

The object of playing a guard is to block your opponent's stones from getting to yours. Sometimes you play a guard *before* you play the stone that it's supposed to be guarding. How does this work? Chapter 14 explains a great deal about this type of strategy, but in simple terms, you throw the guard first and then throw the stone to be guarded so that it ends up behind the guard. This strategy is quite common in curling.

There are many different types of guards. A stone that is just over the Hog line is referred to as a *long guard*, while one that is close to the rings is called a *tight guard*. A stone that is very close to the house is called a *short guard*. And in another great example of confusing curling terminology, a stone that is off to either side of the sheet, out by the edge of the 8-foot, is called a *corner guard*. There's no real explanation of how a stone guarding a circle can be called a corner guard, but it is an accepted term, nonetheless.

The first rock thrown in a game is often a guard, usually played so it comes to rest on the Centre line about four or five feet from the house. But guards are played throughout an end, depending on the situation.

A good guard can make or break a game. One that comes too close to the house can be trouble, but so, too, can one that isn't close enough. Just as with draws, guards need to be precise if they are to have the desired effect.

Some people say the perfect guard is the toughest shot in curling. I don't agree with that, but it is definitely one of the most important.

The Freeze

The reason I said the guard wasn't the toughest shot in curling is that, in my book, the *freeze* is tougher. A stone thrown as a freeze comes perfectly to rest *directly in front* of another stone, without moving it (see Figure 10-5). The skip calls for it by tapping the ice directly in front of the stationary stone he wants the shooter to cover.

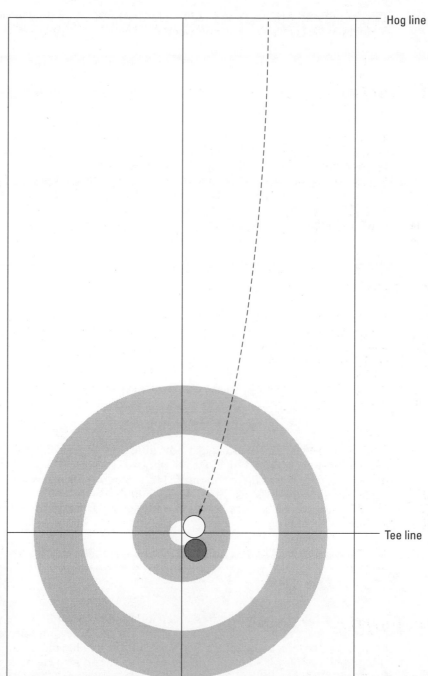

Hog line

Tee line

Back line

Figure 10-5:
The freeze
is probably
the most
difficult shot
in curling.

It's difficult to throw because your weight has to be absolutely perfect. A perfect freeze leaves no space between the shooter and the stationary stone.

If thrown perfectly (much, much easier said than done), the freeze is a very effective shot. See, once it's there, you can't remove it. Your rock is sitting up against another rock and that means there's really nowhere for it to go, no matter how hard it's hit.

The perfect freeze really is between a rock and a hard place. Sometimes, however, you want to play what's called a *corner freeze*. This is a stone that sits at either a 10:30 or 2:30 position (imagine the stationary stone as the face of a clock) in relation to the stone behind it. It sits in front of only part of the stationary stone. The corner freeze is often played on a rock that is off to the side of the sheet. It's still effective because the angled position the shooter ends up in makes it difficult for the stone behind it to be removed.

The Split

The *split* is sort of a two-for-one shot. If you play it properly, you can put two of your team's stones into the rings. To call for this shot, the skip taps the stationary stone to be hit and then moves the broom from one side of the stone to the other.

If you have a stone sitting just out in front of the house — perhaps no more than three feet or so — you can hit a quarter or less of it and spill both it *and* your shooter into the house, as shown in Figure 10-6.

It takes some practice to know just how much of the stationary stone you need to hit to get both of them into the house. Too thick, and only the stationary stone will end up in the rings. Too thin, and only the shooter will get in. The split also needs just the right amount of weight (a little heavier than a draw), because you've got to move the stationary stone as well as the shooter.

The Run-back

This is another shot that requires precision to execute well. When you throw a *run-back,* your shooter hits a stone in front of the house and drives it back onto an opposition stone inside the house, as shown in Figure 10-7 (just flip the page). You play it with takeout weight. You could also call this shot a *raise takeout.*

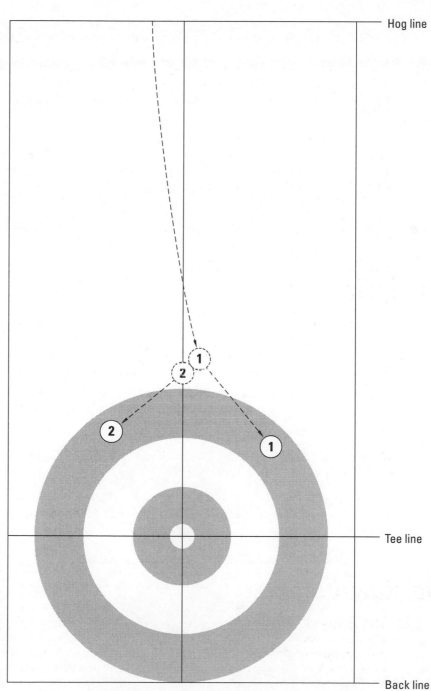

Hog line

Tee line

Back line

Figure 10-6:
The split is
tough to
execute but
can leave
you with
two rocks in
the house.

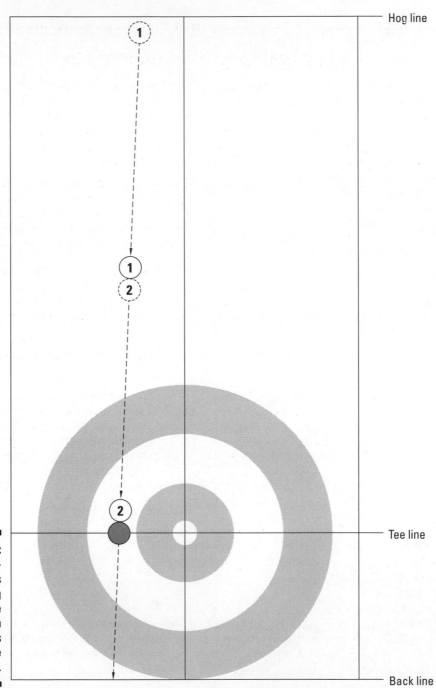

Figure 10-7:
The run-back is becoming a more common shot, thanks to good ice conditions.

Perfection is hard to come by

The perfect end in curling is an eight-ender. That's when all your stones end up in the house, closer to the centre than any of your opposition's stones. It means you've made all your shots. It's sometimes likened to a hole-in-one in golf, but in my book, it's much more difficult. Why? In golf, no one is trying to stop you from getting the ball in the hole. In curling, you have eight opposition stones attempting to prevent you from scoring one point, let alone eight. It's sometimes tough just to throw eight stones into the house consecutively, without anyone trying to stop you.

One team, however, enjoyed the most remarkable feat of scoring in the history of the game. In 1992, Kim Gellard (who would go on to win the 1993 World Junior Championships, as well as

the 1995 women's world championship), skipped a rink playing in a Toronto high school competition. During one game, she and her teammates notched the perfect eight-ender. It was a great moment — one that left the team in awe of its own achievement.

But then, during the very next end, something miraculous happened. The team scored another perfect eight — 16 points in two ends. You can get an idea of how remarkable that was when you consider that some of the most accomplished curlers have never scored an eight-ender. In all my years of curling, I have never seen one! In scoring back-to-back eights, the Kim Gellard team did something that had never been done before (and may never be done again).

There are lots of possible combinations with the run-back. Sometimes, you hit one of your own stones back onto an opposition stone. Other times, you hit one of the opposition's back onto another opposition stone, attempting to remove both of them. Most times, the instructions are relayed verbally down the sheet because they can be complicated if there are lots of rocks in play.

The improvement in ice conditions has made the run-back a much more achievable shot. For this reason, it has become more popular in the past few years, even though it has been around for a long time.

The Raise

The *raise* is sort of like the run-back — except you are just gently bumping one of your stones from in front of the house into the house, as shown in Figure 10-8, on the following pages. Some precision is necessary here also, because you have to direct the stationary stone back on the proper angle.

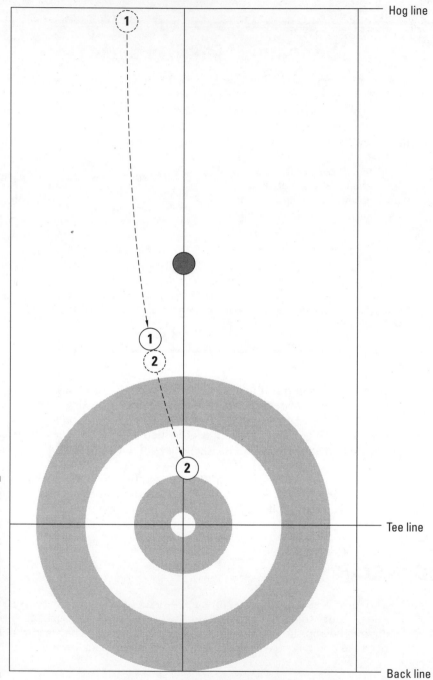

Figure 10-8:
A raise is a good way to get a rock behind cover if the ice is straight and you can't draw a rock behind the guard.

Hog line

Tee line

Back line

That angle depends on the situation, but you need to know where the stationary stone must be struck — and with how much force — to get it to move properly.

The raise can be as simple as bumping a shot from the centre of the sheet into the 4-foot when no other stones are in play, or as complex as moving a stone from way over on the side of the sheet into the 4-foot. If a stone is being promoted from the side of the sheet to the centre, it is referred to as an *angle raise*.

Chapter 11

Sweeping

● ●

In This Chapter

▶ Realizing that you're not just cleaning the ice

▶ Getting the hang of the push-slide step (no, it's not a dance move)

▶ Positioning your hands correctly on the broom

▶ Sweeping with your teammate

▶ Timing the rocks to gauge their speed

● ●

Sweeping is one of the most unusual and least-understood actions in sports. I can't tell you the number of times I've taken someone to see their first curling game, only to have them nearly burst out laughing when they saw the players sweeping.

"Why are those people cleaning the ice?" they say, through their chuckles.

Well, they're not actually cleaning the ice — although to be sure, that *is* one reason for sweeping. They're helping the rock reach its target. And you know what? It does look a little silly to see two grown adults furiously sweeping a stone as it travels down the sheet. But there is good reason for all this brushing.

Sweeping the ice accomplishes two things:

✔ It makes the rock travel farther.

✔ It makes the rock curl less.

A pair of good sweepers can make a stone travel 15 to 20 feet farther down the sheet than if it wasn't being swept at all. And, if a stone is bending too much, sweeping can help keep it straighter.

I really can't say enough about having able sweepers on your team. A good sweeper can be as advantageous as having an extra stone in each end. I played for years with a curler who was easily the best sweeper in my club. I can't tell you how many times he changed the course of a game just because he was able to sweep a rock that extra two or three feet.

How to Sweep

All this sounds great, but how do you actually sweep? Sweeping requires skills such as strength, balance, footwork, not to mention a keen eye. It's not quite as simple as just plopping your broom down in front of the stone and moving the brush back and forth.

Slip-sliding away

For a new curler, the most important thing to get the hang of is keeping up with the stone as it moves down the ice. This goes back to your shoes and the relationship between the gripper and the slider.

After you learn the delivery, the next most important movement you can learn is the *push-slide step*. It's a way of propelling yourself down the sheet. You'll eventually do this holding the broom, but for now, just focus on getting the foot movement down. Put your broom aside. You can pick it up later.

To do the push-slide step:

1. **Turn your body so it is at a 90-degree angle to the end of the sheet where the stones are being played.** If you are right-handed, your slider is on your left foot and your gripper is on your right. You want your slider foot to be the foot closest to the target end, while your gripper foot is closer to the end from where the stones are being delivered. If you are left-handed, reverse this stance, facing the other way.

2. **With your gripper foot firmly planted and your knees slightly bent, push yourself towards the far end of the sheet, keeping your body turned at a 90-degree angle to the direction of play.** Go slowly at first so you don't lose your balance and fall.

   If you've done this right, you should be able to move yourself four or five feet down the ice.

3. **Push off again just as you begin to slow down.** The action is a push-slide, push-slide, push-slide, all the way down the sheet.

Practise going up and down the sheet until you get comfortable with the movement. Don't worry about other stuff like holding the broom or trying to track where you are on the sheet. I know I don't have to tell you this, but, obviously, don't do this while a game is on.

Holding the broom

Once you're comfortable with the push-slide step, you need to know how to hold the curling broom. I recommend you use a push broom or brush, so that's what I describe in this section.

While there isn't one specific way to hold your brush, there are a few fundamentals that help you brush better.

Although your brush measures about five feet in height, you won't use all of that length to sweep. Assuming you're right-handed, do the following:

1. **Place your right hand about two feet from the top of the shaft — the end away from the brush head.** Grip the handle so that your palm is facing towards your body. Your thumb is on top of the handle pointed towards the head, with your fingers wrapped underneath.

2. **Place your left hand about a foot from the head, in more or less the opposite position.** Your palm is facing away from your body this time. Your thumb should still be on top, pointed towards the head of the brush, with your fingers gripping the handle underneath.

As in Figure 11-1, your hands should be in opposite positions on the broom, mirroring each other.

Figure 11-1: Remember how you position your hands on the rope in a tug-of-war? That's the way you want to grip your broom.

Grip the broom securely and with good pressure, because when you become really good at sweeping, you'll be supporting your entire body weight with that grip.

The positions I describe here for hand placement are just guidelines. You'll probably adjust your own hand positions as you get more comfortable sweeping. Every player has certain tendencies and personal preferences, and you need to find yours.

Brushing the stone

When you sweep, bend from your knees and your waist, keeping your weight on the balls of your feet, as shown in Figure 11-2. Place the broom head on the ice so that it is to the left of your body. At first, don't worry about putting too much pressure on the broom — just try to keep your balance. Standing in place, move the head of the brush back and forth. The actual movement should only be about a foot or two forward and back. Any more than this is wasted movement as you're only trying to sweep the path the stone is travelling. The faster you move the brush head, the better.

Figure 11-2: The more of your body weight you can put on the broom handle, the more effective your sweeping will be.

As you become more confident with this movement, try to put a bit more of your body weight over the broom handle. The more pressure you apply to your broom, the more effective your sweeping will be. As you do this, you might also alter your grip somewhat. Better players keep both hands on the broom, squeezing the top of the broom handle between their upper body and upper arm. This gives them a bit more leverage so that they can transfer more weight onto the broom.

Putting it all together

Bet you were wondering when I'd get around to actually sweeping a rock. So, you've mastered the push-slide step? Your grip on your handle is firm and confident? Great. I'm now going to confuse you again, as we put this all together.

Start with your broom on the ice and move it back and forth. Push off with your gripper foot and move yourself down the ice, still sweeping with your brush. This is a bit like trying to walk and chew gum at the same time, but with more practice, it becomes easy.

Practise going up and down the sheet a few times like this, until you get a feel for it.

When, you have that down pat, you can try actually sweeping a stone:

1. **Position yourself at the near Hog line.** Keep back so you are close to the Sideline.

2. **Have a teammate throw a slow rock.** It should only make it about halfway down the sheet.

3. **As your teammate delivers the rock, you begin to move closer to the path of the stone.** Make sure you're not getting in the way of your teammate delivering the stone.

4. **By the time your teammate is about at the top of the house, you begin your push-slide step.** Try to build up some speed so that you are travelling at the same rate as the rock is when your teammate lets go of it.

5. **Put your brush on the ice in front of the stone, in the path where it's travelling.** If you're positioned properly, your broom head will be right in the stone's path and your body will be to the left of it. Move the broom back and forth as quickly as you can in front of where the stone is moving.

Sweeping dos and don'ts

✔ Do clean your broom off every time before you sweep.

✔ Do replace the synthetic surface on your broom when it wears out.

✔ Do always be ready to sweep; from the moment a player releases the stone until it comes to a stop.

✔ Do make sure you and your sweeping partner know how you will sweep together — who will be closer to the stone.

✔ Don't try to use a vacuum cleaner instead of a broom (the extension cord probably won't be long enough).

✔ Don't *over-sweep a rock* (sweep it so that it goes too far). It's a cardinal sin in curling.

✔ Don't use your broom to sweep your kitchen in the off-season.

✔ Don't sweep anyone off their feet (unless you're planning on marrying them).

When you first try this, you probably won't be able to keep up — the stone moves too fast. As you get more stable with your push-slide step, though, you can stay with the stone and work on your sweeping technique. The key is to learn to keep your balance as you move down the sheet. When that becomes second nature, sweeping becomes easier.

Where to Sweep

Sweeping can help your rock, but only if you sweep the path of the stone. You can be a great sweeper, but if you're sweeping *beside* the stone instead of *in front* of it, you won't be any benefit to anyone. It's sort of like shovelling your driveway after a snowstorm so that you can get your car into the garage. If you shovel off your lawn instead of your driveway, it doesn't matter how good a job you do, because you still won't be able to get your car into the driveway. If you aren't brushing the path of the stone when you sweep, then, no matter how strong a sweeper you are, you won't help the stone reach its intended destination.

In curling, there are two sweepers for every stone that's thrown. You won't help things if you and your sweeping partner don't sort out who's sweeping where beforehand. The two of you must become a team, knowing where to put your brooms and how to move your feet so that you can focus solely on sweeping the stone — and not get tangled up with each other.

It takes some practice and some communication to build a team of sweepers, but once you get into symmetry, it can be almost like poetry in motion.

Stay in line!

When the skip calls for you to sweep, place your broom on the ice in the stone's path and move it back and forth across the entire path of the stone. This is key. Don't sweep just part of the path. Not only can you cause the stone to curl unnecessarily, but you'll break a rule of the game.

Move your broom across the whole path — but not much more. You can waste energy if you make your strokes too long.

A lot of curlers waste energy and lose effectiveness because they don't sweep in the right place. It's vitally important that you sweep the path of the rock — but it's easy to miss when you're worried about trying to stay on your feet and listen to the directions being given by the skip. I've played with and against curlers who thought their brooms were in the right place but, in reality, they were sweeping well outside the line. All that effort might keep them warm in the cold arena, but it doesn't help the stone.

You're not sweeping alone, you know

There are two players who sweep every stone thrown. Now, in a perfect world, one sweeper would be situated on the left side of the sheet, the other sweeper on the right. They wouldn't have to worry about bumping into each other, getting their feet tangled, or burning the stone.

But unless you have a left-handed and right-handed player, or your team members are skilled enough to sweep on either side of the stone, you end up with two players sweeping on one side. This makes it tough for the second sweeper @the one farthest from the stone — to get the broom close to the stone's path.

The other side of the sheet

When you become good enough with your balance and your push-slide step, you may find that you can actually work on a *pull-slide step*, that is, switch over to the other side of the sheet and still move yourself down the sheet and sweep. Your footing becomes a little tricky this way — you have to sort of drag yourself along by using your gripper foot to pull rather than push. Or, you may choose to put the cover over your slider and go down the ice without the benefit of any slider. This requires you to adopt a sort of short jog or hop-step to keep up with the rock and still be able to brush. Experiment with different foot actions and you too might be able to sweep on either side of the sheet.

What does sweeping do?

It's generally agreed that sweeping makes the rocks travel farther and curl less. But exactly how sweeping accomplishes this remains a bit of a mystery.

✔ One theory is that the heat from the sweeping action melts a bit of the ice, creating a micro-thin layer of water that the rock rides on top of.

✔ The other theory is that the sweeping action polishes the pebble, wearing it down and making the ice a bit smoother for the stone to travel on.

Although we still don't know *how* the sweeping action makes the rocks travel farther, research done at Queen's University in Kingston, Ontario, proved beyond a doubt that sweeping *does* make them go farther.

Average club curlers swept rocks thrown by a machine with identical force. On heavy ice, the sweepers could drag a rock an extra two feet. On quick ice, this distance increased to ten feet. The best sweepers would be able to sweep the stones an even greater distance, the study indicated.

It's the second sweeper who generally has the most problems getting the broom in the right path. Being farther away from the stone means it's tougher to get a visual sense of where your broom is in relation to the path of the stone. If you think you might not be getting your broom in the right place, ask your skip for feedback. She'll be able to tell by watching you come down the ice.

Why You Sweep

As I said at the start of this chapter, the reason you sweep is to make the stone travel farther and curl less. That, in a nutshell, is what all this crazy brushing is about.

Special sweeping circumstances

Here are a few specific instances in a game when you need to sweep, and what it accomplishes (or at least tries to):

✔ **Drawing around a guard:** In this situation, you are trying to place your stone behind cover, but you see that it's curling to the point where it will hit the guard. You sweep the stone to make it curl less, taking it past the guard and in behind the cover.

✔ **Drawing into the house:** In this situation, you are trying to deliver your stone so it ends up, say, in the 4-foot, but it looks like it will only go as far as the 12-foot. You sweep the stone to make it travel farther.

✔ **Playing a takeout:** In this situation, you are trying to hit an opposition stone, but your stone starts to curl and it looks like it will move past that target stone. You sweep the stone so it curls less, stays on line, and hits the target.

You can see that there are many situations in a game where you need to sweep. When you first start playing, the skip (or the third when the skip is throwing) actually tells you when to sweep. As you get more experienced, however, a different rule applies. While the skip or third calls the line, the sweepers have to judge the weight. The more you play, the better you become at judging weight. A good lead and second know whether a stone needs sweeping almost from the time a player lets it go. If it requires sweeping for line, the skip barks the orders from the far end of the sheet.

Don't forget your stopwatch

If you play lead or second, you can help your sweeping by carrying a stopwatch. Timing rocks, if done properly, can give you an immediate indication of the weight of a stone. To do this takes a lot of practice and some quick hands. That's because you carry the watch in one hand, your broom in the other, time the rock, and then put the watch away and grab the broom with your second hand. And you thought just sweeping the rock was hard!

I know that sounds a little complicated, but it's not that tough once you get the hang of it. Really.

But why should you time your stones in the first place? You can use a stopwatch to measure how fast or slow the ice is, based on the amount of time it takes a stone to travel down the sheet. Normal ice speed at my club, for example, is about 23 seconds. Given this, I know how hard I have to push from the hack to deliver a stone. When I go to a different club and time the ice at 21 seconds, I know I have to push out a little harder.

So what does this have to do with sweeping? Well, gradually the top players realized that the same principles of timing a stone could be applied earlier in the delivery. They time stones from the first Tee line to the first

Hog line, and, with this number, they immediately know whether the stone requires sweeping. If a player takes three seconds to travel from the Hog to the Tee and that stone ends up on the Tee line, the sweepers know that if the next one takes 3.5 seconds, then it will require sweeping. Most of the time, the differences are in tenths and hundredths of seconds.

Timing rocks is becoming more and more popular. There are even special stopwatches that wrap around brooms to make it that much more manageable.

If you are new to curling, don't worry too much about timing the rocks. However, as you become more proficient at other parts of the game, get yourself a good stopwatch and try it out. It can make sweeping that much easier.

Chapter 12

Stepping onto the Ice

* *

In This Chapter

▶ Limbering up before the game

▶ Trying some practice slides

▶ Observing traditions throughout the game

▶ Ending the game the right way

* *

*N*ow that you know the basics of curling, you can step onto the ice and actually play a game.

But wait! Not so fast. There are quite a few little things you need to know before you get started — several nuances that happen during the match that don't necessarily affect the score but are still integral to the game.

It's as important to know these subtler parts of the game as to know how to deliver a rock, throw a takeout, and sweep properly. Some are traditions, while others are formal parts of playing.

Before First Rock Is Thrown

You've got your shoes on — and you've made sure they're clean. You have your broom, your gloves, and your sweater. You know what position you are playing and who your teammates are. So what's next?

Although it may seem rather obvious, check to see what time your game is at. You should arrive at the club about 45 minutes before the start, so that you have enough time to dress and prepare for the match.

Arrive at your club well in advance of your game. Put on your pants and your shoes. Keep your sweater off until you are ready to go onto the ice. If you wear it beforehand, you'll get too hot, which could leave you chilled when you do eventually go on the sheet.

Take it from me: There's nothing worse than rushing to the club, changing your clothes in a frenzy, and running out to the ice. You're racing, you're off balance, and you don't have time to focus. It's not the way you want to go into your game.

Warming Up

Stretching before the game helps prevent injuries and helps you play better. If your muscles are tight when you first start the game, you won't slide very well, and that affects your shotmaking ability.

Legs

The muscles in your legs are the most important ones to stretch out. Though you should stretch all your leg muscles — your calf muscles, adductors, and abductors — focus on your hamstrings and quadriceps. These are the major muscle groups you use when you slide.

Stretching it out

On a dry surface such as the locker room floor, or on the surface behind the sheet, if there's enough room, get into your delivery position. Gently press down and hold for a few seconds, as shown in Figure 12-1. Make sure you don't bounce up and down — that can lead to injuries. Just feel the stretch in your muscles.

Figure12-1:
Stretching out your leg muscles before the game gets you ready to play and helps prevent injuries.

Quadriceps

Stand and place one hand against a wall. Grab your foot at the ankle and pull it up behind you so that your heel touches your buttocks, as shown in Figure 12-2. Hold this stretch for a few seconds and then switch legs.

Figure 12-2:
This stretch loosens up your quadriceps, a key muscle group in your delivery.

Just hold the stretch without any bouncing or sudden pulls.

Upper body

Loosening up your leg muscles helps you deliver the stone the best you can. You should loosen your upper body, too, to help with your sweeping. I like two particular stretches for the upper back and triceps.

Upper back

Hold your right arm across your chest. With your left arm, take hold of your right arm at the elbow and gently pull it towards you until you feel a stretch in your upper back and shoulder. Hold it for a few seconds and then release. Switch and do the other arm. Avoid any jerking motions.

Triceps

Hold your arm straight up, and then bend at the elbow so your hand is down by the middle of your back and your elbow is pointing straight up. With your other arm, reach up and around and grab the outside of your elbow, as shown in Figure 12-3. Pull your elbow back until you feel the stretch in your triceps. Hold it for a few seconds and then do the other arm in the same fashion.

Figure 12-3:
Stretching out your triceps helps prepare you to sweep.

Reasons you should stretch before you curl:

- ✔ To get your blood flowing and prevent injuries that can occur when you go from a warm area to a cold area, such as from the locker room to the ice.

- ✔ To hit your delivery position and therefore throw better shots.

- ✔ To get you mentally prepared for the game.

- ✔ To avoid being so sore the next morning that you can barely make it out of bed. This especially holds true if you're a relatively new curler or you are playing after a long layoff.

Heading Out to the Sheet

The sheet you're scheduled to play on is posted on a schedule somewhere in your club. You won't play every game on the same sheet, so be sure to check before you play.

Which sheet?

If you're not playing in a regularly scheduled game, ask your skip or the curling manager which sheet you're on. As a last resort, go out onto the ice and find your teammates. They're probably standing in the back of the sheet, wondering where you are. There's no set number of sheets at a club — some have just 1, while others have as many as 16. However, most clubs have between 4 and 6.

Practice slides

You should try a few slides before every game to further loosen your muscles and get a feel for the ice.

I usually slide — without the rock — two or three times on my sheet, trying to imagine I'm throwing a stone in the game. While this warm-up is mostly to get loose, you should still pick out a target and slide at it. The more you can make these warm-up slides like your real delivery, the more effective they'll be. There's no point in just jumping into the hack and recklessly sliding down the sheet.

As recently as 20 years ago, it was taboo to practise on the sheet you were going to play your game on. Though it was actually in the rulebook for a while, it was more of an unspoken agreement between teams to stay off the ice until the start of the game. The thinking was that one team might get an advantage by seeing how the ice was running before the game started. But rules and etiquette have changed in recent years. Today, it's quite common to throw practice stones before the game. You won't be able to do this if there is a game immediately before yours — the ice technician needs those few minutes between games to prepare the sheet. But if there is no game before yours, take the opportunity to practise.

I make a point of getting to the sheet before the game and throwing a few stones up and down.

If you can do this, practise with the same stones you're going to use in your game. Try to accomplish two things:

✔ Get your draw weight down. By "draw weight," I mean the proper amount of force to throw the stone into the house.

✔ Determine how much (or how little) the ice is curling in certain spots.

If I only have time to throw two practice shots, I always draw one to the Button (to try to get the weight down), and one as a centre guard. This gives me not only an idea of weight, but also a good idea of the line I need for that all-important first shot of the game, whether my team has last rock or not. This is one way I can get an edge on my opposition early in the contest.

Shaking Hands

This is one of the great traditions of curling. Before the start of the game, you shake hands with all four players on the other team, and say, "Good curling" to each player — sort of a variation on "Good luck," or "Have a good game." If you don't know the players on the other team, this is also the point where you introduce yourself.

Curling has been built on traditions such as this, and shaking hands before the start of a game is one of the most important. It not only shows respect for your opposition, but also symbolizes a time-honoured belief among curlers: that the personal interaction and camaraderie enjoyed with your fellow players is more important than winning the game. Curlers shake hands before the start of club games and world championships. They do it all over the world — in small rinks and big. Wherever you're playing, don't ever let the outcome of the game take over the respect you have for your peers. In all my years in curling, I haven't met too many curlers that I didn't like or, at the very least, who didn't share a love of the sport. Shaking hands is one way to show this.

Oh, but please remember to take your glove off before you shake.

The Coin Toss

There's one more thing to do before the first rock is thrown — and that's decide which team will throw it. The traditional way of deciding this is to flip a coin. This is the job of the thirds. One third tosses the coin and the other third calls either heads or tails while it's in the air.

It used to be that whoever won the coin toss had two choices:

- ✔ Taking last stone in the first end (meaning the other team would shoot the first stone);

  or

- ✔ Choosing the set of rocks they would play with and throwing the first stone of the end.

Nowadays, however, the winner always takes last rock in the first end.

Other ways to award last rock

Although the coin toss is used in club games to determine who gets last rock in the first end, in major competitions this advantage is actually assigned to one or the other team.

Why is this seemingly arbitrary system used?

In the Brier, the Canadian men's championship, there are 11 games in the round robin. Last rock is assigned to each team a minimum of five times — roughly half of the games in the round robin.

It needs to be awarded using this more structured system because having last rock is a serious advantage for the teams at this level. If one rink was to get it, say, ten times, by luck of the coin toss, it could prove a very unfair advantage.

Still another method of awarding last rock is used when the teams get to a playoff: Whichever rink beat the other in the round robin gets last rock.

In other events, organizers sometimes use skill rather than luck to determine who gets last rock in the opening end. A popular method — that is even gaining acceptance in some club games — is for each skip to throw a draw to the Button. Whichever skip's stone finishes closer to the Button is rewarded with last rock.

Choosing your rocks

Most of the time, if your team loses the coin toss, you get to select the set of rocks you will play with. But instead of simply reaching for whichever set is closest, make an educated selection.

Pull out your record book on each set of stones at your club (I talk about the value of keeping a book like this in Chapter 5), and refer to your notes on the two sets of stones on your sheet. See if either set has any bad rocks. If there are some rotten ones — perhaps one or two that are much slower than the others — then select the better of the two sets. Even if you don't get last rock in the first end, this might be a way to get a bit of an advantage.

Sometimes, the set of stones you use is predetermined, so you don't get to pick. Some clubs use a system based on the game schedule and the rock colours on the scoreboard. Let's say that, on the schedule, your rink's name appears before your opposition's — your name is over top of theirs. You would play with whichever colour rock appears on the top part of the scoreboard. There are times when you have to take what you get and make the best of it.

If you're unsure about what colour to throw, ask your skip.

Courtesy stones

Curling is a game of tradition and respect. That's evident when you shake hands, when you introduce yourself, and even when you step up to throw. Although it's far from universal, there is a practice in many curling clubs called *courtesy stones*. It's also sometimes called *setting up the stones*.

A courtesy stone is one that is set up for you by your opponent. You return the favour for the other team.

When you go to throw the first stone of the game, all the stones are lined up at the end of the sheet, out of the way. You go over to the group and pull out the stone you are going to throw. But before you step into the hack, you go over to your opposition's stones and pull one out for them. You place this stone beside the hack that you're not using (about two or three feet away from it, to make sure it won't get in the way of your delivery). In the same way, when you go to throw, your opponent will set up a rock for you.

The practice of courtesy stones has disappeared at a lot of clubs. That's too bad for those who believe in the traditions of the sport, but understandable in this age of rock selection. Up until about 15 years ago, the stones weren't numbered. You often had no idea which two stones you were throwing — you just grabbed one and then the other, and tossed them down the sheet.

Even though stones are numbered today, players don't always throw the numbers they are supposed to. This is because, in recent years, teams have begun to spend a great amount of time and energy trying to figure out which stone matches up with which, on quests for well-matched sets that will perform better. Numbers don't have anything to do with this selection. So when it comes right down to it, a lead might not always throw stones No. 1 and No. 2, and a skip might not always throw No. 7 and No. 8. This makes it tough to set up courtesy stones — you really have no idea which two stones your opposition is going to throw. Because of this, the courtesy stones tradition is being practised less and less.

If you are unsure whether to set up the stones, then just watch the opposing rink. If they don't do it, then you shouldn't, either.

Let the Game Begin

Now, you're ready to start playing (finally, you're probably saying). The position you play determines what you do at the start of the game and throughout the end. If you're the lead, for instance, you throw the first two stones of the end and then sweep the next six stones. No matter what position you play, if you are throwing stones, then you will either be in the hack (when you're actually throwing) or standing behind the throwing area (when your opposite number is throwing). Table 12-1 explains the responsibilities of each player during each shot of the end.

Table 12-1	Team Members' Actions in an End			
	Lead's Shots	*Second's Shots*	*Third's Shots*	*Skip's Shots*
Lead	Throwing	Sweeping	Sweeping	Sweeping
Second	Sweeping	Throwing	Sweeping	Sweeping
Third	Sweeping	Sweeping	Throwing	Holding the broom
Skip	Holding the broom	Holding the broom	Holding the broom	Throwing

That's quite a pace!

Curling is not exactly played at a leisurely pace. As soon as the other team has thrown its stone — even before it comes to a stop — you should step into the hack and begin preparing for your shot. Get yourself positioned and clean off your rock. You should be ready to throw your stone as soon as the other team's shot has reached its final destination. Doing this makes your game go a lot faster. You can waste a lot of time by waiting for the other team's stone to stop before you start to get ready.

Playing short

Maybe it's due to an injury or perhaps a previous commitment, but from time to time, you might not be able to get four players out to a game.

If you know ahead of time, you might be able to get a replacement for the missing player. In curling, a replacement is called a *spare*. Most clubs will have a *spare list*, a sheet where those curlers who don't belong to a team can sign up. It's sort of a pool of extras, whom you can contact to see if they can fill in.

If *you're* the one who can't make the game, it's up to you to find a spare. Inform your skip (or third if you are the skip) that you won't be coming. If and when you find a spare, give them the details about the team they're playing on and the time of the game. Most of time, the spare fills whatever position the missing team member plays, but some clubs have a rule that a spare must play lead. Check with your club to find out the policy where you play.

If you can't find a spare, you can still play with three players. The first player — a sort of lead-second — throws three rocks; the second-third delivers the next three; and the skip throws the final two. And, there's only one sweeper per stone.

It's obviously not an ideal situation, so try to have four of you as often as possible.

After you've thrown your two shots, go out between the two Hog lines and wait until it's your turn to sweep. Here again, you can help save time by preparing and being ready to go as soon as it's your turn. When the other team has thrown its shot, and the player throwing it has finished his slide, begin preparing for your team's next shot. Take your broom and lightly run it over the centre of the sheet, from in front of the house all the way into the hack. This is called *cleaning the slide path*. You do it to get rid of any debris that might be left on the ice after the previous player's delivery. The two players who are sweeping the next rock should be responsible for cleaning the slide path.

The end of the end

The end may be over after all 16 rocks have been played, but there is still a lot to do.

First, the thirds on each team must agree on the score for the end. Once that's been confirmed, all the players — except for the two skips — clear the stones off the sheet.

There is an area at the end of every sheet, usually marked off by lines or by a coloured area under the ice, where the stones should be placed when not in use. Push all the stones to their respective sides and, if you are an organizer by nature, put them in the order in which they'll be played in the next end.

Notice that the skips don't have to endure all this physical labour. So what are they doing while all the stones are being kicked off? They should be down at the other end of the sheet, getting ready for the first stones of the next end. The skips get off easy; they don't have to sweep and they don't have to clear off all those stones! It's a skip's privilege.

The beginning of the next end

The team that scored in the last end goes first in the next end. If your team scored in the fourth end, for example, then you go first in the fifth end. This order continues throughout the game, and often involves some decisions relating to strategy, which I get to in Chapter 14.

The blank end

You may play an end in a game where neither team gets any rocks in the house, so nobody scores. This is called a *blank end*. It's quite common to have a blank end in a game — sometimes it's done on purpose.

Why would a team intentionally decide not to score? It all stems back to having last rock. Because having the last shot is a decided advantage, you might *blank an end* (deliberately not score) to retain the *hammer* (to retain last shot). Say you're playing an eight-end game. Heading into the seventh end, the score is tied 5–5. When you come to throw your last rock of the end, there is nothing in play. You could draw your stone down to the house and score 1. While you would be ahead by 1, you would give up the all-important last shot in the final end to your opponent.

Most teams would decide to throw the stone through the house — that's generally how an end is blanked — and keep the score tied, while retaining last shot.

Oops...I Did It Again

From time to time in a season, you might make an innocent mistake during the course of a game. These mistakes aren't so much rules infractions, as small hiccups that are more embarrassing than anything else. Curlers are an honourable, sporting lot, however, as I keep mentioning. They understand when someone messes up. In most cases, you just correct the mistake and play on. Here are a few common slip-ups you'll make (we've all made them) if you play the game long enough.

Throwing the wrong colour

When you play a lot of games in a short space of time, it's easy to lose track of what colour stones you are throwing. Once in a while, you throw one of your opposition's rocks down the sheet instead of your own. There's no penalty for this; you merely replace the other team's stone with one of yours.

If the stone is in play, put your feet around the rock, with your heels together — so the stone sits in the V formed by your feet. Carefully slide the rock out of the way, making sure you don't move your feet out of the V position and lose your place on the ice. Put your own stone in the V and move away.

Playing out of order

When you play a lot of games, or maybe just lose track of the progress of the game you are currently playing, you might play out of order. If you're the third and you throw the seventh and sixth stones of the end instead of the sixth and fifth, that's a problem. Whoever missed their turn has to throw the last stone of the end. Sometimes you won't be able to figure out who missed their turn — either your team has short memories or no one admits to it. When this happens, the lead has to throw the final stone of the end for your rink.

Arriving late

Traffic is awful and you end up arriving late for your game. Can you still play? Yes, but you can't throw any stones until the end that's currently being played is over. In other words, you can't join in the middle of the end. You can, however, sweep your team's stones in the end that's being played. They'll always let you on to sweep!

It used to be that latecomers had to enter the game as lead. You weren't allowed to play any other position. That rule has changed, however. Now, if you're the third and you're late, you can still play third. The same is true for all the positions.

Having an injured teammate

If one of your teammates has to leave the game because of an injury or because she suddenly feels sick, the game continues with your team playing with just the three of you (see the sidebar, "Playing short," earlier in this chapter). This does not affect the order of throwing.

It Ain't Over 'Til It's Over

The end of the game is as steeped in tradition as the beginning and middle. Just as you did at the start of the contest, shake hands with your opponents (remembering to take off your glove). If you lost, offer your congratulations with a salutation of "Good game," or "Well played." If you won, thank your opponents for a fun match. Accept any congratulations respectfully.

Five things you do in other sports but don't do in curling

1. Slam-dunking the rocks after a good play.

2. Trash talking.

3. Dumping Gatorade on the skip after a big win.

4. Dropping your gloves and fighting with that second from the other team.

5. Shouting "You da Man!" after a great shot.

There's one more great tradition to attend to at the end of the game. This one, however, takes place off the ice. That's right — it's time for the two teams to sit down together and enjoy a libation. More precisely, the winning team buys the losing team a round of drinks. The best part about this tradition is that the second round is on the losers. Almost every curling club in the world has a bar attached to it. What a game!

As you're shaking hands at the end of the game, ask your opposite number what he'd like to drink. So, the winning lead buys the losing lead a drink, the winning second buys the losing second a drink, and so on.

This is a time to enjoy the company of your opposition. Have fun, talk about the game or anything else. It's a chance to get to know your fellow curlers.

Before You Call It a Day

When the game is over and you've finished your post-game, it's time to call it a day. But before you head home, there are a few last-minute things you should do to prepare for your next game, whenever that may be.

- ✔ **Give your broom a quick cleaning.** If you've been sweeping hard, and you use a synthetic broom, the head will likely be pretty wet. It's a good time to get rid of all the debris your broom has picked up during the game. Use a nail or vegetable brush to give it a quick wipe. The head material will last longer if you do this.

- ✔ **Give your slider a wipe.** You should have covered your slider with a protector before you left the ice. Take it off now and clean any dirt off your slider. Now is also a good time to give your slider a bit of an inspection: Make sure it's not cracking or becoming detached from the sole of your shoe. You might also want to invest in a pair of shoetrees to help your shoes keep their shape.

✔ **Give your clothes some air.** If you notice that people are standing at the other end of the ice when you play, this is an unmistakable clue to air out your clothes. Hang them up in your locker (if you have one) or take them home and wash them.

Chapter 13

Getting a Game

*N*ow that you know how to play the game and throw the rock, and you understand the rules of the game and all the markings on the sheet, you need to know how and where to get your game.

Like most other sports, curling games come in all shapes and sizes. There are very serious curling leagues, where the top players knock heads. There are regular, but less serious games in your local club. There are pick-up games, special events, and *bonspiels* (tournaments, in curling-speak). Each type of game is different, and you need to know how to sign up for and how to play in all of them if you are going to become a curler. No matter whether you're just intending to play with your friends on a Friday night, or you hope to enter the playdowns en route to the world championships, you need to know how to get in the game.

Before we go any farther, there's another curling contradiction I have to tell you about. It's rare in curling that you ever sign up for or play in a single-game event. Most of the time, you play in *competitions*, loosely defined as a group of games. It might last all weekend or all season. But these shouldn't be confused with *competitive curling*. Although all games are competitive in the sense that there's a winner and a loser, competitive curling refers to the matches that are played between top teams, usually with a great deal — either money or significant titles — on the line.

Types of Game

There are four categories of curling game:

- **Club games:** mainly social games held at your home club
- **Competitive games:** more serious games, with money or titles at stake
- **Playdowns:** also fairly serious games that lead to sanctioned titles
- **Bonspiels:** tournaments — both serious and fun

Signing up

In most cases, to enter a competition of any sort, you just sign up to play. Sometimes you sign up as part of a team — that is, you sign up all four players at once. At other times, you sign up individually. Most of the time, a club will have a dedicated section of bulletin board or wall space with sign-up sheets for the various competitions. Or it might send a sign-up sheet to your home and ask you to mail it back.

If you're unsure, ask the manager of your club how to sign up.

You need to take several things into account before you sign up for a game or competition. For example, how long does it run for: all year long or just a weekend? Is it open to all players, or are there certain restrictions? These restrictions might have to do with age or level of experience. There are competitions for *masters* (age 60 and over), *seniors* (age 50 and over), *intermediates* (age 40 and over), and *bantams* (age16 and under). There are also events for those who haven't won anything before, or for those who are new to curling. Also make sure that the date and time of the game fits your schedule.

Drawing conclusions — make sure you know when you're playing

Curling games are divided into *draws*. A draw — not to be confused with the *draw shot* — is a group of games held at the same time. The six games that are held every Thursday night at 6:45 p.m. at my club are considered a draw. Sometimes, a draw is referred to by the time it is played at. So that series of games on Thursday night would be called the *6:45 draw*. It's followed by the *9:00 draw*.

Getting mixed up

Teams sometimes make mistakes when they sign up for bonspiels. That was the case for Toronto curler Ian Robertson. A successful competitive player, Robertson decided to take his team to a bonspiel at a different area club to get in some practice before a big playdown.

The team had been playing well leading up to this bonspiel and was looking forward to it. Imagine its surprise, then, when the four team members walked into the *host club* (the club they were visiting, not their regular club) and saw that all the other rinks were mixed — two women and two men making up each of them.

After apologizing and admitting he probably didn't read the sign-up flyer well enough, Robertson sent two of his teammates home, and asked two of the women from the host club who weren't playing to join his team. Guess what? They went on to win the bonspiel. Despite his success, it was an embarrassing mistake that most of his curling buddies never let Robertson forget.

Some leagues have three or four draws in a night. Others have just one. It depends on the size of the league. Some leagues schedule their draws on a set night of the week, while others hold theirs on different days.

Most often, though, certain nights of the week are reserved for certain types of competition. Monday night might be the men's competitive league. Tuesday night could be the women's league. Wednesday might be reserved for the senior men's league, and, Thursday might be *mixed*, where men and women play together on the same team.

Club Games

As the name suggests, these are games held in your own club. Club games cover a wide range of competitions — from serious to fun, from juniors to seniors. Whatever the type of game being played, though, club games are usually what you play in, week in and week out.

League games

League play is the foundation of every curling club. It might be known as something different where you play, but these regularly scheduled games are the heart and soul of any club. League games are played on a weekly, bi-weekly, or tri-weekly basis, depending on the club. There are about as many different types of league play as there are rocks on a sheet of ice.

Most league play is based on the skill levels of the various teams. You try to play against teams that have the same skill level (and same goals for the season) as yours does. So, if you want to just play in a very fun-type league, you probably can. If, on the other hand, you want to play in a league that brings in the top men's curlers in your club, you can do that, too. If you want to play in the businesswomen's league, that's also possible. The sky's pretty much the limit. You're quite likely to find a league that's right in step with your team's desires.

Each section of the club — men's, women's, mixed, and so on — has its own league, and sets its own standards of play. In most play, the league is run on a *ladder* or *points system*. Teams are divided up into groups and play against other teams in their group. As with European soccer, the number of wins and losses is tallied at the end of a round robin or set time frame. The top teams move up, and the bottom teams head the other way.

One of the more popular systems to use is the *flights* system, where you'll have flights of A, B, C, and D, for example. Each flight, or section, might have six, eight, or ten teams in it (depending on how many players and teams you have in your club). After all the teams within a flight play each other once, the *won-loss records* are compared. If your team finishes first in the C flight, it would then likely move up to the B flight for the next round. If you finish last in the C flight, your next games would be in the D flight, since your team would move down.

This is a good system, since you mostly end up playing against teams of your own calibre. It's no fun to go out and get slaughtered every time you step on the ice.

In regular league play, you sign up as part of a team. You and three other players enter together and play as a unit for the entire season.

If you don't have a team to enter with, you can usually sign up as a *single* — a single player — and the organizers will put you with a team that's looking for a fourth player. This often happens when you're new to the game. While it might be a bit nerve-wracking to come in as a greenhorn and play with three other people whom you don't know, almost every curler has gone through it — your "new" teammates included. Curlers are great people; they welcome new players to the game with open arms.

Skip's draw

Another type of club game is the *Skip's draw*. This format is much like the schoolyard pick-up game you probably played as a kid. All the skips that are entered in the competition pick their teams from a pool of players also entered. The only difference between this and those schoolyard games you remember from your childhood is that the skips don't make their choices with all the players hanging about. So, no one has to feel bad about being the last person picked.

The skips might get together the night before the start of the season and hold the draw, forming the teams based on the players who have entered. Most times, the players are ranked by their playing ability and by the positions they've played in the past. This gives the skips a good idea who to pick to play third, second, and lead.

In this type of competition, you enter as an individual and play with your team for the length of the event. It might last the entire season, or just a few games.

The Skip's draw is usually less competitive than league play. It's a good way for players new to the game, as well as for more experienced ones new to the area, to meet the other players at the club.

Jitney

The *Jitney* or *Tag draw*, as it's also known, is another less competitive club game. Similar to drawing names from a hat, in this format, all the players show up at a prescribed time and enter their name to play. The club will often have the curlers' names on a small tag or coin (the word *jitney* means small coin). These tags or coins are then pulled randomly from a hat, and the teams formed based on the order in which the names are pulled.

This is a fun way to play when there's just one game being held and there's nothing serious at stake. And, like the skip's draw, it's another good way for newcomers to get into the action when they don't know anybody at the club.

Some clubs hold a regular Jitney and keep track of how each player does, awarding points based on whether the team the player is on wins or loses. At the end of the competition — it might be one game or 20 — you see how you fared against all the other players in the club.

This makes it a bit more of an individual competition, but still a fun one.

Doubles

There's no hard-and-fast rule that says every club competition has to be played with four players on a rink. Many clubs hold a doubles event at some time during the season. *Doubles* isn't about playing after having a stiff drink — it's a game where the teams have only two players instead of four.

You're probably wondering how you manage to play a game with just two players per team. You manage, because there are no sweepers in doubles games. One player stays at one end of the sheet and throws the rocks, while the other stays at the opposite and holds the broom for her. After all the rocks in an end are thrown, they switch positions.

I've always found that doubles games are a good way to start the season off. I get to throw a lot of rocks, which I always feel I need to do early in the year, and there's no sweeping, which means I won't get really tired. Doubles is also fun to play with couples.

There aren't many games that let you bend the rules so drastically, playing with literally half a team. Curling is just that type of game. It goes to show you that when there's nothing on the line except fun, you can change the rules to enhance that fun.

Competitive Games

If you want to play at a higher level, you need to understand how the big teams play. Although there are still handshakes and drinks after the game, on the ice, things are taken a bit more seriously. Sometimes there's money on the line; at other times, there's the chance to advance towards significant championships. Many of the best curlers in the world don't play any games at the club level. That's because they want superior competition every time out. Most clubs have a few good teams, but not enough to provide a steady diet of top-flight play. For that reason, competitive curlers tend to look elsewhere.

Super league

The *Super league*, or *Major league*, is much like an all-star league. Players from a bunch of different clubs in a given area, who are at the same advanced level of play, get together regularly to compete.

Super league is generally for very competitive teams. They play against each other to get a quality of competition that they might not get in regular league play at a club. When you are at this level, you want to play teams that are as good or better than you, to gain experience and to learn.

These leagues usually play for cash prizes. Some leagues have sponsorship to help increase the prize purse, while others merely charge an entry fee to participating teams. Despite how competitive Super leagues are, they still hold the spirit of curling close.

Cashspiels

Cashspiels — a combination of the two words *cash* and *bonspiel* — are competitive tournaments played for cash. Just about every weekend of the season, somewhere in Canada (and likely in a lot of places all over the world, too) cashspiels are being held. For the more significant ones, you might have to travel (yes, by that I mean get on a plane), but there are also smaller ones that are usually within driving distance. There are different types of cashspiels. Some are small, with prizes in the hundreds of dollars. Others are quite sizeable, with the rewards running into the tens of thousands of dollars.

Most cashspiels have sponsors that help beef up the prize purse. In return, the sponsor might get its name in the title of the game, such as The XYZ Company Curling Classic.

Cashspiels are usually run with a *field* of teams ranging from 8 up to 128. The more common ones have a field of 24, 32, or 64 teams. The rinks play either a *double knockout format* or a *triple knockout format*. That means that a rink continues to play for the top prize unless it loses two (double knockout) or three (triple knockout) games.

Cashspiels are held all over the world. There is also a *World Curling Tour*, a circuit made up of the richest cashspiels.

If you want to play in a cashspiel, all you have to do is enter. There are no restrictions on who can enter a cashspiel — you pay your money and you take your chances. Entry forms are usually sent to clubs to be posted. Ask the manager at your club where to find them.

Another way to find out about upcoming cashspiels is to look on the Internet. The World Curling Tour Web site, www.wctour.com, has a list of all its events — both big and small — with contact names and numbers. One phone call to the event organizer gets you all the information you need about entering.

Cashspiels can be expensive to enter. You can expect to pay somewhere around $1,000 per team for the privilege of playing in a top-ranked cashspiel. That, of course, is only the beginning of your costs. You have to pay for your travel, meals, and accommodation (if it is out of town). And, since the bigger cash events start on a Wednesday and finish on a Monday, you also need to negotiate time away from work (which may not be such a bad thing).

Cashspiels attract a lot of the best teams, all intent on taking home a share of the purse, so you'd better be prepared to play. For this reason, I'd suggest that you only look at entering cashspiels once you become more of a seasoned player, or become part of an experienced team.

Double rink

This style of curling was very popular back in the early 1900s right up until about 1950. In fact, in some places, like Ontario, double-rink competitions were held in higher regard than single-rink events.

A *double-rink* competition is when two teams take on two other teams. The pairs of teams are usually from the same club, but not always. Although two separate games are played, the scores of both games are added together at the end to determine the big winner. If the score at the end of your game is 5–4 for you and the other team from your club wins its game 6–4, the winning and losing scores are added together, for a final outcome of 11–8. The individual games don't matter on their own; what counts is how they affect the total.

There are still some significant events that use the double-rink format, and the World Curling Federation is considering inaugurating an international event — much like golf's Ryder Cup — that would use this format, as well.

Playdowns

Playdowns are games that lead to recognized regional, provincial, national, or international curling championships. These competitions are usually more formal and organized than club games, but they start in the club, all the same.

There are different types of playdown based on categories such as age group and team makeup. To play in a playdown, you have to determine if you are eligible. There are playdowns for the following:

- ✔ Juniors
- ✔ Men
- ✔ Women
- ✔ Mixed
- ✔ Seniors

And there are plenty of other categories. In Canada, there are playdowns for firefighters, postal workers, and police officers, for example.

Whatever the playdown, there is usually one way to enter, and that's to sign up. There are sign-up sheets posted in each club, which spell out the regulations that allow you to register for a given event. Read these regulations carefully and decide whether your team qualifies. You must then ensure you sign up by the specified date (each playdown has a deadline by which your team must be entered). The playdowns begin shortly after the entries close. Depending on the area and the level of competition, your playdowns might begin in your own club to determine your *club representative* (or representatives, if you have more than one).

In playdowns, there is a limited number of teams that can enter into the second stage of the competition (the first stage past the club playdowns). Each club is given a certain number of positions, usually based on the number of members the club has. In Ontario, for example, the province is divided into 16 *zones* (geographical areas). At each zone playdown, there is room for 16 teams. Those 16 spots are awarded based on a membership formula. My club, a big one in the area, might be allotted four of those spots, while a smaller club might get only one spot.

But if there are six teams in my club that want to enter the zone playdowns, then we play off to determine our four club representatives.

If your team is successful in the club, you progress through a series of games of different levels until you reach the final one.

There can be one or two levels of competition — or ten or more. Each playdown is different, depending on the rules by which it's organized.

What *is* similar about all playdowns is that they are the most serious curling games of each year. Often, a great deal is at stake. The playdowns are what most top teams gear their year around.

Bonspiels and Other Fun Stuff

Not all curling is serious stuff. In fact, the vast majority of curling is purely fun. And nowhere can that be seen more than at the many fun *bonspiels* that take place in curling clubs everywhere. There are also plenty of in-club special events, where you can participate in a specially themed night or day and enjoy the camaraderie of your fellow club members.

Bonspiels range in length from one game in one day, to two or three games in a day, to several games over several days (the number of games and days varies from club to club). Many are held on weekends, starting Friday evening and concluding on Sunday.

Whatever the event, these fun programs are based less on the numbers that end up on the scoreboard than on the social aspects of the outing.

Bonspiels

A *bonspiel* (also referred to by its shorter name, *spiel*) is an event where teams from all over come to a certain club to play in a friendly competition and enjoy some fellowship. The vast majority of bonspiels are purely about having fun. Clubs take great pride in being able to host a successful event — each tries to outdo the other.

For a reasonable entry fee — usually somewhere around $50 or $60 per player — a typical bonspiel will get you three games, a meal or two, and some entertainment. That entertainment might be a dance, a show, or what's known as *home hosting*. This is when members of the host club invite two or three teams back to their home for some post-game food and drink. It's a pleasurable gathering that allows you to mix with other curlers away from the rink. (Heck, it's just a party at someone's house.)

These are some common types of bonspiel you're likely to see at your club:

- ✔ **Juniors:** Events for the younger crowd, usually followed by a dance of some sort.

- ✔ **Men's:** Events for male players only. Some of the more common things you'll find at a men's spiel might be a *Calcutta* on the teams (a betting scenario where each team is auctioned off for a price and the person who holds the winning team gets the money), a stag night, or a dinner-dance, where the players bring their significant others.

- ✔ **Mixed:** Events where male and female players play on the same team. These are, in my experience, the most fun to play in. That's likely because they bring men and women together, and the social atmosphere is a great deal of fun. In addition to the curling on the ice, mixed spiels usually have dances and other party-type events to make the day or days very enjoyable.

✔ **Women's:** Events for female players only. Similar to the men's spiels, some are very competitive, while others are just plain fun.

✔ **Seniors:** Events for older (and undoubtedly much more accomplished!) players.

How do you sign up for a bonspiel? It's easy. Your local club should have an area displaying flyers from other clubs hosting events — usually on a bulletin board or in a binder. As with the playdowns, read the flyer carefully to see what type of bonspiel it is. Again, there are events for men, women, mixed teams, seniors, juniors — just about every size, shape, and type of curler.

You might also find some listings on the Internet. Check for curling Web sites devoted to your area. The Ontario Curling Association, for example, at www.ontcurl.com, has a list of spiels in clubs that fall under its jurisdiction. You can also check out www.curling.com for a list of bonspiels posted by organizers all over the world.

Once you find a spiel that looks promising, you also need to check the dates and the location of the event to make sure your team can make it.

After you have all this information, and if it suits the needs and desires of your team, mail your entry in to the host club — there's usually a portion of the flyer that you send back, with your team information and other pertinent details. Don't forget to include payment of the entry fee! If your team is accepted to play in the bonspiel, you will get a phone call, or notification in some other way, and be told when the game starts and what to expect.

"And tonight's theme is...": Themed bonspiels

Many bonspiels are themed events. Some are based on special days or holidays, such as New Year's Day, Valentine's Day, St. Patrick's Day, or Thanksgiving.

Others have themes that have nothing to do with the calendar. One particularly successful event I used to play in, near Toronto, had a different theme every year. For the opening game, you were required to dress up according to the theme. One year it was the circus. Not only were their curlers that looked like clowns and acrobats and lion tamers, but the entire club was decorated to make it look just like the big top. The highlight of this event came when a live Bengal tiger was brought onto the ice in the middle of the competition. (No one tried to tame it!)

The ten most memorable bonspiels I've played in

I thought I'd recount these David Letterman-style, in descending order from 10 to 1.

10. **The Weston Junior Men's:** This was the first bonspiel I ever played in. I was 13 years old and I won a belt. It doesn't fit me anymore.

9. **The London (Ontario) Harvest Spiel:** I played in this as a university student. We won the event, and I received a blender as a prize. Like any student would, I traded it for a case of beer.

8. **The Royal Canadian Curling Club Three-Day Mixed:** I won this one, too. For some reason still unknown to me, the trophy, on which my name is engraved, is a radiator at the Royal Canadian Curling Club. Yeah, the kind they use for heating. I should probably ask what's up with that trophy.

7. **The Thornhill Curling Club Junior Mixed Spiel:** This one was always held right after Christmas. No one cared if they won or lost — it was just a big party (hey, we were all 16 and looking for fun).

6. **The Blind River (Ontario) Men's Spiel:** This bonspiel was in the hometown of a good friend. We drove to the spiel — a 14-hour drive — and made it to the semi-final. The final was to be held late Sunday, and we realized if we played in it, we wouldn't make it back home in time for work on Monday. So we tried to lose the semi-final game. Unfortunately, our opposition was equally terrible (maybe they were trying to lose, too) and it wasn't until the final end that we finally prevailed — by losing. I made it back in time for work on Monday.

5. **The Bacardi Cashspiel:** I played in this one with two-time world champion, Ed Werenich. We won the spiel and picked up a nice cash prize. Oh yeah, it was sponsored by the world's leading rum company — need I say more?

4. **The Sarnia (Ontario) Men's Cashspiel:** This was a very competitive event. Our team defeated Ed Werenich in the quarter-final, another two-time world champion, Russ Howard, in the semi-final, but ended up losing in an extra end to a local club curler! I think that after we beat the two world champs, we thought we'd just walk all over the local team. Oops!

3. **The Chatham (Ontario) Men's Beef-o-Rama:** This was an event put on in a farming community with all the prizes consisting of meat and poultry. I don't remember how we did, but I do know that late one night, after perhaps one too many, we went out on the ice and had a game using frozen turkeys instead of stones.

2. **The Thornhill Men's Spiel:** A great event with a different theme each year. One year the theme was Expo 86, the world's fair, which was held in Vancouver that year. My team dressed up as terrorists who planned to take over the event. The organizers of this bonspiel were probably the best-organized, best-prepared group of people I've ever seen.

1. **The Chicago (Illinois) Men's Spiel:** This is the best spiel I've ever played in, bar none. It had great fellowship, good competition, and home hosting (where curlers from the host club take you back to their house for a party). The best part, though, came after the first draw. My team won its game and I went to buy my opposition a drink. When I went to pay for the drinks, the bartender said: "The bar is free all through the bonspiel." When I regained consciousness, we went on to lose in the semi-finals.

In-club events

It's fun to compete against your fellow club members, and your local club or curling facility probably offers a wealth of in-club events where you can do just that. Most are fun, annual competitions that, while offering a bit of serious curling, lean more towards providing a few laughs on the ice. Here are a few of the events you might see where you play:

- ✔ **Battle of the sexes:** A bonspiel where men's teams take on women's teams. Chauvinism and chivalry (all in fun) go hand in hand here.

- ✔ **Club championship:** A bonspiel to determine who will be tops in the club for the given year. There are club champions declared in just about every category where there are curlers: men's, women's, juniors, seniors, and mixed.

- ✔ **End-of-season spiel:** A bonspiel held as a last-gasp final event of the year. Because the ice is removed from the sheet right after this spiel, some clubs do things such as freeze tires into the ice and play *bumper curling* (where you bounce your stones off the tires and into the rings like bumper pool). You also might curl a game and then skate on the ice.

- ✔ **Family bonspiels:** A bonspiel where families take on other families, as the name suggests.

- ✔ **Inter-club:** A bonspiel held between two clubs, with a group of teams from one club taking on a group from the other. It's all about bragging rights.

Your club should provide all the information you need to enter one of these events. There is usually a sign-up sheet in the club, or you may get notification of the in-club events in the mail. Most events are held annually — that's certainly the case for club championships.

As with other events, you need to ensure that you and your team qualify under the event format, and that you can make the dates and times of the games. If you're at all in doubt, speak with the event organizer or club manager about the rules and regulations.

Don't forget that in-club bonspiels are about having fun. Don't take them too seriously. Enjoy the competition; play to win, sure, but remember that curling — especially in-club curling — is a game, above all else.

Part IV
Getting Better

In this part . . .

You delve into the strategic part of the game. After all, why settle for just throwing rocks down the ice when you can deliver them with a purpose? This part is also full of ideas to get you practising your game regularly — both on and off the ice. Come on, it's time to take your game to a higher level.

Chapter 14

Strategy

- -

In This Chapter

▶ Understanding curling strategy in theory

▶ Appreciating last rock advantage

▶ Making smart shot choices

▶ Applying curling strategy in practice

▶ Learning how to think strategically

- -

Strategy is involved in every sport to some degree, and curling is no exception. In fact, without strategy, curling would just be bowling on ice. Toss the stones and see where they end up. But that isn't the case. A great deal of thought goes into planning and plotting exactly where the stones finish.

You may know *how* to throw the rocks, but *where* you throw them is an entirely different matter. Proper placement of the stones is the lifeblood of the sport. Your team might throw all its rocks perfectly, but if they aren't placed perfectly (or almost perfectly), then you might still lose the game.

Curling Strategy in Theory

In a nutshell, curling strategy involves the decisions a team makes regarding what shots to play and where to play them. Sounds easy enough, right? Actually, nothing could be more deceptive. Strategy is a key part of your game if you want to take it to the next level. See, there's a reason why I devote an entire chapter to this, one of the game's more intangible aspects.

This is the reason why curling is so often referred to as chess on ice. You have to know when to play certain shots, to think ahead and try to guess what shots your opponent will play, and to adjust your strategy accordingly.

Good strategy beats good shotmaking every time. If you play a perfect draw but really should have played a hit, then the shot is no good. If you throw a guard when you should have played a draw into the house, well, your strategy needs a bit of an overhaul.

When you get down to it, though, there really is no such thing as a set curling strategy, and that makes teaching it on the ice or writing about it in a book such as this a bit difficult. The reason no such textbook patterns exist is that every situation is different and every sheet of ice is different. The configuration of the stones in the house changes after every stone is played, and, therefore, so does your strategy. As well, the ice conditions might not be suited to allow you to follow a certain type of strategy. If it's very heavy, then it makes it tough to play draws, because you have to throw the stone so hard. I will give you some basics and some examples later, but this is no textbook. Such a book on curling strategy belongs in a perfect world. Understanding the theory is one thing; applying it in practice is quite another. There's really no substitute for real-game situations, so I encourage you to just get out there and play.

There are, however, some common situations from which you can learn (hey, you didn't think I'd have an entire chapter on strategy if I wasn't going to tell you anything did you?). There are also some common theories regarding what you should do in certain situations that crop up often in a game:

- ✔ When you have last rock
- ✔ When you don't have last rock
- ✔ When you're behind
- ✔ When you're ahead
- ✔ When you're playing aggressively
- ✔ When you're playing defensively

There are others, but these are the main ones you run into during the course of a season. Not only is it important for you to understand these situations, but it's also vital that you learn *when* to put each into practice and how to play your stones accordingly.

But before I get into describing just where you should put your stones, there are several other factors to consider when talking about strategy. These are not exactly the rock-by-rock movements you need to know, but the intangibles that may affect where you place the stones.

- ✔ **Your team:** You have to play to your team's strengths and recognize its weaknesses. Don't try to play a lot of takeouts if your team doesn't throw them very well. Also, if you have a choice of shots or a choice of turns on a particular shot, choose the one your team throws better.

- ✔ **Your opposition:** Your strategy can be affected by the strengths and weaknesses of the team you're playing against. If they aren't good at hitting, use that to your advantage by playing your stones right into the house and guarding them afterwards.

✔ **Your ice:** The ice plays a big part in dictating what kind of strategy you employ. For instance, if it's very swingy, draw shots are usually better because they curl behind guards. If it's slow, hitting is easier than drawing. Size up the ice quickly and consider its condition when thinking about what shots to play.

Last Rock

The biggest single influence on the strategy you employ in a game is determined by whether or not you have last rock in the end. Your entire strategy can change based on this.

✔ When you have last rock, you try to score two or more points, and you want to keep the centre of the sheet open.

✔ When you don't have last stone, scoring one point is considered a "win," plus, you want to control the centre of the sheet.

With last rock

Having last rock means you get to throw the final shot in an end, or have the final say in the end's outcome. It's a huge advantage — you often build the entire end around that last shot. That means you set things up throughout the end, playing certain shots knowing that with your last rock you can finish things off.

With last rock, you are attempting to score two or more points. Having the last rock should give you enough of an advantage to score two points, so you always strive to score more than one. It's certainly not the end of the world if you only get one point, but in curling circles, there is a general understanding that you'd like to get two or more.

So, how do you do that?

The best way is to keep your rocks apart from each other. This is referred to as *splitting the house*. This means that you'd like to have one stone on one side of the house and the other on the opposite side, as shown in Figure 14-1 on the next page. The reason you do this is to prevent your opposition from performing a double takeout and removing both stones at once. If all he can do is take out one, then you can simply trade takeouts with him throughout the end. Because you have last rock, when you play your final takeout, you will still have two stones in the house and, hopefully, score two. That's a rather simplistic explanation, but it does hold true in a basic sense.

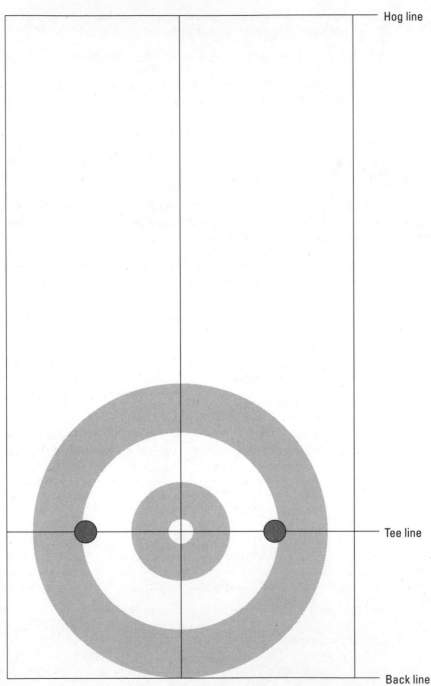

Hog line

Tee line

Back line

Figure 14-1:
Splitting the
house is
the most
common
strategy for
scoring two
points.

Splitting the house accomplishes something else. It keeps the play to the sides of the sheet, which allows you to keep the centre of the sheet free.

Why is this so important when you have last rock?

If there is a clear path for your final stone to reach the centre of the house then there is always a way to save the end. In other words, if your opposition has six stones in the house after her last shot but you still have a clear path to the Tee, then you can draw a stone to the centre and count one. If, on the other hand, your opposition has six stones in the rings, but all in the 4-foot and hidden behind a centre guard, you might not score. There's no way for you to get your last shot closer than the six opposition rocks.

Once again, I emphasize that situations like these happen in a perfect world. No strategy can be lifted right from a textbook. Shots may be missed and others will be only partially made, all of which will affect your strategy.

But in general terms, when you have last rock, you want to try to split your rocks up in the house and play away from the centre.

Without last rock

When you don't have last rock, you play a more defensive end. It is key that you try to control the centre of the sheet. For that reason, your first shot of the end is almost always a guard, close to the rings on the centre line as shown in Figure 14-2, on the next page.

By placing your stone in this position, you are doing the one thing that your opposition doesn't want — gaining control of the centre of the sheet. The team that is in charge of this part of the ice, more often than not, will score. That's because if you can take ownership over that part of the ice, it's easy to get your stone to the very centre, and if you do that, you will score. Remember, the objective of the game is to get more of your stones closer to the centre than the other team.

And with the *free guard zone rule* (any rock that lands there cannot be removed from play until the fourth rock of the end), that stone that sits out in front of the house can't be removed with the next shot (another advantage to playing a guard).

When you don't have last stone, your objective is to make it very difficult for the opposition skip to get closer than yours with her last shot. Most often, this is accomplished by having a stone near the centre of the house and one in front of the rings guarding it. That prevents the opposition from playing a takeout to remove it and makes it difficult (if your *shot rock* is very close to the centre) for the skip to play a draw to the centre and be closer than yours. The shot rock is the rock closest to the centre of the house.

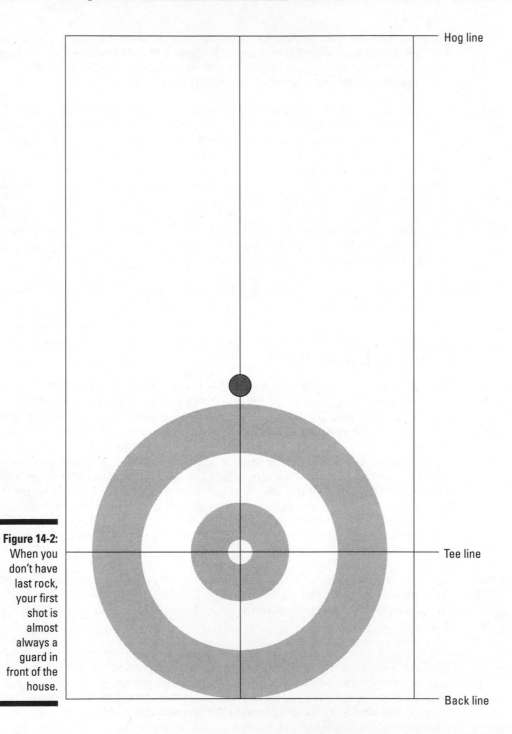

Hog line

Tee line

Back line

Figure 14-2:
When you
don't have
last rock,
your first
shot is
almost
always a
guard in
front of the
house.

In Figure 14-3 on the next page, you can see how the team with last shot would have a tough time scoring if you have a stone guarded in the 4-foot. The route to the Tee has virtually been blocked off. It would be very difficult for the opposing skip to get her final rock closer to the centre than yours.

When you score a point (or more) when you don't have last rock, it's called *stealing a point*. It's regarded as a significant achievement, as the term suggests. That's because you've done it while the other skip has the last shot, meaning she likely missed that shot.

Curling Strategy in Practice

Now you know the two most basic forms of strategic theory based on whether you have last rock or not. But what happens in a real game? In other words, how do you take this theory and put it into practice? First of all, put the textbook away. I'd almost advise you to put this book away, too, but I won't, because it's not a textbook, and because I'm about to describe some actual game situations where you can see strategy in practice. Of course, nothing replaces getting out on a sheet and playing a game. You should definitely do this — just finish this book first.

In a game, both strategies concerning who has last rock are in play at the same time. The team with last rock is trying to keep the front open and score two points, while at the same time the other team is attempting to clog up the centre of the sheet and steal a point. Obviously only one team can prevail.

It becomes complicated — but exciting — because you often have many choices. To give you an example, I'll walk you through the first four shots of a typical end so you can see what happens. Here is a list, in order, of shots played in this hypothetical end. The corresponding illustrations of these shots occur one after the other on the next four pages (Figures 14–4 through 14–7). Just flip ahead to see what I'm talking about. In these examples, Team B has last rock, and is the white rock in the illustrations. Team A is the first to shoot, and is represented by the shaded rock.

Shot #1 Team A plays a guard on the Centre line (Figure 14-4).

Shot #2 Team B can't remove this stone because of the free guard zone rule, so it elects to draw one into the rings at the side of the house (Figure 14-5).

Shot #3 Team A now has a choice to make. It can play aggressively and draw around its own guard, or it can play defensively and try to hit Team B's shot, attempting to roll the shooter in behind the guard. Team A decides to hit and roll behind the cover (Figure 14-6).

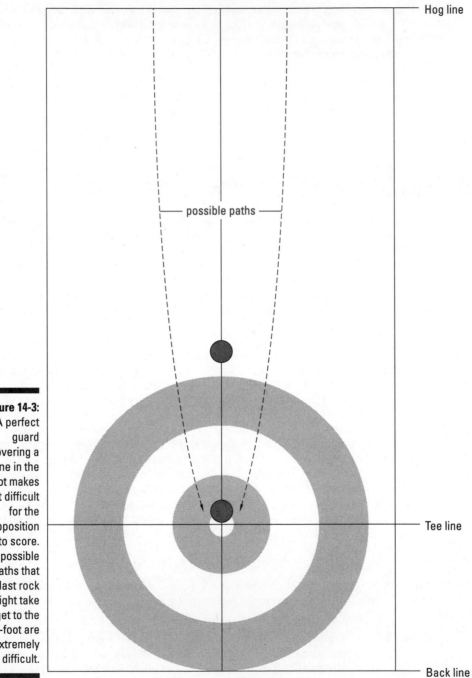

Hog line

possible paths

Figure 14-3:
A perfect
guard
covering a
stone in the
4-foot makes
it difficult
for the
opposition
to score.
The possible
paths that
the last rock
might take
to get to the
4-foot are
extremely
difficult.

Tee line

Back line

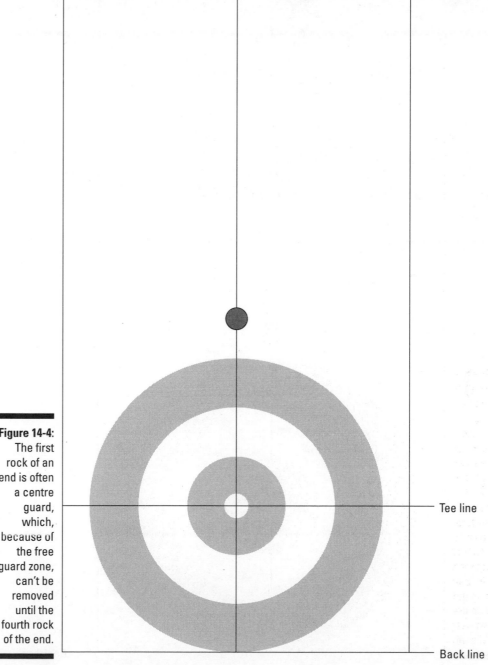

Figure 14-4:
The first rock of an end is often a centre guard, which, because of the free guard zone, can't be removed until the fourth rock of the end.

Hog line

Tee line

Back line

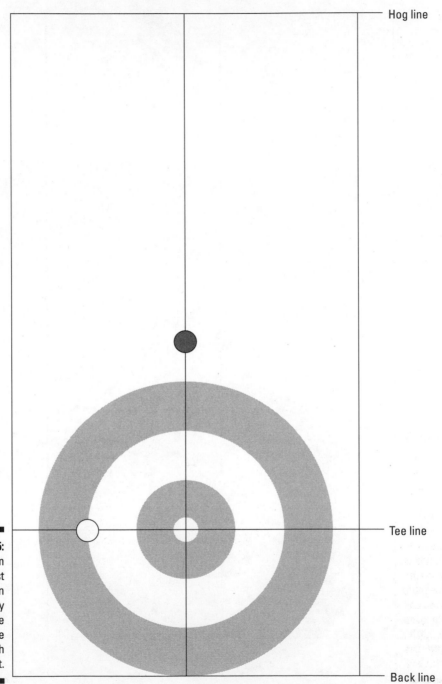

Hog line

Tee line

Back line

Figure 14-5:
The team
with last
rock often
plays away
from the
guard, in the
rings, with
its first shot.

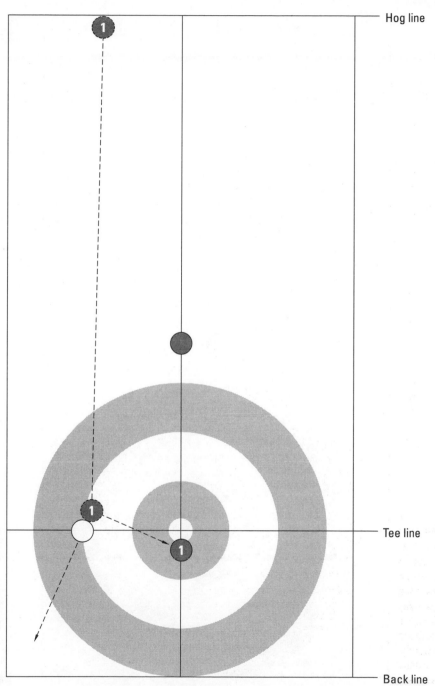

Figure 14-6:
Team A
plays a hit
on Team B's
stone and
rolls its
shooter in
behind the
guard.

Tee line

Back line

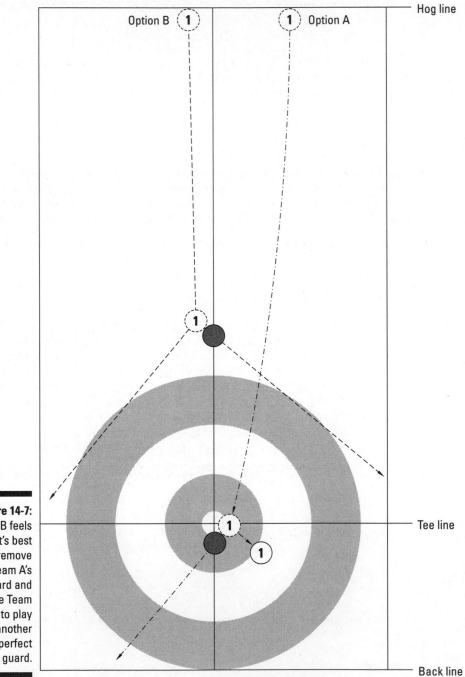

Figure 14-7:
Team B feels
that it's best
to remove
Team A's
guard and
force Team
A to play
another
perfect
guard.

Shot #4 Team B can't see Team A's rock because it's protected by the guard. Now it has a choice. It can try to play a very delicate hit — say, with enough weight to just push it through the house — or it can play a takeout on the guard, hoping that if Team A replaces it, the next one won't be quite as perfect. In this example, shown in Figure 14-7, it plays the hit on the guard.

Game Situations

Because things change so quickly and so frequently, it can be tough to determine which shot to play in a particular situation. Instead, what I suggest is to look at general game strategies as they pertain to your position in that game. They won't always be textbook cases, but you can find some clues to help you play your next shot.

When you're behind

When you trail in a game, you obviously need to score points. That's more or less a given. But how you do that often depends on what part of the game you're in and how many points you are behind your opposition. You will likely behave one way if you're early on in a game — quite another if it's later.

Early in the game

When it's early in the game, say, the third end of an eight-end game — and you find yourself behind by three points, my first piece of advice is this: Don't panic! Also, don't think you have to make up the difference in just one end.

The key is to stay patient and stick to the basics. If you score two points in the fourth end, limit the opposition to one point in the fifth and take two more in the sixth. Suddenly, the game is tied up.

You have lots of time left to make up the difference. Don't try anything rash, just stick to your plan and keep it simple. You'll be surprised at how often a sure and steady strategy works out in the end.

Here are three strategic keys when you're trailing early in the game:

- Stay patient.
- Stick to the game plan.
- Try to score two when you have last rock and only give up one when you don't.

Late in the game

When the game is nearing the end and you are trailing, then it's time to panic. Well, maybe not panic, but it *is* the time to try some things you wouldn't do early in the game.

In my mind, it doesn't matter whether you lose a game by ten points or one point — it's still a loss. That's why I always feel that you should throw caution to the wind in trying to come back late in the game.

Here's an example: I'm behind by three with two ends to go and have last rock. My opposition throws a centre guard. I won't hesitate to draw behind it. Early in the game, I probably would draw to the open side, but because I only have two ends to make up three points, I must play aggressively. By electing to draw behind the centre guard, I am taking a risk. If the stone is heavy and goes through the house, my opponent can now use the guard and draw behind it. If he makes that shot, then I'm really in trouble. But if I make it, then I'm one step closer to scoring a big end.

Get the idea? You have to take chances, and, if you have a choice, play offensively — even if you don't have last rock.

When you're behind without much time left, guards are your friends. The more guards you can get in play, the more rocks you can hide behind them. If your opponent can't see the stones, she can't remove them. Your other friends are opposition stones behind the Tee line. If there's no guard up front, but there *is* an opposition stone at the back of the 8-foot, I'll play a *freeze* (that's a stone that sits right in front of and up against another stone) on this shot. That makes it tough for my opponent to remove it, which is exactly what I want.

Don't worry so much about how many stones the other team has in the house, just keep playing yours in there. If you're behind late in the game, draws are always better than hits. That's because draws are more likely to remain in play than hits. You want as many of your stones in play as possible — be they guards or *counters* (any rocks that would count as a point if the end were to finish at that point) — in the house. The more of your rocks in the house, the better.

Here are three strategic keys when you're trailing late in the game:

- ✔ Play aggressively.
- ✔ Try to get guards in play.
- ✔ Throw more draws than hits.

When you're ahead

You've built up a lead in your game and now you want to maintain it. Sometimes that's tougher than it might seem. It's not always easy to protect a lead, especially against a tough opponent. She's always hungry — one miss can often lead to a big end being scored against you. There are several things you can do to prevent that.

Early in the game

It's always nice to get off to a good start. So if you get up early in the game, give yourself a pat on the back. But right after you do that, get back to work. You want to extend that lead and prevent any comebacks by your opponent.

When I'm in this position, the first thing I do is assess both teams. Do I have a big lead because my team is playing really well? Or is it because the other team just isn't playing well at all? It can be both, of course, but it's important to know because it affects your next moves. If your team is playing well, then just stick with the strategy you've been using. In other words, if it ain't broke, don't fix it. If the other team has just curled poorly then be wary. Maybe they've just missed one or two key shots, which has allowed you to get a lead. In this case, I like to change my strategy a bit and try to play very simply. I try to keep guards out of play because they can often lead to big ends. I try not to have too many rocks in play. These moves make it tougher for the opposition to score.

Here are three strategic keys when you have a lead early in the game:

✔ KISS (Keep it simple, stupid).

✔ Assess how you got the lead and play accordingly.

✔ Try to keep guards to a minimum.

Late in the game

When you have a lead late in the game, your strategy is to try to remove every opposition stone that you can. It's full-out defense here, and the name of the game will be takeouts. Your opponent can't score if her rocks are out of play, so try to get as many as you can off the sheet.

This, of course, can be tough, thanks to the free guard zone. No matter who has last stone, one in the free guard zone can't be removed until the fourth stone of the end (under Canadian rules).

So, let's say, for example, that I have last rock in the last end and I'm leading by two. My opponent puts up a centre guard. What should I do?

There are two strategies I might consider. One would be to intentionally have my lead throw his stone through the house and out of play. The fewer stones in play, the better. The less complicated I can make the end, the better. The other strategy is what's called the *tick shot*. This is to try to just tick the guard over to the side of the sheet without removing it. This requires precision and perfect weight. To do it, you would throw a takeout with about hack or board weight (that's just enough weight to push the stationary stone to the hack or the boards at the end of the sheet). You want to hit just a sliver of the stone and push it to the side. Remember, if it goes out of play, my shooter comes off the sheet and the opposition stone is replaced.

Why do I want to move that centre guard away? With last rock, I want to keep the centre of the ice open. At the very worst, I want to have a clear path to the button for my last shot if absolutely necessary.

Here are three strategic keys when you have a lead late in the game:

✓ Remember that the fewer rocks you have in play, the better.

✓ Try to keep the centre clear.

✓ Don't be afraid to throw your stones through the house if they are only going to complicate matters.

Head games

Not all your strategizing takes place between you and the rocks. Psyching out your opponent is a time-honoured way to give your team a better chance at winning a game.

I remember playing in the provincial junior finals one year and employing an effective "game" on one of our opponents in the eight-team round robin. The team in question was one of the rinks that was favoured to win the title. During a practice session prior to the start of the competition, our rink found ourselves practising on the sheet next to this team. When we knew they were watching us, we intentionally slid well past the Hog line before releasing our rocks — a violation if it had occurred in a game.

This immediately caught their eye, although we pretended that we didn't notice their raised-eyebrow glances over to our sheet.

Why did we do that? When we faced that rink in the competition in the big game, their players were all wrapped up in trying to see if we went over the Hog line with our shots. Whenever we were shooting, early in the game, a couple of their players raced to stand at the Hog line and observe us closely. Of course, we reverted back to normal and had no problem letting go of the stone before the line. But our plan worked — the other guys were more worried about us than about their own shots, and we went on to win easily.

Not scoring

Most of the examples I've outlined so far deal with scoring points. But sometimes, it's beneficial not to score any points at all. When you don't score points in an end, it's called *blanking the end*. And believe it or not, from time to time, you do it intentionally.

Why would you blank an end when you have the chance to score a point? When you have last rock, you are trying to score two points or more. If you get down to the final shot of an end and find that you don't have a chance to score two, you might elect to forgo the chance at scoring a single point and try it again in the next end. When you blank an end, you keep last rock the next end. That's the main reason you'd elect to blank the end. Keeping last rock can help you control the game.

Situations when you might want to blank an end:

- ✔ **In the second-to-last end of a close game:** If the game is tied, it's better to keep last rock for the final end than to be one ahead without the last rock.

- ✔ **In the first end of a game:** Most times, you want to score two points when you have last rock. I find it's always better to do this early on rather than give up the last rock. If you don't score two in the first end, you can blank the end and try to score two in the second end. You're now two up with only six ends left to play.

- ✔ **In an odd-numbered end:** It's always better to have last rock in the even ends. The reason for this is that if both teams trade scoring for the rest of the game, you have last rock in the final end, which is always a big plus.

Strategic Thinking

Curling strategy is all about thinking. Thinking about what shot to play. Thinking about what shot your opposition is going to play. Thinking ahead to the next shots. Thinking ahead to the next end.

The skip is the head thinker on the team. It's her job to constantly run all the options and ideas through her head, while at the same time keeping all her other duties (such as reading the ice) flowing. It's important that a skip thinks long and hard about every move she makes and assesses each one before the rock comes sliding down the sheet.

Get inside your opposition's head

It's not enough to just think about what shots you want *your* team to play; you have to think about what shots your *opponent* is going to play as well. I remember a former Canadian champion, Alf Phillips, saying that his team used to try to think five or six shots ahead when deciding how to play.

Look at Figure 14-8. My team is the dark rocks. I have a guard in front and one stone on the 4-foot. My opponent has one in the 8-foot. He can't see my stone in the 4-foot and therefore can't remove it. I might be tempted to play a takeout on his stone in the 8-foot because that would leave me sitting two points and also remove one of his stones from play.

But if I look ahead, I see that a takeout is not the correct shot. Right now, my opponent has no way to get at my shot stone in the 4-foot. If I *hit and stick* (play a takeout and have my shooter remain in the house) on his outside one, I have suddenly set up a double takeout for him. He can hit the outside one and then roll his shooter in and hit my shot stone, which was untouchable before I played.

A better shot might be to draw another stone around the centre guard and sit two behind the protection.

Before you play any shot, ask yourself what your opponent will do once you have played your shot. Try to think of what you would do if you were her. Try not to think of a shot as being a single action, but rather part of the whole end. Where will it leave you? How does it help you — and hurt your opponent?

This is what you need to consider. You can also help yourself in this type of situation by knowing the tendencies of your opposition. If they prefer the draw over the takeout, or if they play defensively rather than aggressively, use that knowledge when you decide which shots to play.

Play to your strengths

You get choices at certain times of the game. Whether to throw the in-turn or the out-turn? Whether to throw the draw or the hit?

For me, when these situations are 50-50, the final decision often comes down to my personal preference.

Here's an example: It's the last end of a meaningful game against a tough team and the game is tied. The only stone in play is one of theirs, sitting in the 8-foot. I have my last rock left to come.

I am facing a choice: I can hit and stick to score one point or I can draw the 4-foot to score my point.

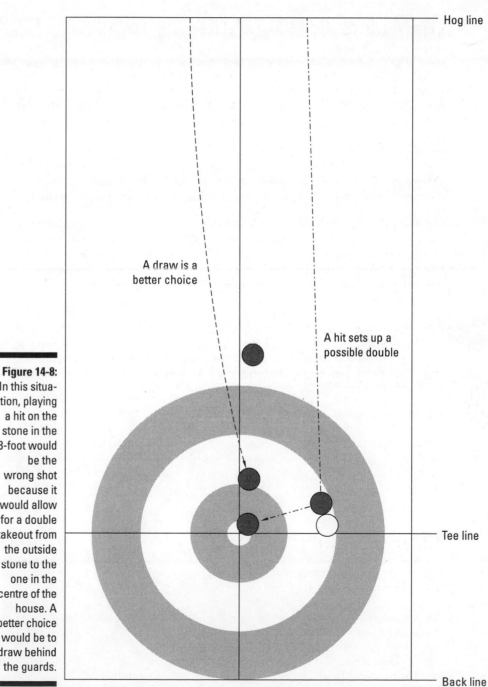

Hog line

A draw is a
better choice

A hit sets up a
possible double

Figure 14-8:
In this situa-
tion, playing
a hit on the
stone in the
8-foot would
be the
wrong shot
because it
would allow
for a double
takeout from
the outside
stone to the
one in the
centre of the
house. A
better choice
would be to
draw behind
the guards.

Tee line

Back line

I have a few things to consider before I throw this rock. How have I been playing tonight? Have I been making all my draws or been inconsistent with the weight? Is the ice tricky where their stone is sitting or will it run true to form? If I hit their stone and roll out to blank the end, there will be an extra end. If I miss the draw, however, the other team scores a point and I lose.

I know that my choice would probably be to throw the draw because I feel comfortable throwing draws. Most nights, I feel confident that I can draw the 4-foot by the end of the game. The decision is based on my personal preference.

You might elect to play the hit because you are better at those shots. But whatever your choice, you have to feel confident when you step in the hack to throw it.

I've been on the other side of these decisions. I've talked with my teammates and they have wanted me to play a shot that I didn't agree with and didn't feel I could make. For some reason, I decide to meet their wishes, and more often than not, I miss the shot because I don't feel right about it.

Being confident in your ability to throw a given shot is often the determining factor, even for many of the game's top players. Two-time world champion skip Wayne Middaugh goes so far as to allow his team to call their own shots at any time during the game. He feels they are talented enough and knowledgeable enough to do so. The only catch is that if they miss, they forfeit that benefit for the rest of the game.

Chapter 15

Practising

*T*he great golfer Gary Player once said, "The more I practise, the luckier I get." That not only holds true for golf, but for just about any sport. Including curling. Practising your shots, your sweeping, and even your strategy, will help you become a better player all around.

As a newcomer, practising makes it easier for you to get proficient at the game. As a seasoned player, practising allows you to get better and take on — and hopefully beat — better players and teams.

If you want to become a better curler, you simply have to devote some time to practising. And not all of that is done on the ice. You can spend some time working out off the ice, as well as managing your diet, to help your curling. More and more of the top players are realizing that to be among the best, you have to work at your game 365 days a year. Well, maybe not *every* day of the year — I'll let you take Sundays and holidays off.

Why You Need to Practise

Simply put, practising makes you better. You can apply the old saying, "Practice makes perfect," to curling, but it might be better to say, "Perfect practice makes perfect curling." It's great to practise, but unless you do it properly, you could be wasting your time.

There's another reason why you need to practise. If you play two games a week, you're only throwing 32 stones down the ice. That's not nearly enough to keep your game in top shape — or even in adequate shape. Especially when you're starting out, you should throw as many stones as your body can handle, working on all the shots — and even just on your slide alone — without throwing a stone.

All of this will make you a better curler. It takes some time and dedication, but is vital if you want to curl at a decent level.

Your Basic Routine

You know you should practise, but just how should you go about it? A good deal depends on what level of curling you're currently at. Your routine will also be determined to some extent by whether you practise alone, with another teammate, or with your entire team. In this chapter, I give you ideas for all three scenarios.

But, most practice routines cover off a number of areas, including the following:

- Working on your shots
- Working on your delivery fundamentals, such as your set-up and slide
- Working on your strategy (This mostly occurs off the ice.)

Training Alone

Here's what I suggest you do if you are practising by yourself (which is how you'll likely practise most of the time):

1. **Work on your slide:** Slide at least 24 times — without any stones — to groove your delivery.

2. **Work on throwing rocks:** Throw a minimum of 64 stones. Fewer are acceptable, but only if your body can't take it. If you can handle more, by all means, do so. Just don't wear yourself out.

3. **Work on different turns:** Throw half your stones with the in-turn and half with the out-turn.

4. **Work on different shots:** Make sure you go through a full repertoire of shots — draws, hits, splits, raises, and others.

When you practise by yourself, try to set up a regular schedule that allows you at least one hour of time on the ice. Check with the club manager to find out when the ice is free. At busier clubs, you may have to do it late at night or at other less convenient times.

Practising your slide

Once you arrive at the rink, get dressed and stretch, head to the ice, and begin to slide. Each time, set yourself up properly in the hack, pick out a target at the far end — maybe a spot on the wall or a chair leg — and slide to it as if it were the broom. If you have access to them, take a couple of extra brooms and put them at the far end of the ice against the back wall to use as targets.

Try to slide a couple of times down the left side of the sheet, a couple down the centre, and two more down the right, trying to slide directly at the targets each time. Go through this until you've done it a total of 24 times.

Every time you slide, work on your fundamentals. Check the position of your foot in the hack, your sliding foot as it moves back and through, and your balance. Keep your eyes locked on the target and try to keep the centre of your body sliding up the broom.

This should take place after you stretch, but before you throw any rocks.

Practising shots

Now get ready to throw some stones. When I practise, I like to work with eight stones and the same eight stones, keeping them in pairs, so that I have some knowledge of how they'll react, and can therefore stay focused on my shots. If I just pick any old stones, it's tough to know what's affecting the shot more — the ice, the rock, or me. Practising consistently with the same set of rocks lets me detect any inconsistencies that are attributable to the rocks and not to my throwing or the ice conditions.

Practising draws

The draw being one of the more common shots, it's the one I practise first.

Rocks 1 and 2: I like to work on my draw shots with my first rocks. I generally start off by throwing my draws in pairs — throwing the same shot twice, attempting to replicate it. That is, I throw an in-turn draw down the centre of the sheet so it curls to the side, watch it slide and stop, and then try to throw the exact same shot again, with the same weight. If I'm doing well, the second stone will come to rest just in front of the first one or might bump it slightly.

Rocks 3 and 4: I then try to do the same thing with the out-turn, throwing two stones right down the centre, attempting to get them to stop almost on the same spot on the opposite side of the house.

Rocks 5, 6, 7, and 8: I throw two in-turns from the outside in, trying to hit the Button, and then two out-turns from the outside in, also trying to get them to stop on the Button.

With these first eight stones, shown in Figure 15-1, try to hit the Tee line every time. It likely won't happen, but that should be your goal.

You're aiming for consistency here — that ability to throw the exact same shot twice in a row. With these opening shots, don't worry too much if you aren't right on. You need to get a feel for the ice first. Concentrate on your delivery and on sliding at your target, the imaginary broom. You're also working on your slide, ensuring you're sliding in balance, right at the broom. By throwing practise rocks, you build up your balance and your curling muscles, especially in your legs.

If you practise enough, you won't even have to worry about your balance when you're delivering the stones during games. It will just happen naturally, which leaves you to focus on your line and weight.

Throw these same draw shots three times, so you have a total of 24 draws. Do the same thing each time and try to measure your improvement from the first round of eight to the third.

Practising hits

If you're pleased with the results, switch over to hits. This will require a little more effort on your part, because if you do this correctly, there will be rocks skittering all over the ice and possibly onto other sheets. You don't want to disrupt anything that's happening on the other sheets, be they games or someone else's practise, so make sure you either let the players on the other sheets know what you're doing, or work with a friend or teammate who can catch the rocks as they head for the sides of the sheet.

To practise takeouts, I take three rocks and arrange them on the sheet. I put one in the centre of the sheet, another on the left side of the sheet, at about the edge of the 8-foot, and the third on the right side of the sheet, also on the 8-foot, as shown in Figure 15-2 a page ahead. These rocks should not be part of the set of eight you were throwing draws with. Use different ones — either from another sheet or from the other eight on your own sheet.

Once you've set the rocks up, start throwing your hits. Next, throw a takeout on the rock in the centre of the sheet with an in-turn. Then, throw a takeout on the rock on the right side of the sheet with an out-turn. Throw a takeout on the rock on the left side of the sheet with an in-turn. Do the same thing again, but this time throw the opposite turns. Depending on how you did the first time around, you may have to set up the positioned rocks again.

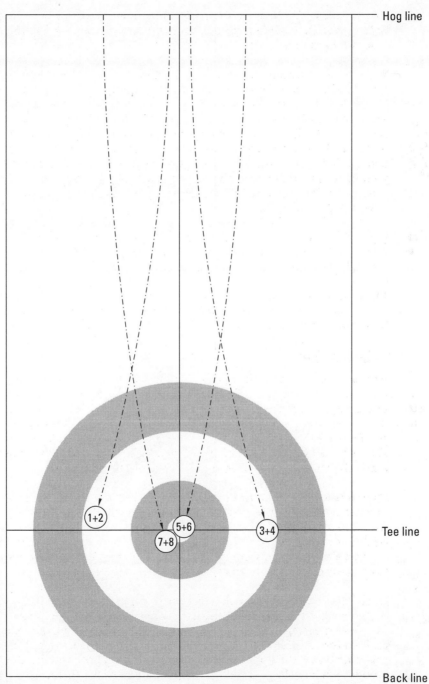

Hog line

Tee line

Back line

Figure 15-1:
Your
practise
draws
should
give you a
workout on
both turns.

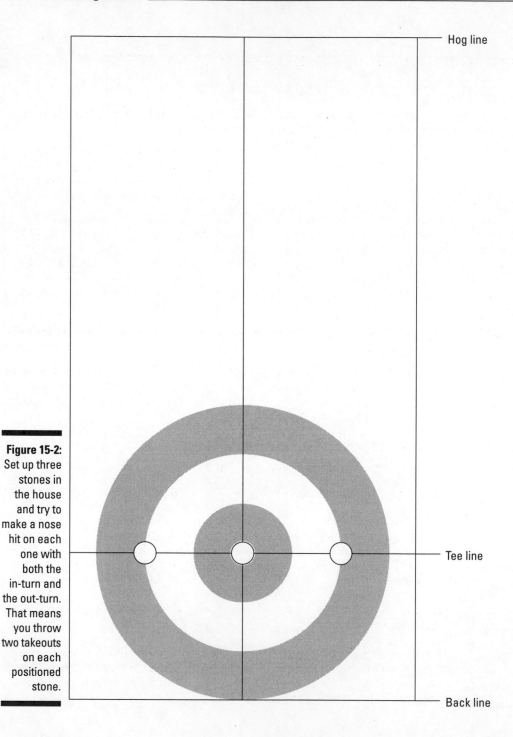

Figure 15-2:
Set up three stones in the house and try to make a nose hit on each one with both the in-turn and the out-turn. That means you throw two takeouts on each positioned stone.

Hog line

Tee line

Back line

Trouble shots

Assuming you're a right-handed curler, you may find the out-turn takeout on a stone on the left of the sheet (assuming you're a right-handed curler) a tough one to throw.

That's because you have to throw across your body.

Your natural body movement pulls you more towards the outside of the sheet, meaning you miss the rock on the outside. It's a shot I find tough to throw, and for that reason I spend a little extra time in practice working on it. I have to concentrate on keeping the centre of my body

sliding right at the broom, and not on the line, as shown in Figure 15-2.

I also have to resist the temptation to try to adjust the rock's line with my hand. If I slide right at the broom and have a clean release, then the shot generally ends up on target.

You may find that you have a trouble shot — one that frequently gives you problems. If so, spend a little extra time and work on it until you feel comfortable throwing it. It may add a little extra time to your practice regimen, but the next time you encounter it in a game, that effort will have been worth it.

On each hit, try at first to make contact on the nose. Go through each shot as described, then do each one with the opposite turn. You want to try and make each nose hit with both turns. Try to make it so there's very little roll, or — best case scenario — none at all.

Do this exercise three times, as well, bringing your total of practise stones thrown to 42.

Once you go through straight hits and you're happy with the results, try some hit and rolls. For this, I like to set one rock right at the top of the rings. I first play a hit and roll to the left. If I make that, I try to hit and roll to the right, aiming to get it back to where I first placed it. If that's successful, I do the same thing on the right side of the sheet, trying to hit the centre stone and roll it to the right. I'm not always spot on with this, but unless the shooter rolls completely out of play, I always play my next shot on the stone I've just thrown.

I practise my hit and rolls eight times, which means I've now thrown 50 practise rocks.

The next training is for your softer weight hits. To do this, I first throw two draws — an in-turn and an out-turn. I try to get them to stop on the Tee line if I can, and then I throw two in-turns and two out-turns at each, trying to just gently push them through the house.

I've now thrown 60 practise rocks and covered a variety of shots.

Before every rock, however, I make sure I know exactly what I'm trying to do. Never throw a practise stone down the ice without deciding what shot you're going for. You wouldn't throw a rock like that in a game, so don't do it in practise. There's nothing worse than throwing a rock with no intent. It's a waste of time and energy.

Finishing up

After I've completed practise draws and hits, I like to finish up by throwing four more shots. With these, I try to draw right to the Button. I throw an in-turn up the sheet, and then an out-turn. Then I go to the other end and do the same thing.

I do this for mental reasons as much as anything. When I throw these last four stones, I try to visualize being in an actual game (why not the world championships?). I pretend I need to draw to the Button for the win. I don't always make the shots, but it's a fun way to end a good workout.

There. I've thrown my 64 practise shots. If I've worked out properly, I should be a better player for it.

Any practise is good practise if you begin with good intentions. You don't have to go through as formal a process as I've described here. Often, you don't have time, can't get any ice, or maybe your body just won't allow you to throw 64 stones. If you want, just throw some draws up the sheet and a few hits back down. Just try to have a goal in mind when you arrive. That might be to throw at least half your draw shots into the house, or to make at least half your takeouts. Whatever your goal, be firm about it and practise with a purpose.

Training with Your Team

Practising can be fun — and often more effective — when you do it with your team, or even just with another team member. Among other things, you can get valuable feedback on your shots — and believe me, your teammates won't be shy about giving it.

Whenever possible, try to work out with another person or with your full team. It will give you a better indication of how you are progressing as individuals and as a team, and allow you to work more on weak parts of your game.

Just as when I'm alone, the first thing I do is stretch and then slide to loosen up. I go through my 24 slides, varying among the left, the centre, and the right of the sheet, each time trying to slide at a target. Now I'm ready to go to work on my game.

Work in pairs

When I'm with my team, I start out by working in pairs. One person holds the broom at one end of the sheet, while the other delivers their stones. Start out by throwing draws in groups of twos. Throw two in-turns down the centre of the sheet to the side and then two out-turns also down the centre to the side. Throw two in-turns to the centre of the sheet and then throw two out-turns to the centre of the sheet.

Your partner should be giving you immediate feedback on whether or not you're hitting the broom. This information can be relayed down the sheet verbally, or via signals with the broom. When I'm holding the broom for my partner, I show him where he's coming out by moving the broom to that spot on the ice. If he's hitting the broom, then I lift it slightly, pointing the end at him. Our team has worked out this signal to identify that we're hitting the broom.

After one person has thrown eight draws to one end of the sheet, the roles reverse. The player who was holding the broom now becomes the shooter and the other curler is now the broom-holder.

After throwing 16 draws, you can vary things slightly. Have the person holding the broom call draw shots to different parts of the house and attempt to make all eight shots. These shots might be guards or draws to the far edge of the sheet. By mixing them up, you better replicate actual game conditions and build your stamina as you work at throwing different shots one after the other.

Next, work on your hits. When I have someone to work with, I have him set up one rock and then call a certain type of hit on that rock. He might put a stone right on the Button and then call for me to play a nose hit with the in-turn. Next, he might have me throw a hit-and-roll with the out-turn. Keep mixing it up, varying the calls and the shots. Play hits on stones in the house and in front of the house. Play nose hits, hit and rolls, and peels.

Just as with the draws, once you throw eight hits, change and have the thrower become the broom-holder and vice versa.

Work as a team

After you throw 16 hits, it's time for the four players to come together. One effective way to organize this part of your team practise is to have the skip hold the broom and the other three players throw shots in order. The skip stays at one end of the sheet and calls shots, holding the broom. The lead, second, and third then take turns throwing stones, in that order. The skip tries to vary the shots, so the lead might first be asked to throw a centre guard, then the second has to play a hit on that, and the third plays a draw around that.

Note to skips: Go through different shots with each player. In this part of the practise, I like to get my teammates to work on their weaknesses. If I know my lead has trouble with his out-turn draw, I ask him to play that a few times.

All through this part of the practise, communication has to be free flowing. Everyone should be allowed to comment and offer suggestions on how to help each player. Make it constructive, though. You don't want to knock someone's confidence down.

Sweeping

Most times, on-ice practise is just for throwing stones. The top teams don't spend that much time working on their sweeping. But that doesn't mean you can't. If you're just starting out, it pays to go up and down the sheet sweeping stones, trying to get your balance and your sweeping motion down.

Besides, you can really only practise your sweeping when you're with another player, so take advantage of the opportunity. You can sweep his practise shots as they travel down the sheet, concentrating on keeping your broom in the rock's path, and on your form.

Don't worry too much about where the rock ends up when you're practising your sweeping. Just work on getting your broom in front of the rock, keeping your balance, and moving the brush. It doesn't matter if the stone eventually ends up going through the house. You're not working on weight judgement, just on sweeping fundamentals.

Finishing up

Just as when you practise alone, make the end of your team practise fun as well. To do this, I like to play a mini-game, between two teams of two. On my rink, it's always the *front end* (the lead and second) against the *back end* (the third and skip).

Getting help

Unlike golf or tennis, there really aren't many curling professionals out there to give you lessons. That's not to say that there aren't people who won't give you help — it's just that the lesson-giving part of the game is much different than in other sports. You can't book a lesson with a curling professional, and have her watch over you and offer help, as you can in golf or tennis.

In Canada, curling instructors are just regular curlers who have taken some classes on how to teach. There are different levels of instructors, with the most basic starting at Level 1. A *Level 1 instructor* is qualified to work with beginners and novices. He can help you get started in the game and help you get better.

Level 2 and *Level 3 instructors* work with more advanced, competitive players, all the way up to world champions.

Unfortunately, these instructors are not resident at every club. Only a handful of curling clubs have "curling pros" on staff. Most of the teaching by these people is done through group clinics held throughout the year, but primarily in the early part of the season. Fortunately, most of these instructors don't charge for lessons. You might have to pay a small fee to attend a clinic, but compared to others sports, it's a paltry sum.

Ask at your club when the next clinic is scheduled for, or, if your club doesn't hold them, find out which clubs do.

My team likes to play a four-rock end with each player shooting two stones. We don't have any skips, just throwers. The two players alternate throwing one stone each, until all four on each team have been delivered. We play two ends of this, with the winning team getting bragging rights until the next practise.

Drills

Practise doesn't have to be just about throwing rocks. There are lots of drills you can do to improve your game. The next time you're on the ice, try a few of these to help groove your game.

- **Run-the-Gauntlet drill:** A drill to help you slide straight. Starting at the Tee line, take eight objects that won't freeze into the ice (like tissue boxes or wooden blocks) and place them on the ice in two lines, about four feet across from each other, at intervals of two feet. They should form two lines down the sheet. Try to slide between the lines, making sure you don't touch any of the objects. If you do knock the objects, it could be that you are drifting in your delivery or not sliding at the broom. As you get better, move the objects closer together.

- **The Short Broom drill:** A drill to help you slide at the broom. Sometimes, because of perception, it's tough to gauge whether or not you're hitting the broom. Have a teammate hold the broom inside the near Hog line and try to slide right at the broom, extending your hand out to actually grab it. Have the person holding it first hold it on one side of the sheet, then on the other, just a foot or so off the Centre line. Do a few right up the Centre line, as well.

- **The Balance drill:** A drill to help you slide in balance. If you're having trouble keeping balanced in your delivery, try sliding without the aid of a broom. By taking away your crutch, you are forced to use your muscles to stay in balance. Don't slide with a rock for this one.

- **The No-Look drill:** A drill to help you slide in balance, at the broom. This one is for more advanced players or those with a little daring. First, pick a target at the far end. Without the stone, slide out with your eyes closed. When you stop sliding, open your eyes and see whether you are in line with the target. This is a great way to check your balance and alignment.

  You should only perform this drill with someone else standing alongside you, just in case an errant rock comes into your path while you have your eyes closed.

Adding an Element of Fun

Let's face it: Practise routines can often get boring. Throwing rocks up and down the sheet, one after another, probably doesn't make it onto your list of top ten fun activities. But it doesn't always have to be that way. While I recommend that most of your practising be regimented, you can spice things up with a few fun games, which will still get you throwing rocks but with a little more competition tossed in. You can play these either one against one, or two against two.

The Howard game

This game was devised by Russ Howard, a two-time world champion, who is credited with being the originator of the free guard zone rule.

In this game, you can't play takeouts. You can bump rocks back or to the side, but not out of play. If you do accidentally push a rock that goes through the rings or touches the Sidelines, your shooter comes off and the rock that was hit is replaced. This game gets you to be precise with your weight. It also requires you to find creative ways to move the stones around the house. If you can't take them out, you have to find different methods of getting to the centre of the sheet. It's fun and you get lots of rocks in play.

The Short Game

An after-game party during a major cashspiel at the Royal Canadian Curling Club, in Toronto, was the genesis of this game. As the party wore on late into the night, some of the curlers tried to find a way to have a fun game without getting back into all their curling gear. The result was the Short Game. It is played from the hack to the near house. You play it just like any regular curling game in terms of scoring, but you "throw" the rocks by just gently sliding them from the near end. The only catch is that you have to keep one foot in the hack. It doesn't necessarily have to be the gripper foot in the hack — you can use either hack or either foot. You can stretch out as far as you want to get a better angle at the rings.

This game gets you thinking about strategy and angles. It helps you see what can develop in a house filled with rocks.

Speed Play

This curling game is played just like a regular game, except that you only have three seconds to play your next shot after the previous one stops. It forces you to think quickly and to be ready for anything. It's amazing how fast you can play an entire game (although I usually only play four ends), and how speedily you have to make decisions. Talk about thinking on your feet.

Raises

This is another game where you have to get creative. Start by placing six rocks in front of the house, as shown in Figure 15-3, on the next page. Now play a regular curling game, except that you can't put a rock in the house unless it has been raised there. If you draw one in on its own, take it out of play. If at any point in the game one player has no rocks in front of the house left to raise, he loses. You don't have to play a raise on every shot — just on stones that enter the house

Dryland Training

You can improve your curling prowess without even stepping onto the ice. There are several ways to get better without having to slip on your slider and pull your sweater over your head.

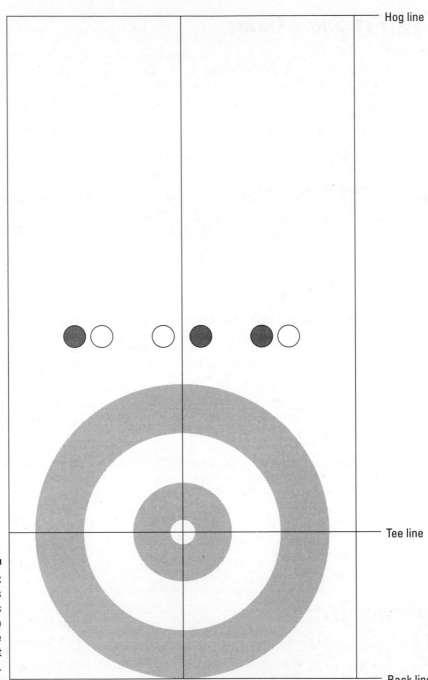

Hog line

Tee line

Back line

Figure 15-3:
The Raises
game helps
develop
your sense
of weight
and angles.

At the Gym

It used to be that curlers personified the "before" people in those before and after pictures used to promote gyms. Curlers were the anti-athletes, so to speak. In fact, in the early days of the Canadian championships, the players used to smoke (and a few used to sneak the odd drink) on the ice while the competition was taking place. The fact that the sponsor of the men's championship was a tobacco company had something to do with that, but it was also an indication of the prevailing mindset of the time — that curling and fitness didn't go hand in hand.

To many non-curlers, those who play the sport are stereotypically fat, old, and out of shape. But nothing could be farther from the truth. Go to that same championship today and you'll see slim, strong, trim, and fit players. Today's top curlers know that to excel, they have to be athletes and train like athletes. That's why you see more and more of them working out.

There are three kinds of training that are good for curling:

- ✔ Cardiovascular training
- ✔ Strength training
- ✔ Flexibility

Each benefits different parts of your game. Together, they increase your overall advantage. Before beginning any fitness program, however, check with your doctor or an experienced trainer to ensure you are doing the exercises properly and that your body can handle it.

Cardiovascular training

Cardiovascular training, or *aerobic training,* is training that conditions your heart. It improves your endurance, a necessity for good curling. This is especially important for the front-end players, who do a lot of sweeping (an aerobic activity). You need to build up your capacity to maintain a good sweeping effort throughout the game.

Good aerobic activities that will help you build endurance are walking, swimming, biking, cross training, low-impact aerobics, and skating. Any one of these will get your heart rate up, which is the key. Once you have your heart rate up, you should sustain it at that pace for a good 20 minutes. That's when you start to get the maximum benefits. Notice that I didn't include exercises like skipping, running, high-impact aerobics, or working on the Stairmaster. Although great for your heart, these exercises are also tough on your knees.

Believe me, curling is not a sport that's kind to your knee joints. More than one player has been forced to give up the game because of a bad knee. For that reason, keep your aerobic activities limited to those that are nice to knees.

Strength training

Curling is a game that requires you to use your muscles. Just to move the 40-pound rock can be a task for some players, while sweeping and sliding are also demanding of various muscle groups in your body.

You can improve all of these parts of your game if you keep your muscles toned. The main areas you want to work on are your legs — especially your quadriceps, hamstrings, and glutes — and your arms and chest — including your pectoral muscles, biceps, and triceps.

 Your legs play a major part in your delivery. You want to keep them strong so that they can support the weight of the rest of your body as you slide. It also makes pushing from the hack when you throw the stone, easier. Your upper body helps most with sweeping. For this reason, building muscles in your arms can be important.

When I suggest you build muscle tone, this doesn't mean that you have to become like Joe Weider, with rippling muscles all over your body. But keeping them in shape, and even building a little, can go a long way to helping your game.

Flexibility

Flexibility is, in my opinion, the key fitness element in good curling. If you reach and maintain the optimum level of flexibility for your own body — and this varies widely from person to person — you'll play a better game. For example, you'll be able to deliver the stone without cringing in pain or suffering a pulled muscle.

Over the years, I've seen many people injure themselves because they didn't have the flexibility necessary to bend down to get in the hack, to extend in the delivery, or even to push with their broom. A regular stretching program can be a big benefit to your curling success. This goes above and beyond your normal pre-game stretches — I'm referring to a complete series of stretches that works all your muscle groups, getting them ready for the sometimes awkward and unnatural positions you assume during the game (think of the slide position in the delivery).

Slimming for gold

In 1988, curling got a chance to be included in the Winter Olympics as a demonstration sport. With the Games in Calgary, a curling hotbed, it was hoped it could be a showcase that would boost the sport's chances of being upgraded to a full medal sport.

The Canadian Curling Association (CCA) held trials to help pick Canada's representatives at these Games; the prospective participants, in addition to playing many games, were put through a battery of physical tests. The tests revealed that a few of the better-known players were in such poor physical condition that the CCA was forced to tell them to either shape up or ship out. Ed Werenich, a two-time world champion and the best known of the group, couldn't do a single sit-up and was asked to lose weight.

Werenich complied, losing 18 pounds in a few short months and increasing his flexibility. But for him, the weight loss was counterproductive. He said that dropping the pounds threw off his delivery and he never felt good curling at his new, lighter weight. With his success — he regained the weight and went on to win the 1990 world championships — it's hard to argue.

Your Weekly Workout

Many of the game's top players train regularly to improve their strength, flexibility, and overall conditioning. If you're going to undertake such a program, consult your doctor first and a physical trainer second. I describe these exercises the way I perform them at the gym. You may need to vary them to suit your individual fitness level. In any event, again, I suggest you work with your trainer to learn these properly and have her set up a program for you.

Divide up your body into three sections:

- Legs
- Chest and back
- Arms and shoulders

Monday

On Monday, work on your legs. Great exercises include squats, dead lifts, leg curls, and calf raises. Try to do four sets of 12 to 15 repetitions each.

Leg squats

See Figure 15-4. Place the barbell on the upper portion of your back (not your neck) and your hands in a wide grip. Keep your legs shoulder-width apart and point your toes slightly out. Slowly bend your knees and lower your hips until your thighs are parallel to the ground. Then push up from your heels to the starting position again.

Figure 15-4:
Leg squats:
Don't bend
forward at
the waist;
you could
hurt your
back.

Dead lifts

See Figure 15-5. Start with your feet shoulder-width apart, with a dumbbell in each hand. Your palms should be facing inwards towards your body. Bend forward at your hips and slowly lower the weights until they touch the top of your shoes. Return to the starting position.

Leg curls

See Figure 15-6. Lie down on the leg curl machine so that the bar is across the back of your ankles. Curl your legs up against the bar, trying to bring it up as far as possible. Return slowly to the starting position.

Figure 15-5:
Dead lifts: Keep your back straight and try to keep the weights close to your legs all the way down.

Figure 15-6:
Leg curls: Try to touch the back of your legs, if possible.

Calf raises

See Figure 15-7. Hold a dumbbell in your right hand and place the ball of your right foot on a step or other raised area. Lift your left foot and hook it around the back of your right ankle. In a smooth, continuous motion, slowly lower your right heel as low as you can and then raise it up as high as you can. Hold that for a count of two and then start again. Switch feet and do the same thing on the left side.

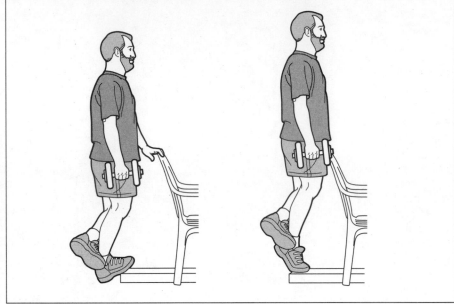

Figure 15-7:
Calf raises:
Remember
to give
your calf
muscles a
good stretch
after this
exercise.

Tuesday

Tuesday is a cardio day combined with some abdominal and flexibility training. Start by spending 20 minutes in the pool or on the bike. When you finish, do four sets of two different abdominal exercises, such as crunches and leg extensions. Conclude with a full stretching workout.

Crunches

See Figure 15-8. Lie on the floor with your back pressed down and your hands behind your head, elbows out to your sides. Gently roll up, raising your shoulders off the floor, keeping your knees and hips stationary. Try to hold for two counts, then go back to the starting position and do it again (and again and again).

Leg extensions

See Figure 15-9. Sitting on the leg extension machine with the bar across the bottom of your shin, place your hands on the handles to keep your hips from sliding up or out. Straighten out your legs and lift the weight up and then back down.

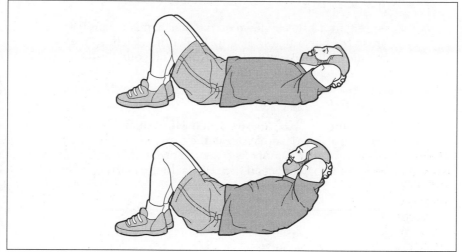

Figure 15-8:
Crunches:
Start with
your back
flat on the
floor and
roll up in
a small,
isolated
movement.

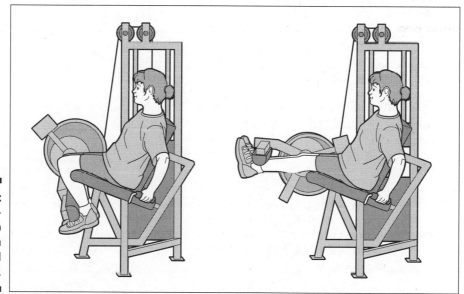

Figure 15-9:
Leg exten-
sions: Keep
the motion
slow and
continuouc.

Wednesday

Your chest and back get a workout today. Start with the bench press, and then move on to dumbbell flyes. You can throw in some push-ups, a good exercise for your pectoral muscles. For your back, you're going to do a series of one-arm rows followed by four sets of lateral pull-downs. Shoot for four sets of 12 to15 repetitions each, increasing the weight in each set.

Bench presses

See Figure 15-10. Lie down on the bench, place your feet on the floor, and grasp the bar with a wide grip. Lower the weight to your chest (about in the middle of it) and (without bouncing it off your chest) push it back up to the starting position. Repeat.

Dumbbell flyes

See Figure 15-11. Lie on the bench with a dumbbell in each hand. Extend your arms straight ahead of you, so they are pointing up. With your elbows slightly bent, lower the dumbbells out and down until they are even with the bench. Hold for two counts and then return to the starting position.

Figure 15-10: Bench press: It's a good idea to have someone spot you when you do these.

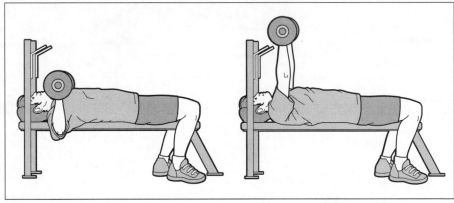

Figure 15-11: Dumbbell flyes: Think of hugging a tree when you bring your arms back to the starting position.

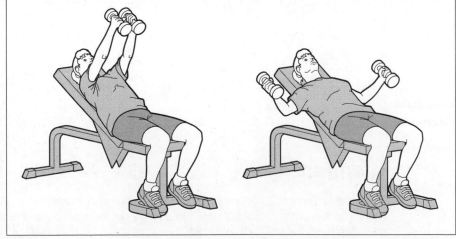

Push-ups

See Figure 15-12. Lie on the floor with your hands just outside your shoulders and your toes pointing down at the floor. Without taking the weight off your arms and chest, push your body off the ground and then lower it back down.

One-arm rows

See Figure 15-13. Place your left knee on a bench and your right foot flat on the floor beside it. Lean forward so that your left arm rests on the bench and your back is flat. With your right hand, grasp a barbell. Looking straight ahead, lift the barbell by pulling your elbow up. Feel the squeeze in your back muscles. Keep your arm close to your body at all times. Lower it and start again. Do a set with each arm.

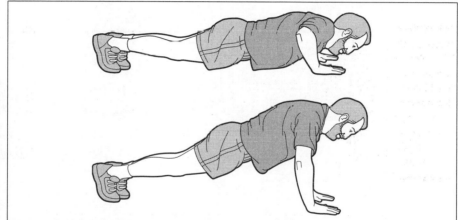

Figure 15-12:
Push-ups: To modify this exercise, bend your knees and let them rest on the floor.

Figure 15-13:
One-arm rows: Keep your arm close to your body throughout this exercise.

Lateral pull-downs

See Figure 15-14. Sit at the pull-down machine with your knees under the pads and your arms grabbing the wide bar near the ends. Pull the bar down to the top of your chest, hold it, and then return it to the top and start again.

Figure 15-14:
Lateral
pull-downs:
You'll feel
this in
your back
muscles
tomorrow!

Thursday

Thursday should be a repeat of what you did on Tuesday, although you may want to mix up some of the exercises. If you swam on Tuesday, try working out on the bike today. Do the stretching and abdominal exercises again, as well.

Friday

This is arms and shoulders day. Start working your shoulders with a shoulder press, and then do front and side arm raises, finishing off with a set of shrugs to help your trapezius muscles. For your arms, do exercises that focus on your biceps (such as curls) and triceps (such as dips).

Shoulder presses

See Figure 15-15. Sit on a bench with a dumbbell in each hand. Push the dumbbells up and in so they finish over your head. Don't let your elbows lock. Lower your arms and then start again.

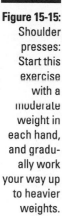

Figure 15-15: Shoulder presses: Start this exercise with a moderate weight in each hand, and gradually work your way up to heavier weights.

Front arm raises

See Figure 15-16. Stand with your legs shoulder-width apart and a dumbbell in each hand. Your arms and hands should face inwards, towards your body. One arm at a time, raise the dumbbell straight up until it is at shoulder height. Lower it all the way back down and raise the other arm. Keep your arm straight but don't lock the elbow.

Side arm raises

See Figure 15-17. Stand with your legs shoulder-width apart and a dumbbell in each hand. Your arms and hands should face inwards, towards your body. Raise both arms up and out to the side until they reach slightly above shoulder height. Try to hold them there for one count, then lower them and start again.

Shrugs

See Figure 15-18. Stand with your legs shoulder-width apart, a dumbbell in each hand. Keep the dumbbells in front of you, with your arms and hands turned inwards. The dumbbells should be touching your thighs. Keeping your arms still, move the dumbbells up by bringing your shoulders up to your ears. Hold for one count and then lower them again.

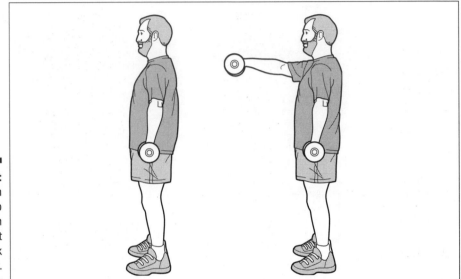

Figure 15-16:
Front arm raises: Keep your arm straight, but don't lock the elbow.

Figure 15-17:
Side arm raises: Avoid "swinging" the barbells up by moving your torso down and up.

Curls

See Figure 15-19. Stand with your legs shoulder-width apart, holding a barbell with both hands in an underhand grip. Slowly raise the barbell up to nose level. Lower it and start again.

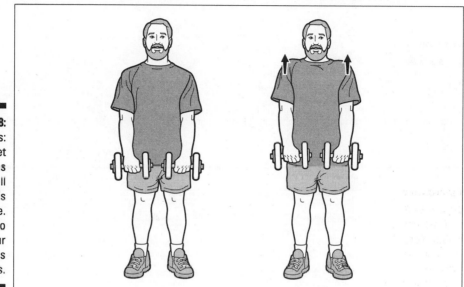

Figure 15-18: Shrugs: Don't let your arms swing at all during this exercise. You want to isolate your trapezius muscles.

Figure 15-19: Curls: Keep a slow steady pace while doing this exercise.

Dips

See Figure 15-20. Lean on a flat bench with your hands resting on the bench and your legs out in front of you, slightly bent. Your arms should be close to your body. Keeping your elbows in, slowly lower your body down until the upper part of your arms is parallel to the ground. Raise yourself back up and do it again.

Figure 15-20:
Dips: This exercise works your abdominal and glute muscles, as well as your triceps. It's a great overall endurance builder.

The weekend

Do a full flexibility workout on Saturday, mostly allowing your body to recover. Sunday is your day off.

This is just a sample workout. Work with a trainer to come up with one that will help you benefit not just for curling but also for your overall well-being. The exercises may vary, but the payback will be worth it.

Eating Right

Curlers can help themselves by adopting a good diet. There's no such thing as a "curling-specific diet," but good, healthy food choices keep your body fit and improve your chances of playing a better game.

Your curling diet should be well balanced with lots of fruits and vegetables, some carbohydrates, and plenty of protein. Try to keep the fat to a minimum.

Not many overweight curlers have success (although some, such as Ed Werenich, might beg to differ). It can also be stressful to your knee to be sliding with all the extra weight on it. Through proper diet along with a good fitness program, you can keep the weight off and help your curling.

Before a big competition, you might want to try a little extra carbohydrates, such as pasta or rice. This will provide you with the energy you need to survive a long, gruelling bonspiel.

Here are some eating Dos and Don'ts:

- Do stay away from fatty foods: In addition to adding weight, these will make you sluggish during the game.

- Do sip water throughout the game: Keep yourself hydrated during the game. As you perspire, your body craves more water to keep your muscles from seizing up.

- Do eat something for energy during the game: You might want to snack on some grapes or an orange slice to give you a little fuel during the game.

- Don't drink coffee before a game: As with alcohol, you get dehydrated from coffee.

- Don't drink alcohol before (or during) a competition: This will dehydrate you and when that happens, your performance will drop.

- Don't eat just before a game: It's tough to curl on a full stomach and tough to digest your food as you curl.

Part V
Behind the Glass

In this part . . .

You discover that you don't have to actually play the game to love curling. There are lots of other ways to get involved in the sport without competing. You can help out with junior curling as an instructor or coach (Chapter 16). If you want to coach more competitive teams, you can move up to the senior level and work with all sorts of teams — from the club level all the way to world-class calibre (Chapter 17). Maybe you're an armchair curler at heart. There are plenty of ways to heighten your enjoyment of the game as a fan (Chapter 18). This part shows you how you can be a curling lover without actually being a curler.

Chapter 16

Kids and Curling

*T*here's one thing kids love to do — and that's have fun. And curling can be a whole lot of fun. It's no surprise, then, that one of the fastest-growing segments of curling is Juniors. In the past seven years or so, the number of curlers 19 years old and under has risen steadily. There are a number of reasons for this:

✔ It's easier for kids to play the game, with the creation of *Little Rocks*, a smaller version of traditional curling stones.

✔ It's an inexpensive alternative to other winter sports, such as hockey or skiing.

✔ It's practically gender-neutral, especially when you curl at a young age.

✔ It's easy to learn.

✔ It doesn't have strict size requirements, as do other sports.

✔ It's accessible for both kids and parents, with plenty of available ice time.

There are lots of other reasons why kids are taking to curling, and one of them is the improvement of the coaching systems. Parents and other adults are devoting time not only to helping kids learn the game, but also to coaching them in competitive situations. That means working directly with the youngsters as well as taking courses on how to coach.

Junior curling development has never been stronger. Kids are becoming better curlers, and doing so at an earlier age.

In Canada, competitions involving Juniors are restricted to curlers who are 20 years of age and younger. In some parts of the world, the age limit is 21 and under. That's for the competitive scene, anyway. In most club curling, you are considered a Junior if you are beneath the age of majority. Once a youngster hits the age where she can vote and drink, she's eligible to play with the adults, and many choose to do just that. If you are around that 18- or 19-year mark, you can have the best of both worlds. You can curl with the adults in club competitions, but still enter playdowns that lead all the way to the World Junior Championships.

As with adult curling, there are many different classes of junior curlers. In addition to a variety of age group classifications, there are those who curl for fun and those who strive to win titles. While there are many very talented junior curling teams — some of which could give the best men's and women's teams a run for their money — the backbone of junior curling is at the club and school level, where the fun, social aspects of curling are emphasized a little over the competitive aspects. This is the time kids learn to love the game.

Youngsters playing for fun is something that's been going on as long as curling has been around. And no matter how old they are when they throw their first stones, young curlers are the future of the game. I can attest to the fact that a great many junior curlers stay with the game and continue playing well into their adult years. At least a dozen of the people I played with as a Junior are still playing at the same club — nearly 20 years later. I was lucky that my club had an active and well-organized junior section. That, I believe, is the reason the attrition rate was so low when the Juniors moved on to become Seniors. The game was made to be fun. We came to associate curling with enjoyment. The same story can be told at countless other curling clubs around the world. Sadly, I know other clubs where the junior section was ignored, and it later cost the facility because these players either dropped out or moved to other clubs.

Building a successful junior program requires dedication, commitment, and a great deal of enthusiasm. But kids and curling are worth it in the long run. Instill the sportsmanship and fun of the game at an early age and you have a curler for life.

Little Rocks

Perhaps the most significant development in curling over the past 20 years has been curling entrepreneur Dave Padgett's creation of smaller, lighter versions of regular curling stones, called — what else? — "Little Rocks." They weigh approximately 20 pounds (compared to the 44 pounds that regular stones weigh) and are about two-thirds the size (see Figure 16-1). The handle is smaller and narrower, often in a V-shape, which makes it easier for smaller hands to grip.

Figure 16-1: "Little Rocks" are two-thirds the size of regular curling rocks and have a special handle better suited to smaller hands.

Before the introduction of "Little Rocks," many young curlers couldn't play because they were physically unable to lift or even move the regular stones until they were 12 or 13 years of age. By the time they were old enough and big enough to curl, they already had five or six years of other sports under their belts. Convincing them to switch to curling was tough.

The idea for these "Little Rocks" is based on an old tradition called *jam can curling,* where cans were filled with sand or cement and then used to play on outdoor rinks. Smaller folks could slide these cans down the ice easily. When curling moved indoors, however, the jam can curling didn't come along. The cans sometimes tipped over, causing sand and grit to spill all over the ice. Adult curlers (not to mention ice technicians) weren't too happy about this added debris, and jam can curling was banished.

With Padgett's "Little Rocks," however, there's no mess to clean up (except maybe on the faces of the curlers themselves after the ice cream and cake they get following the game). And tykes as young as 5 or 6 can curl.

Gathering rocks

Being able to offer the specially developed smaller stones for kids to play with (these are known as "Little Rocks," and were created by curling entrepreneur Dave Padgett) is key to getting them out on the sheet, but what if your club doesn't have any of these pint-sized stones? They aren't that cheap — a pair can run about $400, and you need eight pairs for one sheet.

But there are innovative ways to raise the money needed. Here are a few tried and tested methods:

- Parents can buy them in exchange for a credit on their child's dues.

- Club members can buy them in exchange for having their or another chosen name engraved on them.

- Clubs can increase the adult membership fee by a small amount, so you spread the cost out among many.

You could also hold a fundraising campaign to help raise the necessary funds. Here are a few campaign ideas:

- Have major leagues donate 1 percent of the league's purse to the fund;

- "Charge" everyone one dollar each time they hog a rock and put that money towards the fund;

- Hold a 50–50 draw before every curling draw (of all the money taken in, half is awarded in prizes, the other half is added to the "Little Rock fund").

- Invite some of the "top name" curlers in the area to play a game at your club in a fun night. Hold an auction among your club members, with the highest bidders winning a spot on the big-name curlers' teams. Donate the proceeds to the "Little Rock fund."

Many curling associations and sports governing bodies have funds set aside for matching grants for purchases such as this. The Ottawa Valley Curling Association helps finance area clubs' purchases of "Little Rocks" and other equipment using funds it raised from the several times it hosted the Brier.

"Little Rockers" (the name given to those who curl using the smaller stones) have taken to the game, well, like ducks to water. Some of the original "Little Rockers" have gone on to become world champions. And the "Little Rocks" have themselves become standard fare at clubs all over the world.

"Little Rockers" can begin curling as young as age 5. They usually move up to regular-sized rocks at around age 11 or 12. The move up is based more on physical capabilities than on age. If a 10-year-old is strong enough to handle the big rocks, he can move up earlier.

Juniors

Junior curlers are age 20 and under in Canada, and age 21 and under in most other parts of the world.

Juniors come in all shapes and sizes, and from just about every curling country. They play by the same rules, with the same equipment (except that their brooms usually have the handle cut down for them to make it easier to use) and on the same playing surface. There is no difference between the game that the Juniors play and the one that adults compete in.

Bantams

Bantam curlers are those who are 16 years of age and under. Once they hit age 17, though, they have to move up to the junior level.

Bantam curling is a relatively new development, coming into being in the past ten years. Subdividing the junior level like this lets younger kids take on curlers their own age and size.

Not surprisingly, a large number of curling kids take to the sport because their parents curl (that was the case for me, way back when I was a Junior). That's good and bad. It's good because following in your mother's or father's footsteps makes your parents proud. But it can be problematic when the only kids who take up curling at your club are the kids of other club members. It's difficult to get kids whose parents don't curl into a club. In order to generate growth, curling needs to attract new blood to the game, instead of looking inwards to a necessarily limited source of players.

Here are some proven ways to attract kids to curling:

- **Bring-a-Friend days:** Kids love to do things in packs. If you have one child who curls, chances are she's the best one to encourage other kids to try the sport. These can be organized at your club.

- **Open houses:** Many times (especially in larger urban centres), those who'd like to try curling don't know how to go about giving it a whirl, either because they aren't sure if there's a club near them, or because they aren't sure how to enroll. Advertising and promoting an open house for Juniors lets both kids and parents walk in off the street and toss a few rocks.

✔ **School programs:** Including curling in physical education programs is a terrific way to introduce kids to the sport. Junior curling has traditionally operated through school programs, and while school participation did drop off for a time, it's now back to healthy levels, resulting in impressive dividends.

Teaching and Coaching Juniors

Teaching and coaching are quite different things. In curling, you can teach a Junior to curl and he can be as happy as a clam, throwing stones and sweeping his friends'. From his teacher, he grasps the basics of the game — how to deliver the stone, how to sweep, and how to know which turn to throw.

Coaching comes later on, after the initial teaching. That's when you help guide the player along with help on strategy, delivery, and team play. It's not always for the more advanced players, but you see it more there than anywhere else. Coaching usually also involves a team rather than an individual.

Both are vital to the development of the younger set and both require some commitment and some training.

In Canada, if you want to teach and coach Juniors at any organized level, you need to get some training certification under your belt. The levels of accreditation — broken down into Level 1, Level 2, and Level 3, respectively — are overseen by the Canadian Curling Association, the various provincial counterparts (like the Southern Alberta Curling Association), as well as by Sport Canada, the national governing body for all Canadian sport. You can find information about these courses by contacting your local curling association by phone or mail, or by logging on to Web sites run by these groups.

In Ontario, if you want to coach a junior team at any level, you must have your Level 1 certificate. Courses on how and what to teach curlers (not just Juniors) are offered throughout the year and provide a good, basic understanding of the game and how to teach it. (You can find out about these courses at www.ontcurl.com. Each junior team must have a Level 1 certified coach with it in order to compete at a sanctioned playdown. Other jurisdictions across Canada and around the world have similar requirements.

If you want to coach, though, you need more than these pieces of paper. You need enthusiasm, patience, commitment, time, and a lot of other qualities. It takes a special person to become a teacher or a coach, but the rewards of seeing the youngsters develop are well worth the effort.

School curling

For many years, junior curling in Canada depended on the support of the school system. Curling was part of the physical education curriculums of most school boards. Junior teams that played for national titles were made up of four players from the same school, instead of from the same club, and the national junior champion was referred to as the Canadian Schoolboy Champion. Junior curling and the school system enjoyed a mutually beneficial relationship.

But by the late 1970s, the relationship was suffering, as curling associations turned their attention to club curlers at the expense of the schools. This proved to be somewhat short-sighted, as removing curling from the school system essentially closed off a natural feeder system to clubs.

Many young curlers — including two-time world champion Ed Werenich — got their first taste of the game through a school program or outing.

But school curling is making a comeback. In Ontario, the Schoolboy Championship (usually for high school players) is among the strongest junior events in the province. There's even an elementary school championship. And once again, in many parts of Canada, curling is back on physical education curricula, giving youngsters an opportunity to develop a love of the sport at an early age.

Giving Lessons to Beginners

A wise person once said that children don't like to be taught, but they do like to learn. Loosely interpreted, this means that if you're going to teach kids to curl, you can't just sit them down in a classroom and read from the rulebook. You have to make it fun and engaging. You teach the same fundamental skills to kids as to adults: the set-up in the hack, the delivery, and how to sweep. Later, after they have the basics down, you can go on to strategy. But above all, keep them smiling.

A healthy sense of fun may be the most important thing you can bring to the table when teaching youngsters just getting their start. Here are some other points to keep in mind as you plan your lessons:

✔ **Teach with a "safety first" policy:** Children don't always have the same sense of balance that adults have. The very young should be required to wear helmets on the ice. Bike helmets or hockey helmets are good protection for kids who might easily slip and bonk their heads. Don't give the kids sliders until they are confident with their footing on the sheet.

✔ **Teach in small groups:** Kids get distracted easily. If you put them in a large group where they have to wait a while 'til it's their turn to try something out, they'll get bored and lose interest. Large groups are also managerial nightmares for you, the teacher. Do your kids and yourself a favour: Keep your group size to four or five.

✔ **Teach interactively:** Most youngsters love to touch and feel and try (ever seen a kid at a video arcade?). The more time they can devote to actively practising moves on the ice, instead of listening to you talk, the better. Let them touch the rocks and slip and slide (safely).

✔ **Teach a variety of game aspects:** Don't spend too long on one area of the game. Mix it up a little to keep boredom at bay. For instance, spend 15 minutes on sweeping, another 15 minutes on the slide, another 15 minutes on the turns, then another 15 minutes back at sweeping. As a general rule, your lessons should be no longer than one to one-and-a-half hours.

✔ **Teach with a healthy disregard for the rules:** I bet you're surprised to read this. Well, I say, "rules, schmules." Don't worry if the kids don't play exactly by the rules when they're just starting out. It's more important that they get out on the ice and enjoy themselves. In fact, throw out the rulebook altogether for the first few lessons.

How long?

Whether you're a Junior or Senior, learning to curl doesn't take a huge amount of time. But learning the game properly does require some commitment — on the part of both the player and teacher. As an instructor, you have several options when you're working out the length of your lessons.

For instance, there are many great one-day clinics around that provide good starts for Juniors. A day-long session might be four or five hours long, and be broken down into one-hour segments:

Hour 1: On-ice instruction;

Hour 2: "Chalk talk" sessions where you review the names of the various parts of the ice;

Hour 3: A little more on-ice instruction (30 minutes);

An instructional curling video (these are available from various curling associations — ask the manager at your club for information) (30 minutes);

Hour 4: A brief two-end game;

Hour 5: A social ending (make sure food is involved!).

Regular instruction can be a part of the weekly session for Juniors who join a facility; the instructional part can come before or after the game. For younger Juniors — Little Rockers and Bantams especially — the instructional element actually takes up the entire session. Most of these little ones don't play any regular games until they're 10 or 12 weeks into the season.

I encourage teachers of smaller kids not to worry about including any kind of formal games in your session until well after they have the fundamentals of the game under their belts. Kids aren't too wrapped up in winning, and, anyway, placing too much emphasis on the "winning is everything" aspect of the game can be a real detriment to a child who's just beginning to feel confident on the ice. So don't be too worried about putting the kids into a game situation right away. They won't miss it too much, as long as they're having fun.

Fun takes planning

It can be tough to ensure that Juniors learn how to play properly, and do so in a fun way. What you need to do is arm yourself with that time-honoured friend of every teacher: a lesson plan. Also, get some support. Round up one or two (or more) friends to give you a hand. Plan out the day with your team well before the kids arrive. Know exactly what you're going to do during your time and make sure that *everyone else* understands their roles, as well. Decide how this program is going to run. Will it be a one-day clinic or will it run all year long? Will it be a half-day or a full-day session? Are the kids 6 years old or 16 years old? All these factors have a bearing on how you plan your program.

Before the kids go out on the ice, tell them what they can expect. This will prepare them for what they may encounter during the day. Remember, these kids are nervous and perhaps a bit anxious in the early going. If you take the mystery out of the day, half your battle is won.

It's very important that every junior curling day start off with a reminder about safety — before the kids get on the ice. Drive home the point that, while the game is fun, it's easy to slip and get hurt, especially if they fool around.

How you end the program is often as important as how you begin it. Finish up the day with hot dogs, chips, and pop in a social atmosphere. What does this remind you of? It's exactly the same as when the adults get together for a drink after their games. It ends the day on a high note, and gives the kids a chance to get to know each other better, without worrying about who's sweeping the next stone.

Fun, fun, fundamentals

The best thing you can do when teaching kids is to make the instruction fun. If a child leaves the ice with a smile on her face, there's a good chance she'll come back.

If you do nothing else, it's important that you teach a child the fundamentals of the game. I can't stress this enough. When kids are learning for the first time, much of it will stay with them forever. If they are taught improperly when they start, they will have to "un-learn" the wrong information and then be taught the proper way all over again.

Make sure these game fundamentals are part of your lesson plan:

- The set-up position in the hack with body square to the target
- The no-lift backswing
- The sliding foot goes in behind the rock when leaving the hack
- The eyes stay on the target

How do you teach these basics and still make it fun? Here are a few ideas:

- **Catch the Brass Ring:** Tape some candy or collectible cards lightly to a board. Hold the board up at the end of the house and have the kids slide out and try to grab one of the treats. Keep moving the board farther and farther back, and encourage them to slide farther out to reach it.

- **Relay Races:** Divide the kids into teams of five or six and have them run a "race." For instance, you could have them practise sliding out of the hack. The first team to have all its players slide out and reach the Tee line wins. The kids will like the race format, and will benefit from repeating the movement several times. Remember to put the emphasis on team-work and safety.

- **Simon Says**: Use this game to encourage the kids to memorize every-thing from the names of equipment, to different markings on the ice, to types of shots.

- **Sing-Song:** Make up a song to a familiar tune using curling terms. Kids commit words and ideas to memory more readily when there's a melody and rhythm associated with them.

Give one of these ideas a try, or come up with some of your own to reinforce the "fun" part of the fundamentals.

Good teacher, bad teacher

As in all things, a good teacher can make all the difference in a child's progress as a curler. A bad teacher can snuff out a child's initiative and confidence in an instant. Here are a few things to remember if you are planning to teach kids.

- ✔ **A good teacher listens:** Your ears are as important as your eyes when teaching kids. Listen to what they are saying and react accordingly.

- ✔ **A good teacher is flexible:** Kids have short attention spans and they may not always want to follow the program you've set out. Be prepared to alter your plans if it's in the kids' best interests.

- ✔ **A good teacher rewards students:** Whether it's a pat on the head or a bag of chips after the lesson, let your students know they've done well.

- ✔ **A bad teacher lacks a sense of fun:** Loosen up. If you're a kid at heart, that fun attitude is passed from you to the children you're teaching.

- ✔ **A bad teacher criticizes in an unconstructive way:** There's a big difference between telling a kid she needs to improve as you suggest ways to do so, and simply telling a kid how poorly she's doing without offering any way to fix it. Nothing turns a kid off quicker.

- ✔ **A bad teacher knows it all:** If you teach with the attitude that you're the only one who knows the right way to do things, you do your students a disservice. Even as a teacher, you should still be learning.

Send Me In, Coach

Surprisingly, coaching junior teams is a relatively new phenomenon in curling. A coach was almost unheard of when I played in the junior ranks, a little over two decades ago. If there *was* a team with a coach, it was usually just someone's parent who had driven the team to the game and had been cajoled into staying on to coach them. That's all changed, now. Instead of just making an appearance at playdown time or at important games, today's coaches work with their junior rinks right through the season.

Usually, coaching involves working with a competitive rink — a rink that has aspirations beyond just performing in club games. Although you can coach fun rinks, most of the work a coach does benefits the more serious teams. Coaches do a number of things for a rink, but in junior curling, their principal role is that of teacher, organizer, and motivator. The coach helps to get the rink ready for games and helps it analyze the games played.

Coaches need training and experience. You don't have to be a champion curler in your own right, but you should have some experience dealing with competitive events, so you can relate that experience to the rink that you're coaching.

Information about training courses is available primarily through the game's governing bodies (the Canadian Curling Association at www.curling.ca or the provincial counterpart). Some of these courses deal exclusively with curling, while others are more expansive and cover topics that pertain to sports in general, such as coaching philosophy.

Singing from the same song book

"Singing from the same song book" is a sports phrase that refers to team building; it means making sure that everyone is prepared to work together to achieve whatever goals have been set. It is one of the most important things a coach does — and it takes place before the season even begins. You need to gather the team together, sit them down, and discuss goals.

I usually try to have this meeting in the summer, before everyone gets wrapped up in playing the game. Ask the team members what their goals are and help them set realistic marks. This might require you to give them a bit of a reality check. If the four members of the rink set winning the provincial championship as their goal and they are only in their second year of curling, you have to help them understand that that particular goal might not be possible — this season.

By the same token, don't dash any hopes. By all means, get the team to set high marks, but not so high that they will be disappointed by striving for unreachable goals.

I get my team to write these goals down, to give the goals some substance and make them real. As the season goes on, they can refer back to them to see how close (or far off) they are to realizing them. You and your team should set up a schedule for the season, including which events they intend to play in, when they intend to practise, and how much the season is going to cost. Remind them that school comes first and that they should plan their curling time around it. With all of this done, you and your team can head into the season knowing what to expect.

Head games

Another constant of coaching is the role you play as motivator and "mind coach." This is especially true when you're talking about coaching kids' teams. Kids are susceptible to a wide range of emotions during a curling season; the coach's job is to help them stay on the right mental plane throughout.

Sometimes, that might mean bringing them down a bit — it's easy for them to get too charged up. Other times, you need to get them focused on a particular task. I've found that with junior teams, the long-term goal is in sight but oftentimes they look too far ahead. In other words, they might be thinking of winning the championship of an event, and forget to focus on one game at a time.

If the team you coach is like most, you encounter laughter, tears, and everything in between over the course of a season. These are, after all, kids. They're not just curling, they're growing up, and we all know what a tumultuous time that can be.

At practice

One of the most important tasks for a junior coach is to set out a practice regimen. This should include when the rink practises, what it practises, and how it practises.

Help your rink as much as you can on the ice at practice by being an extra set of hands and eyes. Hold the broom for them when they are practising their shots; look to see if you can spot any problems with their deliveries; and keep them going for the full length of the workout.

One successful coach I know records all the stones each team member throws, what skills they worked on, and how they felt about that particular session. It's essentially a log of the team's progress. It can be useful to refer back to after games, and, as the season moves on, to see which skills they've really got down and which ones need more work.

When you help your rink during practice, do it with the idea that you are there not so much to *direct* as to *assist*. Help them discover what to do on their own, instead of telling them straight out. Be a good listener, offer constructive criticism, and keep the rink's goals in mind.

During the game

Curling is one of the few sports where virtually all the coach's work occurs before the game. Once the match starts, the coach is relegated to the position of spectator — either in a seat in the stands or behind the glass in the club. In other sports, the coach actively participates in the game's outcome. Think of a hockey coach behind the bench changing lines. Or picture a basketball coach directing the defensive plays from the sidelines.

But in curling, the coach has to sit and watch, almost helpless.

I say "almost" because there is still plenty you can do while you're sitting there. And you do get a chance to talk to the team at the mid-way point of the game.

Charting the game is a task that all successful coaches do. When you chart the game, you make a record of the shots that are thrown and the results of those shots, so you can look over the results with your rink afterwards. When you chart the game, you want to record whether a player plays an in-turn or out-turn, whether she throws a hit or a draw, and whether the shot was successful or not and if not, why. (This is different from scoring the game, which I cover in Chapter 8.) Chart the game for both teams so you can refer to situations that arise during the game, to keep a record of the other team that you might play again later in the year, as well as to see if the players on your team outplayed their opposite number. For example, the chart might show you that your lead has more success with his in-turn draws than with his out-turn draws. It might also show that your third is better at draws than at hits. It might also reveal that the opposing skip was unusually heavy with his out-turns.

You can make up your own chart similar to the example in Figure 16-2. The coach is charting the game for both teams. The first end is complete. D stands for Draw; H stands for Hit; I for In-turn; and O for Out-turn.

Curler	1	D	H	I	O	2	D	H	I	O	3	D	H	I	O	4	D	H	I	O	5	D	H	I	O
Us																									
Lead	3	x		x																					
	4	x			x																				
Second	4		x	x																					
	2	x		x																					
Third	4	x			x																				
	3		x	x																					
Skip	4	x			x																				
	4	x			x																				
Them																									
Lead	3	x		x																					
	0		x	x																					
Second	2	x			x																					
	2	x			x																					
Third	3		x	x																					
	4		x	x																					
Skip	3	x			x																					
	4	x		x																					

Figure 16-2: Charting a game reveals the strengths and weaknesses of both your rink and the opposing one during a particular game.

Another time you can help your team out during the game is at the mid-way point — usually the fifth end break. In most competitions these days, whether it be a sanctioned playdown or a major bonspiel, coaches are allowed five or ten minutes to talk with their team. Some inexperienced coaches will simply bring out a snack to recharge their team's energy reserves, such as sliced oranges, but the break has better uses than that. Many coaches mistakenly use the mid-way point to critique the rink's performance during the first part of the game. They go on about the mistakes that were made or the wrong shots that were called. This is about the worst thing you can do. Instead, focus on the remaining ends — the rest of the game. You can review the game when it's over — not while it's still on. Get the rink to understand what its goal is for the next five ends. Set up a game plan and get the team to buy into it. Don't be hard sell, though. Allow the rink to choose its target. You are just the facilitator.

Knowing the rules

If you want to coach, you have to know the rules. I'm not talking about the rules of the game, but the rules for coaches. In most competitions in Canada, there are certain rules that coaches must follow during an event. In play-downs leading to provincial and national championships, for example, you are not allowed to drink any alcohol for the length of the playdown. That means that if it starts Friday evening and concludes Sunday morning, you are dry for that entire time — no matter whether your team is on the ice or in their beds, asleep.

There are other such rules about coaches' conduct particular to each jurisdiction that you should be aware of. Be sure to check them out before the start of the competition. The last thing you want to do is end up being the reason your team is disqualified.

A Few Final Words of Advice

You can be prepared for just about anything, but trust me, something that takes you by surprise will just about always pop up. Whether it's a flat tire on the way to the rink, a last-minute illness, a problem parent, or something else, it happens over the course of a season, and you just have to be prepared to roll with the punches.

The curling mom or dad

Just as in hockey or baseball or soccer, there are parents out there who believe their child is the next world champion. I refer to these people as *the curling mom* or *the curling dad*. You see these parents at just about every major competition, being very hard on their son or daughter, pushing them too hard and too far.

If you end up coaching or teaching a child with an overbearing parent, the best advice I can give you is to lay down the law to that parent, as their child's coach, as early in the season as possible. As soon as you detect a problem parent, tell them what you're expecting of them. You want their support and encouragement, but not in a detrimental way. Abuse of a player, a rink, or another parent, won't be tolerated. As the coach, you are in charge of the team, and if the parent has concerns, he should come to you first. Warn them of the consequences of their actions — which can result in a rink being thrown out of an event or the parent being barred from the facility.

Coaching your own

If, as is quite common, you end up coaching your own son or daughter, be aware that you're in a no-win situation. If you do it, you're open to lots of criticism from other parents who might accuse you of favouring your child over another. If you don't do it, your kid will probably be disappointed.

The quality time you spend with your son or daughter when you coach them usually far outweighs any criticisms you might receive. But make sure that you talk to your child at the start of the season and explain to them what might happen, just so they are prepared.

Legal challenges

I've been in situations over the years where parents and other rinks have challenged the validity of another team's win because of doubts about a player's age. (Regulations call for junior players to be 20 years old or under, as of a date set by the game's organizers.)

To avoid any confusion, many junior coaches carry copies of their team members' birth certificates. You might never have to bring them out, but having them with you can save a lot of hassle if there is ever a challenge.

Chapter 17

Coaching

· ·

In This Chapter

▶ Understanding the coach's role

▶ Getting the necessary tools to coach

▶ Preparing your team physically and mentally

· ·

Coaching in curling is a relatively new phenomenon. It wasn't until 1975 that the governing bodies in Canada began to certify coaches through clinics taught by Warren Hansen, a long-time instructor and contributor to the game. Nevertheless, coaching didn't catch on right away. For example, none of the teams that competed in the 1990 Brier had a coach with them. It's really been in the past ten years that coaching has come into its own. Today, very few top teams go without some type of coaching help.

What that coach does for the rink, and to what degree that rink relies on the coach, depends on the team members' expectations and comfort level. Some teams are very reliant on getting help from the coach in everything from team preparation, diet, and the mental side of the game, while others see the coach in more of a trainer–scout position, looking after off-ice details and *scouting the opposition*, evaluating the play of future opponents.

But make no mistake, coaching is gaining an important role in the game. With each passing season, top teams are realizing that a good coach can mean the difference between winning and losing.

"I would like to believe that improved coaching skills have levelled the playing field among teams either fortunate enough or smart enough to have a [properly] trained coach," said Bill Tschirhart, the Canadian Curling Association's national development coach. Tschirhart, along with other coaches, is finding that more teams are recognizing and accepting the role of the coach. They are realizing that the techniques and practices of top coaches can make a big difference in their performance.

The Role of the Coach

A curling coach has some of the same qualities as coaches in other sports, and several that are unique to curling. In hockey, baseball, or football, for instance, a coach is an active participant during the game: calling plays, making player substitutions, even arguing with the umpires. In curling, however, the coach has to sit in the stands and watch during the game, like one of the fans. There are ways she can help the team's game while she's up there, but much of the play is left to the team.

Most of the work a curling coach does takes place before and after games, and during practice sessions.

Mike Hay, the national team coach for Scotland, lists the following among his duties as coach: managing, organizing, preparing for peak performance, monitoring, troubleshooting, facilitating, debriefing constructively, scouting the opposition, offering technical and tactical input, and above all, helping the players fulfill their potential.

Whew! That's quite a list! And it contains a wide variety of jobs.

Hay, who was also a world-class curler in his own right, and played in several world championships, only worked with a coach near the end of his playing career. But he soon realized the benefits. "I would like to think we could have turned a couple of silvers into golds, had we had the proper coaching support at the height of our playing career," Hay said.

Although a national team coach, such as Hay, and the coach of a less competitive team may have somewhat different responsibilities, the basics are the same:

- ✔ Goal setting
- ✔ Mental preparation
- ✔ Nutritional help
- ✔ Physical preparation
- ✔ Practising and training
- ✔ Skills development
- ✔ Team building

Getting a Team

So, how do you start coaching? It takes training, experience, and commitment (stay tuned, those come later in this chapter). But first, quite obviously, you need to work with a team.

There isn't really a formal way to establish a relationship with a team, unless you happen to be a national team coach. Most of the time, a coach and team get together through word of mouth. A rink might not even be looking for a coach, but if you present your credentials in a way that shows you have something to offer, they just might be swayed. In other situations, a team already knows it needs a coach and will actively look for help.

The best way to get together is to let rinks and clubs know you're available. It doesn't have to be a hard sell, but if you're interested in coaching, tell people in the know — like your club manager or some of the top players in the club. Word will get around.

Another way to solidify a coaching relationship is to help out a team bit by bit. If you know a team is practising, offer to go out and hold the broom for them while they shoot. You might give them a little bit of feedback and show them that you know what you're doing. Start slowly and let the team come to you. The more they desire your services, the better the relationship will be. If you try to impose yourself on a rink, it might backfire, and your coaching career will be short-lived.

Training

Just as you need to train to become a great curler, you need to train to become a great coach. It takes hard work, including plenty of reading, a dose of theory, a pinch of practical experience, all mixed in with some trial and error.

The formal training system for Canadian coaches is based on criteria established by the national governing body of sport, Sport Canada. It consists of three different levels, each a bit more involved and detailed than the last. Each level is broken down into practical, theoretical, and technical components. Participants hone their teaching and coaching abilities as they pertain to numerous aspects of the game — from learning about the delivery and correcting faults, to preparing players mentally, to examining situations that occur in actual games.

You should take these courses, whether you want to coach at a junior or world-class level. Many competitions require certification in order to participate and be recognized as a coach. The courses cost between $100 and $150. They are well worth it if you plan on advancing in the field of coaching.

Contact your provincial curling association to register for one of these courses. Many have their own Web sites with listings of the dates, locations, and costs. You can also check out the Canadian Curling Association's Web site at www.curling.ca for more help.

Similar courses and programs are available outside Canada. Many are actually taught by Canadians living and/or working abroad. Contact your regional or national curling association to learn more about such courses.

Experience

A new coach may feel a bit like a university graduate looking for a job. No one will hire her until she has some experience, but she can't get any experience until she gets a job. This catch-22 situation is familiar to many new coaches. Teams want experienced coaches, but coaches can't get experience without being taken on by a willing team. So, what's a prospective coach to do?

You've got several options. One is to start off working with *junior rinks* (teams of players who are 20 years of age and under). Most of these teams are hungry for help and aren't quite as demanding about the credentials of their coach, as long as the basic training ability is there. As a coach, this match-up is often ideal, as you get to work with a young team that's eager to learn.

Another way to get experience is to work alongside an existing coach, preferably of a top team. You can help the other coach out in many ways and get a taste of working with a first-rate team. You should be willing to do just about anything in this situation — consider it entry-level coaching. In exchange for getting some great experience, you might have to carry the brooms or put the stones away at the end of practice. But if you view it as an opportunity, taking on the dirty jobs won't seem as tough.

There's one other type of experience necessary if you want to develop into a good coach. That's playing experience. The best coaches are the ones who have themselves been players, who have competed at the highest levels and faced difficult situations — situations that the team they coach will also face, eventually. It's difficult to give the proper direction without being able to relate to the experiences that a player faces, such as trying to throw a shot with the game on the line, or making the right decision strategy-wise at the end of the game. This doesn't mean you have to have been a past world champion, but you should know what it's like to play in important games and feel the pressure.

Not all coaches have this type of experience; you may not be able to get it if you are more interested in coaching than playing, which is understandable. However, if you haven't done any competitive playing, I would advise you to get some games under your belt by entering bonspiels, Super leagues, or other top-ranked events. You might not fare all that well, but you will get an idea of what a team goes through in a similar situation.

Commitment

No ingredient goes farther in coaching than commitment. A good coach must be committed to developing and bringing out the talents of his team. He must be willing to work long and hard, usually far longer and harder than the team does. The coach must not only be at all the practices and all the games, but he must also work away from the ice, detailing weaknesses and strengths, going over game results, and finding ways to make the team better.

Make sure you have enough time in your schedule to do a proper job. You won't do yourself — and especially your team — any favours, by going at it hurriedly or half-heartedly. Before you agree to work with a team, scrutinize your own timetable. Jump in only if you know you can do the job fully.

The Head Coach

Once you have made the decision to coach and gained the necessary training and experience, it's time to start working with your team. There's lots of work ahead and it begins right from the moment you and your team first sit down together.

Putting everybody on the same page

The first job of any coach is to bring the team together for a meeting where you think about your goals for the season. Notice my choice of words, here. I wrote, "think about your goals," not "set your goals." Your first meeting should just be about discussing the goals for each individual on the team, and also for the team as a whole. It's probably premature to actually set goals at the first meeting. You need to let things gel.

Get everyone thinking about the team's goals. What do they want to achieve? What are they willing to do to achieve it? How much time do they want to commit to practising and to playing? How many events do they want to play in? Are they willing to travel to play in these events, or would they rather play in events held within driving distance of their homes?

Send everyone home at the end and ask them to think a bit more about the goals you discussed. At your next meeting, write the team's goals down and have everyone sign the list, essentially creating a contract between you and the team members. This will go a long way to setting up the season.

Setting up the season

Now that the team has established its goals for the season, you can move on to the next step — setting up a plan for the season. The plan should be a more or less definitive schedule of when and where the rink will play and practise. It might include, say, 11 events, a regular Super league game once a week, and a weekly practice session. You can also modify the schedule in parts, to allow for more preparation time for an important game. For example, in the weeks leading up to playdowns, you might add another practice session, upping them to two per week, schedule team meetings to formulate the game plan for the playdowns, and maybe, if it can be arranged, set up a practice session at the club where the playdowns are being held.

Be flexible when you're doing up the schedule. Try to chart the entire year, but don't kid yourself and write in pen. Use pencil, because things will happen that will upset even the best-laid plans. You might have an injury on the team, or the team as a whole might go through a bad couple of weeks where you need to increase the practice time. Be ready for anything.

Game Preparation

The objective of coaching, obviously, is to help your team play better, and, hopefully, win. There are many different ways to do this, and few of them are as straightforward as helping players perfect their deliveries or their strategy. Much of it is about getting the team ready to compete. It can be as simple as talking things over, or as complicated as using high-tech equipment to analyze a curler's slide. But it should all be aimed at preparing the rink so that it can take to the ice ready to play.

Before the game

Before a game, competition, or playdown, you, the coach, can do a great deal to prepare your team. Some of the preparation is done on the ice, some of it off. But if it's done correctly, your team should be ready to take on all comers. They won't always win, but they can enter it as prepared as possible. As a coach, your goal before the game is preparation. You need to get the team to a point where nothing is left to chance, when they step onto the ice. They should be ready to play to their full potential — to perform. As Canadian coach Bill Tschirhart points out, the definition of performance is "The ability to do what you know you can do, anytime you have to do it."

Off the ice

There are a number of things a coach should do to help the team off the ice, while the competition you're preparing for is still a ways off. Most of these things are about eliminating distractions. You should remind the team members of their other commitments outside of curling, and in some cases, take over duties that aren't essential to the team's play. Even the best curlers are not professional athletes, and many have a lot going on in their lives. Here's how you can help out as a coach:

✔ Remind the team, well in advance of the competition, of any other obligations they might have, such as schoolwork, family matters, and job responsibilities, and encourage them to complete them.

✔ Book airline tickets, make hotel reservations, and look after financial matters in advance.

✔ Take on driving duty, whether it's to the club, airport, bus station, or train station.

✔ Deal with any personal issues among team members that might affect their game. Does someone on your team have hurt feelings? Maybe even a broken heart? Get these out in the open and try to work through them before your event.

You should work with your team, before the event, to develop a team strategy. Decide, in general, how the rink is going to play. Is it going to be aggressive or defensive? Will it maybe be a mixed bag, with the team playing conservatively for the first few ends, and then switching to a more aggressive mode later on?

Make certain that all four team members buy into the strategy.

On the ice

Practice is the No. 1 ingredient for on-ice preparation for a big game. Your team practice sessions before the game will be different from your regular sessions.

In terms of how you practise, Bill Tschirhart advises that the days leading up to a big game aren't the time for your rink to be messing with, say, the technical aspects of its deliveries. More important is to reaffirm the fundamental aspects of the delivery — the position in the hack, the backswing, the release, and so on — so that they have confidence in their deliveries. Watch them on the ice as they throw rocks and offer encouragement to build their confidence.

As for what you practise, consider something done by the great golfer Tiger Woods. As he prepared for the 2001 Masters tournament, Woods knew one of the most important shots he would have to hit was a high shot that curved from right to left, on the 13th hole. So, what did he work on? Blasting drives down the practice range? No, he worked on hitting that high shot that curved from right to left. When the important final round was under way, he had a lot of confidence when he went to play that shot because he had spent so much time working on it. It helped him win the tournament.

The same can be true for your rink. They should practise the shots they know they will play in the games. This is linked to your team's overall strategy for the game. If it calls for your lead to play draw shots around centre guards, then that's what she should practise. If it calls for lots of takeouts, then play those.

I once had a coach who took that idea one step farther. He would have us practise just as if it were an actual game, emulating the time between shots. We would throw a shot, then wait for a minute or so, and then throw another. Not only were we practising the shots we would likely play in the game, we were doing so in a way that imitated actual game conditions as closely as possible.

During the game

Curling allows coach and players little or no interaction once the game starts. But there are a couple of times during the game when you can discuss things with your rink. These are obviously important moments — a chance to calm things down or pick things up, as the case may be. It's a rare opportunity to deal directly with the players and set the stage for the rest of the end, or game.

Time out

Teams are allowed one or two time outs in major Canadian championships (depending on the jurisdiction and the event). During these time outs, coaches are allowed to come onto the ice and talk things over with the team. In most cases, a *time out* is called when a team wants to discuss a specific situation in the game. It might be a crucial part of the game and the rink needs to decide which shot to play. This is the type of quandary you might find yourself in when you arrive on the ice.

A time out is only one minute long. In some larger arenas or clubs, it might take you 45 seconds just to make it onto the ice. For that reason, I always tell teams to call the coach out first, before calling the actual time out, so she can get there and have time to contribute the proper input. Once a time out is called, the clock stops, and you have one minute to discuss the situation. For a good coach, the time out is about building confidence, not telling the team which shot to play. Ask your team to describe the situation and tell you what they think their options are.

What you really want to do is to get them to pick a shot and agree on it. You want them to feel confident that they can make the shot when play resumes.

Offering an unsolicited opinion about the situation may just muddy the waters more. Unless they ask you, keep it to yourself. You're a facilitator — not a dictator.

Halftime

The other time you can talk with your team is during *halftime,* better known in curling as the *fifth end break.* In championship games, there is a break of about 5 to 15 minutes (depending on the competition) following the fifth end (or following the fourth end of an eight-end game).

Keith Wendorf, a Canadian who coaches the German national team, believes this break can be a crucial time in any game.

"The coach has the advantage of watching the game while being removed from some of the pressures and tensions being experienced by the on-ice players," says Wendorf. "The coach's awareness of various situations can therefore often remain clearer and more logical, since his emotions are not as involved as the players. However, because of this clarity, the coach can become overly frustrated when observing simple strategy mistakes, poor play, or missed opportunities. It is extremely important not to take this frustration to the team during the fifth end break. After all, you want to prepare the team to have a good second half, not put more stress on them for the mistakes or shortcomings of the first half."

"A wise coach will listen to what the players have to say during the break," says Bill Tschirhart. "He will have instructed them to this fact. A coach wants to hear what's happening on the ice. He can see events as they unfold, but the interpersonal dynamics among the team members is much more difficult to assess. The coach is also interested in what plans the team has for the remaining five ends. There [have been] many more fifth end breaks where I have said nothing than there [have been times where I spoke up]." Much of the coach's job is to listen and be a sounding board for the team. He wants to make sure all four players are still in sync, still aware of the game plan, and still focusing on the same goal.

Wendorf adds that the better you know the team, the more you know how to handle various situations. Sometimes you have to be more than a listener. "This is especially true if any problems stem from lack of concentration, over-confidence, or laziness," he says. "In these cases, the team probably needs a 'wake-up call,' and sometimes it needs to be rude to get their attention. At these times make sure you are going to the five end break as their coach, not as their friend."

Because the halftime break is so short, you should know in advance how you're going to use it. This will allow you to maximize the time you are allot-ted, putting it to good use.

Don't get bogged down with what's happened in the earlier parts of the game. Use the time to look forward and concentrate on the game yet to be played.

Mental Preparation

Mental preparation is one of the fastest-growing areas of interest among curling's top teams. It wasn't always so popular, though. As recently as 15 years ago, the mental aspects of the game barely registered on most competitive curlers' radars. But with so many technically good players in the game today, many of these top curlers are turning to mental preparation to gain an edge over their opponents. Many have heard about athletes in other sports who rely on "mental coaches," and wonder what the benefits are.

"Top coaches and their players understand that ignorance of mental preparation skills deals a losing hand to that team," says Bill Tschirhart. "In today's competitive environment, teams hoping to win on sheer technique and practice alone are fooling themselves big time!"

"As an important event approaches, a wise coach switches his/her focus from the nuts and bolts of preparation (technical skills, game plan, physical preparation, nutrition, team dynamics) and concentrates on the mental aspects of the game," Tschirhart adds. "In particular, a skilled coach knows that all his/her work in preparation can be sabotaged if the athletes do not make things right in their 'real' world." Tschirhart is referring to family, work, and other day-to-day distractions that can cause a curler to lose focus.

Good coaches understand the importance of preparing their teams mentally. Just as they must be physically ready for an important competition or game, so, too, must they be mentally ready.

I don't need a shrink

Some curlers are a little reluctant to delve into the mental side of sports. They liken it to going into therapy, and they aren't too thrilled about the prospect. But in my experience, most of the curlers I know who have worked with a sports psychologist have had the same reactions: They couldn't believe how simple it was, and how much it improved their game.

Mental preparation is about examining the way you think, and realizing what happens to your thinking in certain situations. Here's an example. A top curler is competing in the Ontario playdowns. She's in the hack, ready to throw the last shot of the game. To win, she needs to put the rock right on the Button. She throws it very light and not only misses the Button, but ends up short of the house altogether. What happened? Her delivery was fine, she threw the stone right at the target, but she still came up way short. When she analyzed the shot after the game, she admitted that some pretty destructive thoughts went through her head before she threw:

- ✔ She was worrying about the consequences of the shot: make it and win; miss it and lose.
- ✔ She was worrying about what her teammates would think of her if she missed.
- ✔ She was very nervous.

No wonder she missed!

Nervous? Who, me?

If you're thinking about the consequences of a shot, that means you're not thinking about executing it, which is far more important. Just ask Al Hackner, who threw what is probably the most pressure-packed, high-stakes, dramatic shot in curling history.

Playing the tenth end of the final of the 1985 Brier, Hackner needed to score two points to tie the game. His only shot was an extremely difficult double takeout. With the game and the national title on the line, he executed it perfectly. In the extra end, his team scored one and went on to win the crown.

In the post-game interview, when he was asked how he could throw that shot with so much hanging on that one stone, he replied that he didn't think about the consequences of making or missing the shot, just on the fundamentals of executing it.

It was a perfect example of how to mentally prepare to throw an important shot. By eliminating the unnecessary anxiety over the consequences, Hackner was able to focus on just throwing the rock — something he'd done many, many times before.

Mental preparation is all about eliminating this kind of thinking from your game, or at least being aware of it. Of the three problems this curler mentioned, the only one that mental preparation won't combat is nervousness. In fact, being nervous is a natural process, and sometimes improves your performance. But the other two are problematic. They have nothing to do with her ability to make the shot. If you had asked her to play the same shot during practice at her club, she likely would have made it nine times out of ten. Those thoughts laced with anxiety were brought on by the competitive environment she was in when she had to play the shot. The atmosphere, the crowd, the television cameras, and the fact that the title was on the line, crept into her head and caused her to miss.

Mind games that work

There are several techniques that sports psychologists use to help athletes perform better in competitive situations:

- ✔ **Breathing:** You can relax your body and mind through proper breathing techniques. When you are nervous, breathe in through your nose and out through your mouth — slowly. This will relax your mind and your muscles.

- ✔ **Positive reinforcement:** Always try to talk in positive ways. In other words, don't say, "I don't want to miss this shot"; say, "I want to make this shot." Don't think about what happens if you miss, think about what happens when you make it.

- ✔ **Repetition:** Have you ever seen a golfer before he swings? Most of the top players do something called a *pre-shot routine*. That is, no matter what the shot, they get ready to hit it in exactly the same way each time. Curlers should do the same. They should go through the same actions every time they get ready to throw the stone. This establishes a consistent pattern of preparation, which they can rely upon in stressful situations, freeing up their concentration to focus on making the shot.

- ✔ **Visualization:** Many curlers will sit in the hack and visualize their shot travelling down the ice and landing on its target. The power of visualization is remarkable, like a dress rehearsal in your mind.

There's one more tactic I've used in the past to help me prepare for games: music. It started when I was a junior curler. While driving to an important playdown one weekend, the four of us on the team were packed into a car and just about to arrive at the club. "Disco Inferno" was playing on the radio, and we cranked the volume. The song was loud and upbeat; we jumped from the car to the change room to the ice with the beat still in our heads. We went onto the ice and played one of the best games of the year. I'm not sure if we teenagers realized what we were doing at the time, but we got a tape of that song, and before every big game, played it (much too loudly for our own good) on the car stereo. When that song came on, we were like Pavlov's dogs reacting to stimuli. It put us in a winning state of mind.

As a coach, you should investigate other mental approaches to curling. There are many good books about sports psychology out there, and while they might not be tailored specifically to curling, you can adapt many examples and techniques that will help your team.

Chewing on Rocks

In years gone by, if you asked someone what the diet for a curler consisted of, he might say, beer and chips. Curlers have a reputation for drinking a few pints and having the odd fattening snack along the way. But the elite teams realize that nutrition is another area where they might gain a small advantage over their opposition. The coach can help the team develop a strong nutritional program that will help them play better — individually and collectively.

A curler's diet should follow that of most other athletes in sports requiring similar physical output. A low-fat diet with a good mix of food groups is beneficial. During competitions, such as provincial and national championships, the amount of complex carbohydrates should be increased to provide necessary energy. And you know what? Beer doesn't fit on the diet plan. Sorry about that. Instead, the liquid of choice should be water. Curlers should drink as much as they feel necessary during a game, in order to stay well hydrated. Dehydration can result in cramping, sluggish performance, and mental fatigue. A dry mouth is a warning that you are well behind in your water intake.

What about other beverages? (No, I told you before, beer isn't on the plan.) Specially formulated sports drinks are good because they contain electrolytes, which help you stay hydrated, but watch out for high sodium content, which can work against you.

Still want to talk about beer? All right. Here's the skinny. Beer, while certainly a liquid, actually dehydrates you because of the alcohol content (not to mention the fuzzy head factor). The same is true for coffee. Stay away from both before a game. Save the beer for the victory celebration and the coffee for the morning after.

Sometimes, one of the coach's responsibilities is to work out a suitable diet and meal plan for each team member, and monitor it, as well. That might mean issuing weekly menus and, at the end of the week, comparing what was actually eaten to what was on the plan. It might mean monitoring calorie intake and it might mean watching intake compared to performance. You should see if a pre-game meal has a positive or negative impact on the play of the curlers on your team. And you should see what time is best for meals. Is it an hour before (that should be the minimum)? Two hours? It's the coach's job to look after this type of thing.

The Wendorf Rock

Keith Wendorf has coached and instructed in more countries around the world than any other curler. A Canadian who moved to Germany, Wendorf was a world-class player, making it all the way to the final of the 1983 world championships.

When his playing days were over, Wendorf turned his attention to coaching, and has led the German team for many years. But he's also worked with the World Curling Federation organizing curling clinics in countries that are interested in joining the WCF. Wendorf's travels have taken him to Japan, Norway, Sweden, Denmark, Austria, Germany, Russia, Hungary, the Czech Republic, and New Zealand, among others.

The New Zealanders in particular were so grateful for Wendorf's help that they named their national curling championship after him. The winner of the "Wendorf Rock" receives a trophy — also with Wendorf's name on it.

The Numbers Don't Lie

Statistics have become a coach's friend. They allow a coach in any sport to analyze a player's performance and determine where improvement is needed. Thanks to the increasing prevalence of statistics in curling, you can track your team's play and offer suggestions on how to improve.

One useful statistic is the *shooting percentage*, which tracks the percentage of shots the curler makes successfully. After a few games, it's possible to draw a reasonably accurate picture of a curler's performance. For example, you might see that one of your team members needs help with her out-turn, or with her draws, and incorporate that into the practice schedule.

Computerized analysis packages are another tool that can make a coach's job easier. They basically record the game, shot by shot. It can then be replayed afterwards, and a post-game analysis can occur. It eliminates the disagreements that can occur when discussing a game after it's over. A particular end can be reviewed and the exact positions of the stones shown.

"It is invaluable in comparing the way in which the team thinks it's playing and what is actually happening on the ice," says Bill Tschirhart. There are two such packages currently available — one from Switzerland (The Curling Information System) and another from the United States (Curlstat). Both are used around the world by leading coaches.

Another area where statistics are valuable is in *scouting the opposition*, which, during big events, is a coach's responsibility. By looking over the results of the previous games they have played, you can see where your next opponent's weaknesses are. Maybe the opposing skip is better at playing takeouts than draws. You might tell this to your team, which could help them in their strategy.

Chapter 18

Fun and Furor:
Being a Fan

· ·

· ·

*O*ne of the most remarkable statistics to come out of the television ratings in Canada each March is the number of viewers of the Brier, the Canadian men's curling championship. At the height of the event, there are about four million fans glued to their television sets.

Why is this remarkable? Obviously it's a huge number, but it's also about three million more viewers than there are curlers in the country. That means that there are a lot of curling fans out there who don't actually curl. It also means that you don't have to be a curler to enjoy watching the game.

Whether you take in a game at a local club, on television, or perhaps in a major arena for a national or world championship, being a spectator is an art in itself. You have to know what to look for, how to follow the game, and what you can and can't do behind the glass. This chapter is about making the most of being a fan.

Watching a Game at Your Club

There are lots of reasons why you might want to take in a game at your local curling club, not the least of which is that you might simply enjoy one.

Watching a game can be a fun night out, if you do a bit of planning first. Now, I'm not saying that you have to write out a long and involved battle plan just to sit there and watch the stones go up and down the sheet. But if you want some fun, it's not a bad idea to put a little thought into your rock watching.

Know why you're there

Here are some reasons why you might want to go and watch a curling game at your club:

- ✔ **Cheering on a friend or family member:** You can encourage your son or mother or husband or best friend in the big championship.

- ✔ **Enjoying a night out:** Curling clubs are popular social spots in the winter months. Many people like to come out to watch a game more for the fellowship that goes on behind the glass than because of anything serious happening on the ice. (Don't tell anyone actually on the ice that I said that.)

- ✔ **Getting a read on the ice:** This is really helpful if you are playing a game on that sheet later that day (or week). You can get a good idea of how the ice is reacting by watching how it treats other players.

- ✔ **Learning from better players:** The old adage "Watch and learn" applies here, especially when it comes to strategy. Watching how the best teams in your club play can help you improve your own game.

Know when to be there

Just as you would if you were playing a game, it's a good idea to check the schedule — which should be posted somewhere in the club — to determine when the games are and which ones you can come and watch.

You can, of course, just come out to watch a regularly scheduled game, or a special competition, be it a *bonspiel* (an invitational tournament) or a *playdown* (a competition leading to a sanctioned championship). If your club is hosting one of the key events of the season (clubs in certain areas take turns hosting playdowns from year to year, for example) you get the added bonus of seeing other rinks playing on your ice.

One of the best parts of curling is that even the reigning world championship rink has to start defending its title at the club level the following year. Somewhere, at some club out there, that rink and other top-level rinks will be playing. If it's at your club, you've lucked out. Don't miss an opportunity to see them. Check the playdown schedule to see where they are planned in your area.

Of course, you can go to other clubs to watch similar events. It can be fun to go to a different club to cheer on a team from your own facility if they are competing in a playdown of one sort or another.

Curling clubs the world over are generally welcoming spots. When they're hosting an event or a bonspiel, they usually have an open-door policy along with it. There's rarely an admission fee and you don't have to make a reservation or be a member. Just show up and watch. Be aware, however, that some clubs have certain regulations pertaining to dress code, or to buying food and drink. If you're going to a club you don't know very well, phone ahead and find out its particular dos and don'ts. There's nothing more embarrassing than walking into a club where everyone is wearing a jacket and tie and you're in your sweatpants.

Know what you're watching for

There is a sign posted behind the glass at a curling club I visited once that has stayed with me for a long time since. It reads: "Give me the wisdom, and half the class, as those #*!$%^& behind the glass." Although it's meant in fun, it does reveal one of the great parts of watching a game from the curling lounge: You never miss a shot! (Some wags point out that you also never make one, but that's beside the point.)

When you watch a game in a club, you watch it from *behind the glass*. That's a term used to describe being inside the club but not on the ice surface. It refers to being on the other side of the windows, watching the game and staying warm. What usually goes on behind the glass is a lot of armchair commentating, as fans critique the strengths and weaknesses of the teams on the ice. Fans second-guess the team's strategy, where the skip is holding the broom, even the call of the sweeping. It's no different from fans at a baseball game commenting on the manager's strategy or the pitcher's arm.

Of course, it's all done mostly in fun, for the enjoyment of all those watching.

If there is one formal rule about watching a game from behind the glass, it's that you shouldn't tap on the glass or otherwise disturb the players in the game. You might distract them — not to mention leave fingerprints all over the glass! It's no use running away afterwards. They'll know who you are!

Organizers: Make it a big draw

If you are a club organizer, think about special events that will encourage spectators to come to your club. By attracting people to the facility, you not only help the club financially with bar receipts, but also make it a central part of many people's social lives. This will help sustain the club, since people will look to it as an important part of the community.

Over the years, I've been a member of various clubs in various cities. Some of the best ideas to attract people to the club had as much to do with what happened off the ice as on.

- **Battle of the Sexes:** One club I was a member at used to have an event once a year where the men's teams took on the women's. Bragging rights were at stake. The club was usually jammed, as the fun "battle" took place.

- **The Big Invitational:** Hosting an annual invitational bonspiel can be the highlight of the year for many clubs. When I curled at the Windsor (Ontario) Curling Club, its big bonspiel was called the City of Windsor Championship. One year, when I was playing in the final, I looked up about halfway through the game and saw what appeared to be the entire city watching in the stands. Organizers had gone the extra mile to publicize the event — in newspapers and on radio. It attracted quite a crowd.

- **Championship Night:** Another club I curled at held a special night at the end of the season where the finalists in the various divisions faced off. This included the men's, women's, *mixed* (teams composed of men and women) and seniors divisions. It was a big finale to the year and drew one of the largest crowds.

- **Friday Fun:** Friday nights were the special night at still another club I belonged to (I know, I got around). Each week, two teams (usually two that had just played each other) were responsible for coming up with and hosting a theme night. Memorable ones included a trivia night and a skit night. Lots of people came to watch the games and stay for the fun afterwards.

- **The Olympics:** This was another once-a-season night where all the rules were broken in an Olympics-type competition. Teams competed in various events for a grand prize. The events were deliberately as strange and wacky as possible. They included throwing a stone from the hack on Sheet One over to the house on Sheet Four; sliding down the sheet as far as possible; even throwing a broom instead of a stone (well, actually sliding a broom, in this case).

Watching a Game on Television

Televised curling in Canada is among the most popular of all sporting broadcasts. Next to the Stanley Cup hockey playoffs and the Grey Cup football championship, the Brier (the Canadian men's curling championship) is the highest-rated sports broadcast of the year, drawing up to four million viewers at peak times. Although this may seem odd to non-curlers, when you consider aspects of the game such as the set-up of the sheet and the way the game unfolds, you can see why curling is uniquely suited to television. "There is no better sport for television," sums up Keith Pelley, the president of TSN (The Sports Network), the all-sports cable channel in Canada, which regularly broadcasts more than 125 hours of curling during the winter months. Curling has many one-of-a-kind attributes that justify that statement:

- ✔ Curling is played at the right speed for television: Similar to baseball, the game evolves slowly enough that viewers can follow what's going on without getting bored. You can also get up off the couch, get a snack and a drink, and get back without missing too much.

- ✔ Curling's playing surface is very camera-friendly: The size of the sheet lends itself to great camera angles, including an overhead bird's-eye view from a camera positioned directly over the centre of the house at each end.

- ✔ Curling is populated by down-to-earth players: The curlers who play in most televised events are usually just average people with regular jobs. Because of this, they don't have the same swagger that many of today's professional athletes do. They are usually very happy to conduct interviews or help out with the broadcast. This is a win-win situation for television viewers, since you get to watch some of the best curlers in the world, minus the annoying attitude.

There are attributes unique to televised curling games, which also set it apart from other televised sports:

- ✔ Televised curling lets you get close to the players: Because the curlers in televised matches wear microphones, you can hear what they say during the game; whether it's commenting on an opponent's shot or discussing the team's strategy for the remaining ends. In some cases, you hear more of what the players are saying than what the broadcasters are saying!

- ✔ Televised curling lets you see the future: Since the players often talk in advance about the shots they are going to play, you get to be in the privileged position of knowing what's going to happen before it happens. This is rare in televised sports.

Televised curling allows the viewer to get much more involved in the game, almost to the point where you feel like you are right there on the ice. Because you're more involved, you have a higher stake in the outcome.

Few places aside from Canada can count curling as a staple of winter sports television. Televised games in other curling countries are usually relegated to regional broadcasts on smaller stations. Canada has many different curling events on the schedule, ranging from provincial, national, and international championships, to made-for-television events where the teams play for cash prizes.

Whatever the event, curling on television can be fun, and even addictive, to watch. I can't tell you the number of times I've had friends who aren't curlers — but who know I am — come up to me and comment on a game they watched the night before. I always tell them that their days as a non-curler are numbered.

Know what you're watching for

When you sit down in front of the television to watch a curling event, there are several things you need to know about to enjoy the broadcast to its fullest. First of all, reserve at least three hours, if you intend to watch the game in its entirety — a bit longer, if you want to watch the preamble and post-game wrap-ups.

Televised curling games are longer than those you might watch or play at your club. You can thank commercials for that. At some events, there is even a *halftime break*, much like you see in football. Breaks in these big games can sometimes last 15 or 20 minutes (as opposed to 5 or so in regular playdowns), adding to the overall length. So settle in with your favourite beverage and snacks, and get ready for an afternoon or evening of curling.

Player versus player

Get to know the teams in the game you're watching. Most televised games show a breakdown of the rinks, player by player, before the first rock is thrown. In games where the rinks are representing a province or country, cheer on the team that is closest to your heart.

I also like to keep track of how the different players on each team play against each other, comparing the two leads, seconds, thirds, and the two skips. TSN broadcaster Ray Turnbull popularized something called the *plus-minus*. This is a fun way to analyze just these sorts of match-ups. If the lead on Team A curls better than the lead on Team B, Team A receives a plus while Team B gets a minus. You can do this for all four positions, and see if the team with the most pluses actually ends up winning. Most times they do, but not always, owing to fluky shots or one big miss.

The shooting percentage

Once the curling begins, you start receiving a great deal of continuous information about the progress of the game: commentary, predictions, statistics. One especially useful statistic is the *shooting percentage*. This is the percentage of shots a player makes successfully during a game.

Each player on the rink is awarded between zero and four points for each shot he throws during the game (a four is usually awarded for a perfect shot, though it is possible to score five out of four for a truly amazing shot). At national and international championships, the scoring is done by volunteers who are trained to award and record the numbers. The information is fed into computers that can provide a snapshot of how a player is doing at any point in the game. This information will often come up on your television screen. For instance, after the fifth end, you might learn that the lead on one team is shooting 80 percent. That means she is making 80 percent of her shots.

I have watched the scoring done at major events over the years, and found that, although it's a good general representation of how a player is doing, it's really nothing more than that. Despite receiving plenty of training, the volunteer scorers at big games are usually just average curlers who don't always understand the complex strategy being called. What they might see as a made or missed shot might not be how the skip was asking for it. The result is that they give it an incorrect mark. For that reason, I take the shooting percentage with a grain of salt.

Listen up!

You can hear what the players are saying over the course of a televised broadcast because they wear microphones. In most cases, the skips and thirds wear cordless *RF microphones* ("RF" stands for radio frequency). In recent years, the leads have also begun to be miked.

This allows you to get in on the discussion between the teammates. Here are a few things to listen for:

- ✔ **What they say about the ice conditions:** The players may talk about how the ice is changing throughout the game.

- ✔ **What they say about other players:** The players may talk about their opposition's strengths and weaknesses.

- ✔ **What they say about strategy:** The players will talk about upcoming shots. I find it especially interesting to hear the players talk about the shots they have planned — and not just the very next one. Listen to them discuss the ramifications of a certain shot, and how it might affect a shot three or four shots away.

- ✔ **What they say about themselves:** The players will get personal. Once in a while, you'll hear them discussing where they're going for dinner or how their families are. This usually happens when they're losing badly.

Where to throw 'em

If there's one thing you can learn from watching curlers on television, it's strategy. I always enjoy watching top skips such as Ed Werenich, Russ Howard, Kevin Martin, and Kerry Burtnyk, to see how they play in certain situations. I learn a great deal by seeing what shots they call at different points of the game, where they place their rocks for a big end, and how they get out of trouble when things aren't going that well.

Watch for certain situations in a televised game where strategy really plays a role. For example, see how a skip handles trying to steal a point. Or how she plays when she is ahead by one point in the final end without the benefit of last rock. All these are situations in which you'll find yourself during the season. Watch and learn from the experts.

There's something to be said for style

If you're a new curler watching a televised game, pay attention to the players' deliveries. Most curlers who make it to the point where they are playing in televised games are quite accomplished; and while you'll invariably see a few wonky delivery styles, which you won't want to copy, you can learn plenty by watching them slide and release the stone. Watch how they prepare for each shot, how they slide, where their sliding foot is as they leave the hack, and other subtle points of the delivery. By watching the best, you can become better. (Need a refresher? The delivery is covered in Chapter 9.)

Games worth watching

There has been a proliferation of curling events on television in the past five years. That's not really surprising, considering that the viewing audience is so large. The more popular curling is, the more you'll see it on TV.

Here are some of the regular curling events shown on Canadian television:

- ✔ **The Canadian men's and women's championships:** These events receive end-to-end coverage. The competition lasts for nine days, the first six of which have live broadcasts of three games per day. The final three days are taken up by the playoffs, with the finals held on the ninth day.

Championship season

Prior to 1995, the Canadian and World Curling Championships were held throughout the winter months, each operating as an individual entity. But that year, the St. Clair Group, a Toronto-based sports marketing group, secured the marketing rights to five Canadian and two world championships. It was charged with finding sponsors for the Canadian mixed, senior, junior, women's, and men's, as well as the world junior and the world men's and women's championships (held jointly).

As time passed, the company quickly learned that finding sponsors would be far easier if the events were brought together under an umbrella structure that could be presented to sponsors as a package.

So they organized the various events into a single "season," running from January through April, with a week in between. Dubbed the "Season of Champions," not only was it a great way for curling fans to organize their television viewing schedule, but it also allowed the St. Clair Group to sell the events as one big package — which it did, with great success. Today, all curlers know that they won't be straying too far from their television sets when the Season of Champions begins.

✔ **The McCain/TSN Skins Game:** This is a made-for-television event where teams play for money. The rules in this and other events like it are different from regular curling. See Chapter 19 for more on these somewhat non-traditional games.

✔ **The Olympics**: Curling received great Canadian coverage when it made its Olympic debut as a full-medal sport in 1998, in Nagano, Japan. Only a few highlights were broadcast in the United States and other countries, though.

✔ **Other national championships**: These include the Canadian junior, senior, and mixed championships. Unlike the men's and women's championships, which are covered from start to finish, only the semi-finals and/or finals are broadcast.

✔ **The World Championships**: If it is held in Canada, then it receives the same coverage as does the Canadian championships. If it is held in another part of the world, then just the semi-finals and finals are shown.

✔ **The World Curling Tour**: From October to December, weekly cashspiel events are broadcast either nationally or regionally. The final games of major tournaments are usually also shown.

Know who's in the booth

Curling only has a few expert commentators. I know, you might find that hard to believe when you listen to all the talk behind the glass at your club. But there are really only a few people behind the microphones who provide commentary and play-by-play for the televised broadcasts and get paid for it.

Here are the commentators you are most likely to listen to during a televised game. The network each is associated with is beside their names.

- **Don Duguid (NBC):** After winning back-to-back world championships in 1970 and 1971, Duguid became the colour commentator for the CBC (the Canadian Broadcasting Corporation) for 28 years. In 2001, Duguid was signed by NBC, in the United States, to handle broadcasting duties for the 2002 Winter Olympics.

- **Mike Harris (CBC):** An Olympic silver medallist, Harris is straightforward in his presentation and never minces words. He's a talented broadcaster.

- **Joan McCusker (CBC):** A three-time Canadian and world champion, as well as an Olympic gold medallist, McCusker and Harris took over from Duguid at the CBC in 2001. Like Harris, she has plenty of talent.

- **Linda Moore (TSN):** A former Canadian and world champion, Moore works alongside Vic Rauter and Ray Turnbull, drawing from a wealth of experience. Quieter and more reserved than Turnbull, the two work well together.

- **Vic Rauter (TSN):** Unlike some other commentators, Rauter covered the game first, and then started to play it. Rauter has been with TSN for more than a decade, and is now an ardent player at the club level.

- **Ray Turnbull (TSN):** A past Canadian champion and an international instructor, Turnbull is gregarious, extremely knowledgeable, and has a welcome witty style.

- **Don Wittman (CBC):** This play-by-play commentator is smooth and knowledgeable about the game.

Watching a Championship Game

Just as with any sport, there's really nothing like being there. Attending a major curling event is fun for a variety of reasons. Not all of them have to do with the game on the ice.

In the same way that the television audience has grown, attendance at major curling events has grown tremendously in the past ten years. In 1990, the Brier drew a total of 77,000 fans over the nine days of competition. A decade later, that number had risen to 249,000.

For ardent curling fans such as me, it's sometimes hard to believe that there are now scalpers selling tickets to events like the Brier. Although championships such as this have always been popular, they've now become *the* place to be.

Some of these big events are held in arenas that seat 20,000 or more, while others are hosted at curling clubs, where it's common practice to erect bleachers on the ice for additional — albeit cold — seating. Sometimes a hockey arena is revamped to hold four sheets of ice. All four sheets are in use simultaneously for most of the event, but only one or two are used once the playoffs get under way.

Who needs a pair?

So, you've decided to go to a major curling event. What's the first thing you need to do? Get a ticket, of course. Depending on the event, tickets may be simple or not so simple to come by. Most events travel around to different locations each year, so be on the lookout to see if one is coming to a city or town near you. The host location is usually chosen a year or more in advance to allow organizers enough time to prepare. Tickets go on sale well beforehand, and you can often buy them online, as well. Check local papers or your curling facility for dates and times.

Because of the popularity of these events, buy your tickets well in advance of the tournament dates. The earlier, the better.

You also need to decide what type of ticket or *ticket package* you want to buy. Because most curling events last for a week or more, tickets are sometimes sold in bunches. You might get a pass for the entire competition, for a certain series of games, or for just a single game. Most of the best seats are reserved for those who buy the biggest package — the event pass. You likely won't get a great seat if you just purchase a single ticket, even if you buy early.

For events held in arenas, try to get seats in the *ends* (that's the area behind the house). These seats give you the best view of the action on the ice, as you can see the rocks travelling down the sheet from the vantage point of either the player throwing the rock or the skip, depending on which end you are at. You can watch the stones curl and observe their line better than if you sit on the side.

Tickets for club events are usually *general admission tickets* (no assigned seats). You buy a ticket and take the best seat when you arrive. It's often tough to get an end seat at these tournaments, so look for a spot that's close to the action, yet high enough that you can get some perspective on the rock's path.

Rah, rah, sis boom bah

Is the crowd at a curling championship rowdy and boisterous like at a football game? Or is it more reserved and respectful, like you might find at a golf championship?

The answer is, a bit of both. At events such as the Brier (the Canadian men's championship), the crowd can be raucous and loud, with cheers and blowing horns, and plenty of applause. But most of the time, when a player is in the hack ready to throw an important stone, a hush falls over the audience. You can cheer, applaud, or make noise at almost any time during the game. It's considered part of the fun of going to these events. But when a player steps into the hack, clam up. Be quiet and allow the curler to concentrate. As soon as the stone is on its way, you can cheer all you want. It's also a generally accepted rule that you cheer for your team, but not against the opposition. You don't hear many fans screaming out, "You're washed up!" at curling matches.

At most Canadian finals, which involve all ten provinces and the territories, fans make it known whose side they're on. You'll see fans running around waving provincial flags, or dressed up in costume. Fans from Nova Scotia often dress in hats typically worn by Nova Scotia fishermen and paint their noses blue (a reference to their nickname, "Bluenosers," after the *Bluenose*, the famous ship from that province). Fans often have friendly competitions to outdo each other. At some events, they're almost as much fun to watch as the curling itself.

Wet your whistle

One of the best parts of the Canadian men's and women's championships is not the curling ice, but the area next door. At both these events there is a huge bar where curling fans — and sometimes the curlers themselves — will go to talk about the game, enjoy some laughs, and have a few drinks. It's sort of like the lounge at your curling club, only a lot bigger.

At the men's championship, this area is called the *Brier Patch*. At the women's event, known as the Tournament of Hearts, it is dubbed the *Heart Stop Lounge*.

Fans can make a pit stop there between games (there are usually three draws a day with breaks in between) and during the games themselves. (There are usually large televisions inside the bar, so you won't miss a thing.) It's a must after the last draw of the day. The space itself can often hold as many as 3,000 revellers, and always includes entertainment ranging from well-known acts to local talent. It's a great spot to meet other curlers, whether you're renewing friendships, or making new ones.

If you choose, you can also get a meal there. You could arrive in the morning for the first draw of the day, which usually begins at about 9 a.m., and stay in the building, dividing your time among curling, eating, drinking, and generally having a rousing good time, until last call (about 1 a.m.). Whew!

Because championship events last up to nine days, the bars often become the hubs of off-ice activities — the place to be in town while the curling is on. It's not uncommon to see them jammed to the rafters with curling fans as well as average partygoers who know a good time when they see one.

If you're a true curling fan, stopping at the Brier Patch or Heart Stop Lounge is something you simply must do.

That volunteer spirit

It takes a lot of people to run a big event like the Brier. What boggles the mind is that about 99 percent of them do it voluntarily. People donate hours, days, weeks, and months of their time to help put on one of these championships. They do it for a number of reasons, but the primary one is to help raise money for their curling club or association.

In recent years, because of curling's increasing popularity, hosting the Brier has meant a huge windfall for *host committees* (the groups that organize and run the event). They are composed of about 3,000 people doing all sorts of jobs, from taking tickets, to promoting the championship, to serving beer, to selling programs, to cleaning the ice. And when it's all over, the committee gets to share in the profit (along with the Canadian Curling Association), which can be in the neighbourhood of hundreds of thousands of dollars. A few have even managed to make it over the $1 million mark. The money is most often used to help out the area curling clubs, where it is put to good use. So, when you *do* attend a curling championship, remember that all the folks you see helping to make it happen are doing it out of the kindness of their heart and to help make curling better.

A great way to be part of a major curling event is to become a volunteer. You don't even have to be a curler to take part. There are jobs with flexible hours for just about everyone; you can usually work as much or as little as you want during the event. If you know a championship is coming to your city or town, check with the manager of your club to see about lending a hand. She'll point you in the right direction.

Part VI
The Events

In this part . . .

You find out about all the curling championships you can win, all the countries you can travel to, and even about getting that gold medal around your neck. This part covers curling's biggest events — their history, how they're run, where they're played, and, yes, how you can win them.

Chapter 19

Canadian Events, Eh?

●●●

In This Chapter

▶ Grasping how important the Nokia Brier is to curling in Canada

▶ Charting the rise of the Scott Tournament of Hearts, the Canadian women's championship

▶ Finding out why the Canadian Junior Championships breed champions

●●●

*W*ith the most curlers in the world within its borders, Canada enjoys the distinction of holding what most people agree are the biggest curling events worldwide.

Men's, women's, and junior teams have their own championships to decide the national winners. Each event is quite large, very significant (as it decides the champions of the largest curling country), and draws huge crowds to watch the action. As much as any event can, these curling championships have transcended the sports world to become part of the cultural fabric of the nation. Curling is as Canadian as our one-dollar coin, the "loonie." As winter winds down, curling heats up; the country is awash in talk of brooms and stones.

Some of the events have long histories with many legendary games, players, and stories attached to them. Other events are somewhat younger, but the opportunity to compete in them is no less sought after. They too enjoy great involvement at many levels — players, officials, media, and spectators.

The Nokia Brier

Few would disagree that the Nokia Brier is the greatest curling spectacle in the world. Held in a different Canadian city each March, the event draws the top teams from each region of the country to battle for the right to be the national champions.

What is it?

The Nokia Brier is the Canadian men's curling championship. Known originally as "The Brier" it now includes the name of its current sponsor, mobile phone manufacturer Nokia. (Nokia signed a five-year contract as title sponsor of the event in 2001.)

In many ways, the Nokia Brier defies the standard logic for major sporting events:

- ✔ It lasts for nine days.
- ✔ It has 12 teams in the competition, all Canadian.
- ✔ It has had just three sponsors in more than 70 years.
- ✔ It isn't plagued by agents, trades, trash-talk, lockouts, or strikes.
- ✔ It has no prize money attached to it.

The Brier was created largely as a way of nation building. In 1925, the Macdonald Tobacco Company (which prided itself on philanthropic and nationalistic ventures) provided financial support for the winners of a major curling event in Manitoba (the Manitoba Curling Association Bonspiel) to travel to Ontario and Quebec to play exhibition games against the top teams in those locales. These tours were such a success that two years later, in 1927, Macdonald Tobacco sponsored the first Canadian curling championship, held at the Toronto Granite Club, a posh facility located in mid-town Toronto. The Brier was born.

The teams in the event were selected by invitation that first year. The Nova Scotia team, skipped by Dr. Murray Macneil, won that first Brier, from a lineup of eight rinks.

Today the lineup consists of 12 teams. There is one team from each of the ten provinces, plus a combined Yukon/Northwest Territories/Nunavut entry. I know, that only adds up to 11 teams. The twelfth team is in fact another team from Ontario, which gets to send two teams because of its geographic size and large curling population. (One team is from northern Ontario and can be from anywhere in the province north of Parry Sound. The other team can be from anywhere south of this demarcation.) In this sense, the Nokia Brier is a true Canadian event. Each province or territory holds a provincial playdown to decide on the rink it will send to the championship. The province or territory is divided into a number of regions. Within each region, playdowns start at the club level, where teams try to become the club's representative (or one of a handful of representatives), and then progress onwards through similar playdowns until the provincial final. A few provinces have alternative

What's a Brier?

The name "Brier" has become synonymous with curling, but that's not where it originated.

Back in the 1920s, before the days of pre-made cigarettes, people bought *plugs* (a small portion of tobacco) and rolling papers and made their own. One of the most popular brands of plug at the time was called "Brier," manufactured by the Macdonald Tobacco Company. They came in a little heart-shaped tin and carried the slogan "The Tobacco of Heart." In what may have been one of the first title sponsorships on record in Canada, Macdonald Tobacco named the championship The Macdonald Brier, when it was inaugurated with the company's financial support in 1927.

Every participant received a heart-shaped crest, a tradition still in place today. Known as the Purple Heart, it has come to represent participation in the grandest of all curling championships.

routes to get to the provincial championship, should a team be knocked out along the playdown route, such as winning important bonspiels.

Where is it held?

The Brier was held at the Toronto Granite Club from 1927 through 1941 (with the exception of 1940, when it was held in Winnipeg). But as the event grew in popularity, and in fan base, larger venues were sought. Nowadays, fans can watch their favourite teams battle it out in arenas with seating capacities of up to 20,000.

Today, the Nokia Brier is held in a different Canadian city each year. Cities that want to host the event apply to the Canadian Curling Association. The CCA carries out a site inspection of the venue the prospective host city has proposed, along with other facilities such as hotels, transportation, and parking, to determine if the location has the necessary facilities and infrastructure in place to be a host site. The CCA awards the event based on a number of factors (such as facilities), but attempts to rotate it to different regions of the country. It goes from West to East, with perhaps a little extra time spent in the West because of the rabid curling population there.

The Brier has been held in every province in Canada at least once. Ontario has been the most popular location, hosting it 29 times.

Who runs it?

Two groups organize the Nokia Brier. One is the Canadian Curling Association, a government-funded body that oversees the sport in Canada. It "owns" the national championship, on behalf of the curlers of Canada. Among other things, the CCA is responsible for the marketing, administration, and overall operations of the Nokia Brier. But the actual day-to-day running of the event is handled by an army of volunteers, which can number as many as 1,500.

This volunteer organization — called the *host committee* — does everything from sell hot dogs and programs to clean the ice. It looks after the finances, the opening and closing ceremonies, transportation for the teams, the signage in the arena and many, many more tasks.

At the end of the championship, the CCA and the host committee split the lion's share of the profits. A small but significant portion is also given to the competitors. The CCA uses its portion to run other programs, as well as operate its day-to-day business. In most years, the CCA takes home between $300,000 and $500,000 (the host committee takes home an equal amount). The host committee uses this money to help curling in the local area, through funding improvements to clubs in the area and purchases of equipment.

Only two Briers have not earned a profit since 1980.

The format

The Nokia Brier is a long and arduous event. Teams play a minimum of 11 games in the round robin in the first six days of the competition. The top four teams then advance to a complicated playoff structure known as the *page playoff system.*

Under this system, the fourth-place finisher and the third-place finisher in the round robin play off. The winner of this game advances to the semi-final, while the loser is eliminated. The first-place finisher and the second-place finisher also play off. The winner of this game goes directly to the final. The loser drops back into the semi-final and plays the winner of the contest between the third- and fourth-place finishers. The winner of that game then goes on to the final. The winner of the final is the national champion.

Got all that?

If, at the end of the round robin, there are teams tied for the last playoff spot, games to determine that final spot are necessary. These games are called *tiebreakers.* Tiebreakers only increase the number of games a team must play to eventually win the crown, adding to the difficulty.

The spoils

When you win the Brier, you do not receive a cash prize. In fact, all you get is a trophy, a medal, and a ring. Oh yeah, you also get your name on the *Brier Tankard*, something akin to the Holy Grail for curlers. The winners also represent Canada at the world championship.

That's the formal part of the prizes, and, to be honest, it's not much, considering just how big the championship is.

However, most teams also receive some ancillary benefits. For instance, most of the top cashspiels try to get the Canadian champions to their events. Sometimes, that can involve paying their expenses as well as slipping the rink a little *appearance money* (money given to the team for showing up, regardless of how it does in the competition). If the event is in Europe, it means a holiday (of sorts), as well.

Some of the recent Brier champions have also received endorsement money from companies in return for aligning themselves with certain products. But those deals are few and far between, and pale in comparison to similar endorsement contracts in sports such as hockey and basketball.

The road to the Nokia Brier

Making it to the Nokia Brier and playing for the Canadian championship is a tough task. However, one of the best aspects of this great event is that any rink can sign up to play down.

A team from Ontario would follow a route similar to the one I outline here. The approximate number of games the rink would play at each stage is in brackets.

1. **Win the *club playdown* — the competition that determines the club's representative(s) in the next stage of competition (2 to 4 games).** Move on to represent the club at the *zone playdown* (the next step up, where the team faces off against the top teams from other clubs in its geographical area).

2. **Win the zone playdown (4 to 7 games).** Move on to the *regional playdown* (where the team faces off against the top teams from other zones — usually four).

3. **Win the regional playdown (4 to 7 games).** Move on to represent the region in the Ontario championship. If the team loses either the zone or the regional playdown, it can play in the *Challenge Round*, a last-chance shoot-out that provides two berths in the Ontario final (7 to 11 games).

> # MacDuff the magnificent
>
> It's sometimes difficult to appreciate just how significant winning the Brier is for the championship rink. They become immediate celebrities in their hometowns and are fêted far and wide. But perhaps no rink ever received more plaudits for its Brier win than the Newfoundland rink from the St. John's Curling Club, for its 1976 win.
>
> The unheralded rink, skipped by Jack MacDuff, surprised every curling fan in the country by capturing the Brier, held in Regina that year. Not only was it the ultimate underdog tale of a group of inexperienced, nervous curlers who defeated some of the best rinks in the world, it was also the first time a team from Newfoundland had won the national crown.
>
> The rink immediately became heroes in their native province and enjoyed the splendours that come with such a victory.
>
> The four players were met by cheering fans at the airport when they returned home. A parade was held in their honour, and MacDuff even had his curling shoes bronzed. They are on display today in the St. John's club.
>
> The MacDuff victory is still regarded as one of the greatest stories in the long history of the Brier.

4. **Win the Ontario championship (11 games).** Move on to represent the province at the Nokia Brier.

5. **Win the Nokia Brier (13 to 15 games).** Move on to represent Canada at the world championships.

More than a curling event

The Brier has come a long way since it first started back in 1927. At that time, it was a mere curling event. Now it is bigger than that. Much bigger. When the Nokia Brier comes to town, it really comes to town. In many places, in fact, it takes over the town. Signs advertising the championship are everywhere. The media make it huge news; it usually appears on the front pages of newspapers and leads the sports headlines. Reports estimate that the Nokia Brier pumps in excess of $20 million into the local economy of the host city. Many people travel great distances to attend the event. Traditional parties are held annually, no matter where the host city is. And everyone gets into it. The clergymen get together the week of the event and hold their own bonspiel, called the Friar's Brier. Lemon gin is served at an early morning party held every day of the event. Known as "Morning Classes," it's a spirited way for curling fans to kick-start their day. There are other traditions that have carried on year after year, adding to the lore of the event.

Lights out

Alberta skip Matt Baldwin was an extremely talented curler who skipped his team to three Brier titles. He was also one of the biggest jokers in the game, always ready to jump on the opportunity to create a laugh.

One of Baldwin's more famous pranks occurred during the 1971 Brier in Quebec City. A snowstorm raged outside while the curlers battled indoors. The power went out during the game — plunging the arena into darkness. When the lights came back on, the Baldwin team was nowhere to be seen. But there on their sheet were all eight of their stones, neatly gathered around the 4-foot.

Baldwin and his teammates emerged from the bar to roars of laughter and applause from the fans. The incident became known as the Baldwin Blackout.

The Nokia Brier has become as big an event as there is in Canada. It's similar to football's Grey Cup, in that it is a national championship and big party rolled into one. But the Nokia Brier lasts for nine days, while the Grey Cup is a mere one-day event. It's also likely as prominent as hockey's Stanley Cup playoffs. And while hockey surely takes precedence over curling in the hearts of most Canadians, the Nokia Brier can claim that it always takes place in Canada and features only Canadian participants. The Stanley Cup can't say that anymore.

The Scott Tournament of Hearts

The Canadian women's curling championship is called the *Scott Tournament of Hearts*. Scott Paper has sponsored the event since 1982, and its name has become part and parcel with it. In fact, the championship, held every February, is more popularly known as "the Scott."

But there were sponsors before Scott Paper.

The Canadian women's championship was first held in 1961. It was known as the Diamond D, and was sponsored by the Dominion Group, the grocery chain. The association lasted until 1967, at which point the event went four years without a sponsor. Macdonald Tobacco picked up the title of the event in 1972, naming it the Macdonald Lassie, and kept it until it pulled out of both men's and women's curling in 1979.

Scott Paper, which came on board in 1982, has been the longest-serving sponsor; the company has greatly enhanced the image of women's curling.

Although it doesn't have the grand history that its male counterpart does, the Scott does have many grand moments. Its format is similar to that of the Nokia Brier, specifically regarding the selection process for the host site and structure of play. It, too, is a nine-day event consisting of an 11-game round robin, followed by a playoff that adheres to the page playoff system.

The spoils

Like the Nokia Brier champions, the winners of the Scott don't receive a nickel for their efforts. They get a trophy and a diamond ring or necklace. They also get to represent Canada at the world championships. And the Scott champions get something else that the men don't: a chance to defend their title.

After the 1985 championship, Scott felt that the top Canadian women curlers didn't have a high enough profile. It couldn't count on a recognizable name making the field, and that made it tough to promote the event. Many of the other participants were making their first trip to the national final, and were largely unknown to curling fans. So, Scott adopted a policy of bringing back the defending champion the following year. The public was familiar with the defending champs, who got to compete the second time around, as "Team Canada."

However, the addition of Team Canada didn't increase the size of the field. Just as with the Brier, there are still 12 teams that compete. There is Team Canada, one team from each of the ten provinces (only one from Ontario), and a combined entry for the three territories (Yukon, the Northwest Territories, and Nunavut).

The event

The Scott Tournament of Hearts is not as big an event as the Nokia Brier. It draws significant crowds, however, usually in the range of 5,000 to 7,000. And while it does have a considerable impact on the host community, the impact is not quite as substantial as that of the Nokia Brier.

However, what it may lack in numbers, it makes up for in enthusiasm. The crowds are boisterous and the teams committed. The host community draws on a large number of volunteers to operate all the necessary details of the championship, which takes more than a year of planning to pull off. And let's not forget the Heart Stop Lounge, the large on-site bar that's open for the length of the event. It's often *the* place to be during the nine-day event. Entertainment coupled with lots of good cheer is the common theme.

A big draw

The crowds at the Scott may not rival those at the Nokia Brier, but on television, they often surpass them. "Some years, depending on the teams, we get bigger ratings for the Scott than the Brier," says Keith Pelley, the president of TSN (The Sports Network), the Canadian all-sports channel. "I think that's a tribute to the quality of women's curling." Women's curling has proven attractive to television audiences because they are usually close and exciting games.

The same, but different

The Scott Tournament of Hearts and the Nokia Brier have much in common, but they also have some major differences. Table 19-1 shows you the similarities and differences between the two events.

Table 19-1 The Scott Tournament of Hearts Versus the Nokia Brier		
	The Scott	*The Nokia Brier*
When it started	1961	1927
When it's held	February	March
Who plays	Teams from 10 provinces, 1 from the territories, and the defending champion (total teams: 12)	Teams from 10 provinces (2 teams from Ontario), 1 from the Territories (total teams: 12)
Qualifying procedure	Provincial champions and the defending national champion	Provincial champions
Playdown procedure	11-game round robin	11-game round robin
Playoff procedure	Page playoff system	Page playoff system
Average crowd	5,000–7,000	8,000–12,000
Televised	Yes	Yes
Champion	Represents Canada at the world championships	Represents Canada at the world championships

Schmirler the curler

One woman and one team have become recognized in recent years as the best in the history of the Scott Tournament of Hearts, the Canadian women's curling championship.

Saskatchewan native Sandra Schmirler led her team to three Scott titles as well as three world championships *and* an Olympic gold medal. The record is unmatched in the game's history. Along with teammates Marcia Gudereit, Joan McCusker, and Jan Betker, Schmirler dominated women's curling for almost a decade.

In March 2000, the curling world was stunned when Schmirler, the mother of two young girls, passed away after a battle with cancer. The country was touched by her death; statements were issued from far and wide, from the likes of Wayne Gretzky and Prime Minister Chrétien. Her funeral was broadcast nationwide.

Schmirler may be gone, but her presence will be felt in curling circles for many, many years to come.

The Canadian Junior Championships

Juniors are curlers 20 years of age and under. These youngsters have their own national championship with a significant history.

There are events for male and female Juniors, the *junior men's championship* and the *junior women's championship*, respectively. They have been held concurrently for the past few years, alternating draws between junior men and junior women. Holding them together shares the expenses as well as provides a social atmosphere that can only come when young people of both sexes congregate.

The format

As with the men's and women's championships, the field in the Canadian Junior Championships is made up of provincial representatives. Each event has a team from each of the ten provinces, including two from Ontario, and one from the territories. The junior women's championship doesn't have a returning champion, the way the Scott does.

As opposed to the men's and women's championships, which are held in large arenas, the junior championships most often take place in clubs, although arenas have been used in some locations. The crowds are smaller, usually numbering in the hundreds, and many of those are parents and friends.

The finals of both male and female events are broadcast nationally by the CBC (Canadian Broadcasting Corporation), and draw significant audiences.

Boys will be boys

The junior men's championship started in 1950, and is the second oldest Canadian curling championship. Junior boys' curling was known as *schoolboy curling*. In its early days, teams that competed in the championship were made up of players from the same school. It was the most reliable and popular way of forming teams. From 1958 to 1975, the event was actually known as the Pepsi Schoolboy Championship. In 1976, however, that changed to allow teams of players from the same club to compete. That improved the quality of play; the teams were stronger, not having to worry about attending the same school in order to play together.

The quality of the junior men's championship has always been high. Many of the competitors have gone on to stellar careers at different levels of curling. However, only a few have managed to complete the double national victory of winning the Canadian junior and Canadian men's titles.

Here are the male curlers who have won the junior men's championship and the Brier:

- John Ferguson (Junior: 1977; Brier: 1986)
- Neil Houston (Junior: 1975; Brier: 1986)
- Ed Lukowich (Junior: 1962; Brier: 1978, 1986)
- Kevin Martin (Junior: 1985; Brier: 1991, 1997)
- Jonathon Mead (Junior: 1986; Brier: 1999)
- Dan Petryk (Junior: 1985; Brier: 1991)

A girls' thing

The junior women's championship was started in 1971, 21 years after the junior men's. Despite its relative infancy in relation to other Canadian championships, it has produced many exciting moments. It is also safe to say that the calibre of play in this event has improved more than any other national championship.

Players such as Cathy King (now Cathy Borst), Kim Gellard (now Kim Griffin), and Julie Sutton (now Julie Skinner) have all won Canadian junior crowns as well as women's national and world championships.

Another sign of the improvement is the rapid advance that many of the top junior women curlers make directly into the women's ranks. Heather Godberson won the Canadian Junior in 1996 and two years later captured the Scott Tournament of Hearts. In 1999, Marie-France Larouche was the national junior champion and 24 months later was representing Quebec in the national women's finals. The junior competition is very, very good.

Even if they don't win a Canadian women's title, a number of junior champions go on to successful careers at higher competitive levels.

Chapter 20

Rocking around the World

●●

●●

*E*ven though the Canadian events that I cover in the last chapter usually draw larger crowds, bigger television audiences, and more overall talent in the field, a number of international curling events also have a great deal of prestige. In this chapter, I take a look at the World Curling Championships and the World Junior Championships. Outside of the events held in Canada, they are regarded as the pinnacle of curling achievement.

In 1998, curling joined the world's largest sporting family: the Olympic Games. How could we forget about that? Players, coaches, organizers, and fans hope that being a part of this event will put curling on firmer footing in parts of the world where, right now, it only has a toehold.

The World Curling Championships

The *World Curling Championships* are held annually, either in late March or early April. The event brings together the top teams from ten World Curling Federation member nations to battle it out for the international title. The men's event began in 1959, with the women's following 20 years after that, in 1979. Up until 1989, the two events were held separately, but they are now a joint affair. That has helped in many aspects, including easing the financial burden of hosting such an event.

Although various curling countries take turns hosting the World Curling Championships, Canada is the most popular host country, usually undertaking hosting duties and privileges three years out of five. The event is well attended in Canada, Scotland, and a few other European countries, as great throngs of curling fans congregate to watch the best curlers from around the world. In other locations, however, it's a fairly minor affair that attracts small crowds.

The format

Teams competing in the World Curling Championships play a nine-game round robin with the top four rinks advancing to the playoffs. The playoff structure is less complicated than the one used in Canada, known as the *page playoff system* (see Chapter 19 for that explanation — it's too long to repeat here!). At the World Curling Championships, there are two semi-final games and one final. In the semi-final round, the first-place finisher takes on the fourth-place rink, while the second-place finisher meets the third-place rink. The winners of these respective games meet in the final, with the winner being declared the world champion.

Upwards of 30 countries play down annually to try to make it to the World Curling Championships. The qualifying system, developed by the World Curling Federation, divides the globe into three distinct regions, in which the teams compete. Each region can contribute a certain number of teams to the final ten that compete in the championships. The number is based on the region's curling population:

- ✔ Europe has seven spots
- ✔ North America has two spots
- ✔ The Pacific region has one spot

A playdown is held to determine who gets the world championship spot(s) if there are more teams competing than there are spots available. This happens frequently in the Pacific region; you'll often see the teams from Australia, New Zealand, Japan, and Korea vying for that one coveted spot.

In Europe, the top seven finishers at the European Curling Championships advance to the World Curling Championships. In 2001, for the first time, Scotland failed to end that competition in the top seven and missed the world championships. That was like having a World Series in baseball without an American team.

Canada and the United States are lucky in that, to date, no other North American curling countries have entered the running for the world championships. If Mexico were to elect to enter a team, for example, a playdown would be necessary. For now, however, Canada and the United States pretty much have a free ride into the world championships.

There is one exception to the regional qualifying rule I've been telling you about. A complicated *relegation system* allows a country not in the field to get a spot the following year. If Italy finished in tenth spot, it would have to play off to regain its spot the following year. The challenging team comes out of a playdown of all those countries trying themselves to qualify for the world championships. It's a match between the tenth-place finisher and the winner of the so-called "B pool."

The women's world championship has many of the same ingredients as the men's. It uses the same format for selecting teams, with a regional breakdown and qualifying structure. It also has a nine-team round robin followed by two semi-finals and a final.

However, it is a separate and distinct qualifying set-up. The final field for the women's and men's championships is not linked and is usually quite different.

The history

Unlike many other sports that can trace their histories back a century or so, curling's World Curling Championships are a relatively new affair. It wasn't until 1959 that any sort of global championship was held. And it more closely resembled a boxing title match, with just two participants, albeit both heavy-weights: Canada and Scotland.

The Scotch Cup

After a few years of lobbying, three-time Brier winner Ken Watson, of Manitoba, along with several interested Scottish parties, organized a series of matches between the Canadian champions and their counterparts from Scotland. The event was sponsored by the Scotch Whiskey Company and became known as the Scotch Cup. Held in Scotland, it is regarded today as the first world curling championship.

Canada took its opponent by surprise at that inaugural event, winning all five of the games played, claiming the title. It was represented by the Saskatchewan-based Richardson rink, made up of two brothers and two cousins. This team would go on to win a record four Brier titles as well as four Scotch Cups. The Richardsons played an aggressive takeout-style game, knocking out every stone the Scots put in. This wasn't unusual in Canada, but it was a strategy that was almost unheard of in Scotland. Hits were rare in Scottish curling up until that time. It wasn't uncommon to have 13 or 14 of all 16 stones thrown remain in play for every end. The Richardsons' play upset many Scots, who felt they weren't playing by the rules. But the Scots soon came to adopt a similar style of play.

The combined intrigue of different styles, the international element, not to mention great curling, sowed the seed for the world championships, and curling hasn't looked back. The passing years have seen more and more nations participate in the event, including the United States, Sweden, Norway, Switzerland, and Germany.

The Silver Broom

While the Scotch Cup was the official start of a world curling championship, it became solidified in 1968, when Air Canada took over as the title sponsor of the event. It became known as the Air Canada Silver Broom. The winners received — you guessed it — a two-foot silver broom.

But Air Canada did much more than come up with a neat little trophy. It put plenty of marketing dollars behind the event, which gave it some prestige. The world championship became recognized as something more than just a curling event between teams from different countries, and inherited the ancillary trappings and happenings of other high-profile sports events. These included parties and other functions where spectators could meet and mingle with other curlers and curling fans from different countries as well as some of the competitors — when they weren't busy curling.

The Broom is swept aside

Air Canada ended its sponsorship of the Silver Broom in 1985 under less than ideal circumstances, when an outside group of six curling entrepreneurs took over. Known as Hexagon, the group hoped to advance the world championships even farther than Air Canada had, but the dream fizzled.

Up until 1994, the world championships operated without a sponsor and sort of wallowed in mediocrity. While the championship was still well regarded, it lacked the sizzle that Air Canada had brought to it, as it suffered through a slew of sponsors.

Things finally began to look up in 1995, when the world championships (both men's and women's events, which were held jointly by this time) became part of the Season of Champions, a series of Canadian and international curling events brought together under one advertiser-friendly banner. The world championships suddenly found itself benefiting from the support of the Ford Motor Company, since it took over as title sponsor. I discuss how the women's world championships formed and came to be held jointly with the men's a little later in the chapter.

The first year that Ford sponsored the world championships (held in Hamilton, Ontario) was not a total success, as the local host committee lost hundreds of thousands of dollars. That, however, was the only dark mark. Today, the event

Why the Brier is better than the men's world championship

Canadian curlers like to boast that the Brier, the Canadian men's championship, is better than its counterpart at the international level, the men's world championship. Although there may be some disagreement from other parts of the world, a strong case can be made to support this. Here goes:

At the world championship, there are ten teams in the field. Usually, only about six of those have a realistic chance at winning. The other four teams are just too far behind the top teams in skill to pose any kind of serious threat. At the Brier, however, even with a larger field of 12 teams, it would be easy to say that 10 of them have a shot at the title, raising the overall level of competition. Why is that? It's likely because most of the top curlers are in Canada, with access to a great many resources. There are more than 1,000 curling clubs across the country and hundreds of thousands of players who curl in them. Canada also has great development and training programs, and competitive events just about every weekend of the season.

In order to win the Brier, a Canadian team may be required to play as many as 40 or 50 games from the time it starts out at the club level all the way through to the Brier final. To win a similar national title in one of the countries where curling isn't as established may only take 3 or 4 games.

See the difference? Many of the teams competing in the world championships just can't compare to the calibre of Canadian teams competing in their own national championships.

While the best teams in the rest of the world can compete with any in Canada, the depth of talent in Canada means that, for my money, the Brier is more competitive than the world championship.

is well recognized, well attended, and well played. The quality of play has also improved significantly. It was once thought to be Canada's title to lose, but in recent years, thanks to plenty of good instruction and development programs put in place around the world, it is anyone's game to win.

Joining forces

The women's world championship only started in 1979. The first event was held in Perth, Scotland, and was won by a Swiss rink, skipped by Gaby Casanova.

The championship had rather inauspicious beginnings, starting slowly, with small crowds, and a wide variance in the quality of the rinks competing. But it gradually gained recognition around the world, to the point where today, it is a well-challenged event that attracts top talent.

The men's and women's world championships operated as separate events until 1989. This didn't affect the better-established men's event as much as the women's. Although the competition was good and the title highly sought after, organizing and hosting the women's world championship was a difficult challenge. Crowds were not large enough to sustain the event. Making a profit was tough. For many years, it was break-even, at best. It was difficult to find a location interested in hosting the tournament.

This changed for the better in 1989, when curling's global governing body, the *International Curling Federation* (which would become the World Curling Federation in 1991) decided to amalgamate the men's and women's championships and hold them jointly. It wagered correctly that there was strength in numbers. Both events received a boost and the plan was judged a success.

The World Curling Championships, consisting of both men's and women's events, are held at the same time in the same facility. With four draws a day — two men's and two women's — a great deal of scheduling is necessary to complete all the games. Although this puts a fair amount of strain on everyone from the curlers to the ice technicians and staff at the rink — even the fans — it's worth it to be able to pull off such an event.

Canada dominates

Canada has cleaned up, particularly at the men's championships, over the years, winning 26 out of 43 titles. It's the leader by a healthy margin; the United States and Sweden are next in line, with four wins each.

Because Canada is regarded as the top curling nation, its teams always go into the world championships as favourites. It's a bit of a double-edged sword, in fact. Canada is expected to win, and it's no big deal if it does. But if it loses, it's a big upset. Canadian curling fans wonder what went wrong. "When I lost, it was the longest summer of my life," said Kerry Burtnyk, who won the Canadian men's championship in 1981, but then lost the world title. "All summer, everyone just asked me what went wrong." Burtnyk went on to win a world championship in 1995.

Here are the countries other than Canada that have won the men's world championship:

- ✔ Sweden (4 times)
- ✔ United States (4 times)
- ✔ Norway (3 times)
- ✔ Scotland (3 times)
- ✔ Switzerland (3 times)

Sweden's curling queens

The winningest team in women's world championship history and arguably one of the best teams in the sport's history is that of skip Elisabet Gustafson, and teammates Katarina Nyberg, Louise Marmont, and Elisabeth Persson. This rink has won four world championship titles: the first in 1992, and three others between 1995 and 1999.

How does a rink get and stay this good? Practice and commitment.

It's nothing for this team to practise four or five hours a day. That in itself is quite an achievement. But when you consider that the team has to travel a couple of hours to get to the rink — a very rudimentary facility — scrape and pebble its own ice and haul out its rocks, it really puts the word "commitment" into perspective.

No wonder they're world champs four times over!

Canada hasn't dominated the women's world championship to the extent that it has the men's. While they've won 12 of 23 titles, there seems to be more depth and competition in women's international curling than in men's.

Here are the winners, by country, of the women's world championship:

- ✔ Canada (12 titles)
- ✔ Sweden (5 titles)
- ✔ Norway (2 titles)
- ✔ Switzerland (2 titles)
- ✔ Denmark (1 title)
- ✔ Germany (1 title)

The World Junior Championships

The best curlers in the world have to start somewhere, and for many, it comes at the *World Junior Championships*. Many of those who have gone on to win regular world titles and Olympic gold, first made their international mark at the global championship for the younger set. It's well played and exciting, and boasts some excellent curling. The exuberance that comes from the youthful curlers makes it unlike any other event.

The format

The World Junior Championships are run similar to the men's and women's championships. There are separate junior men's and junior women's components, but they are held jointly.

There are ten teams in each competition. There is a nine-game round robin followed by playoffs among the top four rinks. The first-place rink plays the fourth-place rink, while the second-place rink plays the third-place rink. The winners of these contests face off in the final.

Both world junior championships are open to curlers 21 years of age and under, although some countries impose their own age limits. The Canadian team, for example, is made up of players who are 20 years old and under.

Canada sends the winners of its national junior titles to the World Junior Championships — a pretty easy selection process. For a few years, the Canadian champs were sent a year after winning their national title. The thinking was that giving them a year to prepare for the world final would be beneficial.

But it didn't prove to be any significant advantage, and because the four players had to miss a great deal of school to deal with the year of training, that system was dropped. It was also felt that sending a rink that had just won a national final and was playing well at that time would prove to be a benefit.

Some other countries handpick their entries to the World Junior, using it as a yardstick to see how some of the best young curlers are progressing.

The history

The best junior men in the world have knocked heads for a global title since 1975. It began in 1974 with an invitational tournament in Toronto. Several of the top junior teams in the world came out to compete. That planted the seed for the world junior men's championship. The next year, with the sponsorship of the tire company Uniroyal, the event was officially sanctioned.

The first winner of the world junior men's was Jan Ullsten, of Sweden. In the next 26 years, Canada won 11 titles, followed closely by Scotland, with 8.

The junior women's championship began in 1988. In 14 years, Canada has won 7 of the titles. Scotland is next, with 4.

You're holding it where?

Because the World Junior Championships are a significant but somewhat small event, they have been used as a precursor to bigger events. The junior championships tend to be held in unusual locations — places where curling isn't all that well known. The hope is that the smaller event will generate excitement about curling and lead to larger events being held there eventually.

In 1994, curling was trying to get a foothold in the countries that were formerly part of the Eastern bloc. As a test, the World Junior Championships were held in Bulgaria, a country that had very few curlers, and perhaps even fewer resources to host an international curling event. The event was a success; and though the competitors said they missed the comforts of home — such as familiar food — the game was exposed to many that had never before experienced it.

In 2001, the World Junior Championships were held in Ogden, Utah. Again, Ogden isn't exactly a curling hotbed, but it allowed the World Curling Federation, the organizer of the curling portion of the 2002 Olympic Winter Games, to do a dress rehearsal for the big championship a year away. It got a feel for how the ice would react, made a note of any facilities it might have overlooked, and got a sense of how it would have to handle the crowds.

Looking after the world

The World Curling Federation (WCF) is curling's international governing body. It was created in 1965 with six member countries: Scotland, Canada, the United States, Sweden, Norway, and Switzerland. At first, it was merely a subcommittee of Scotland's Royal Caledonian Curling Club, which was, at that time, in charge of curling internationally. (It is still in charge of curling in Scotland and commands a great deal of respect around the world.) Shortly after, the committee broke away from the Royal Caledonian Curling Club and became an independent body. In 1991, it changed its name to the World Curling Federation.

The WCF is responsible for growing the sport internationally, developing the rules for international play, operating world championships, and representing the sport in international sporting organizations. One of its biggest achievements was getting curling into the Olympics.

Despite the fact that Canada has the majority of the world's curlers and resources, the WCF doesn't have that much Canadian content. Other curling nations, it seems to me, do that on purpose. Many seem to see Canada as the big, bad bully of the curling world, trying to impose its ideas on everyone else.

Although the WCF has done some wonderful things for the sport, it seems mired in bureaucracy most of the time.

Although the junior competitors serve a bit as guinea pigs, taking this route allows the World Curling Federation to break new ground and prepare for the future.

The Olympics

Curling has a long association with the *Olympic Winter Games*, despite the fact that the first official Olympic medals for curling weren't handed out until 1998, in Nagano, Japan. In fact, curling was first showcased at the Olympics back in 1924 in France, but it was a long time until it became a part of the family.

The format

Curling in the Olympic Games observes the international rules that are practised at the World Curling Championships. For example, the ice surface is 14 inches wider than Canadian ice. There is also a four-rock free guard zone rule, meaning a stone that comes to rest in the *free guard zone* (the area between the Hog line and the Tee line, not including the house) may not be removed until the fifth stone of the end. The lineup of teams is smaller, with eight men's and eight women's teams qualifying. The qualifying procedure is a complicated points system based on the teams' performance at the World Curling Championships over the four years between Olympic Games. The format at the Olympics is a seven-game round robin, with the top four teams advancing to the playoffs. The first-place finisher plays off against the fourth-place team, while the second- and third-place finishers meet in another semi-final. The losing teams play off for the bronze medal, while the winners battle it out for the gold and silver medals.

The history

Curling was on the roster of sports included in the first Olympic Winter Games, held in Chamonix, France, in 1924. It was dropped after that first appearance, however, and didn't reappear until the 1988 Games, in Calgary, when it was added to the list of exhibition sports. Exhibition sports are treated just as regular full-medal sports (with medal winners and all), but they aren't counted in the official standings and there's no guarantee that the sport will get to return to the next Games.

The winners of that exhibition contest in Calgary were the Canadian women's rink, skipped by Linda Moore, and the Norwegian men's team, skipped by Eigil Ramsfjell. Although it was great to see curling among the other winter sports, that exhibition showed the Games' officials that there was still a lot of work to do if the sport was to become an official part of the Olympic family.

Let's qualify that

Curling needed to qualify under Olympic regulations in order to be added to the roster of full-medal sports. There were a number of things, both official and unofficial, that needed to be done:

- The World Curling Federation needed to have 25 member nations on three different continents.

- The WCF needed to join various international sporting associations, such as the General Assembly of International Sporting Federations.

- The sport needed to pass the scrutiny of the International Olympic Committee's Program Commission.

The full medal

Thanks to the work of people such as Gunther Hummelt, WCF president, Jack Lynch, a retired Canadian Olympic Association employee, and Warren Hansen, a tireless curling enthusiast who works for the Canadian Curling Association, curling overcame many roadblocks and was finally accepted as a full-medal Olympic sport in 1992. It wasn't supposed to have its official start as a full partner in the games until 2002, but the Japanese organizing committee for the 1998 Nagano Games decided to add it to the lineup then.

The champions

When curling appeared in the Olympics — with full-medal status — it was, in many ways, another coming of age for the sport. Everyone who competed was, in one sense, a winner. But there were medals handed out, and here's who they went to:

On the men's side:

- **Gold:** Switzerland (Patrick Huerlimann, Patrick Lorchester, Danielle Mueller, Diego Perren)

- **Silver:** Canada (Mike Harris, Richard Hart, Collin Mitchell, George Karrys)

- **Bronze:** Norway (Eigil Ramsfjell, Jan Thoresen, Stig Arne Gunnestad, Tore Torvbraten)

On the women's side:

✔ **Gold:** Canada (Sandra Schmirler, Jan Betker, Joan McCusker, Marcia Gudereit)

✔ **Silver:** Denmark (Helena Blach-Lavrsen, Margit Portner, Dorthe Holm, Jane Bidstrup)

✔ **Bronze:** Sweden (Elisabet Gustafson, Katarina Nyberg, Louise Marmont, Elisabeth Persson)

Part VII
The Part of Tens

In this part . . .

I round up some of my favourite games, players, and shots in curling, in chapters neatly and handily broken down into lists of ten. Read what I have to say and then form your own opinions. After you've done that, turn to Chapter 24, which suggests ten other places you can go to learn even more about what is now (I'm presuming) your favourite winter sport.

Chapter 21

Ten Top-Notch Curling Skips

In This Chapter

▶ Discovering what sets these great skips apart

*B*ecause they call the strategy and throw the last shots, the skips tend to get all the glory. But they can also be the goats if they mess up.

Over the years, some skips have stood out for their superior play and their exceptional strategic calls, as well as their off-ice actions. Here are the ten best to ever lace up a pair of curling shoes.

Matt Baldwin

Matt Baldwin, of Alberta, was known for many years for his outrageous sense of humour. That often hid his remarkable curling talent. A three-time Brier winner (1954, 1957, and 1958) with three different lineups, Baldwin could draw better than any competitor in his era. He was also a master of the psych-out, often using his showmanship to distract the other team.

Don Duguid

Known as "The Digit" because of his diminutive stature, Don Duguid skipped back-to-back winners in the Brier (the Canadian men's championship) and the World Championships in 1970 and 1971, respectively. He also won another Brier in 1965 playing third for Terry Braunstein. Duguid retired after winning his third championship and became the colour commentator on curling for the Canadian Broadcasting Corporation, a job he held for 29 years. In that role, he became an icon to a generation of curling fans who tuned in each year to see the national finals.

Elisabet Gustafson

The only woman curler to skip a rink to four world championships, Sweden's Elisabet Gustafson, along with teammates Katarina Nyberg, Louise Marmont, and Elisabeth Persson, had to make many sacrifices to get to the world championships. That included driving great distances to their rink, preparing the ice themselves, and travelling around the world to play in competitive events. Gustafson trains tirelessly, and always seems to have the big shot necessary to win games.

Russ Howard

One of the most talented players in the game's history, Russ Howard has thrown so many remarkable shots that he could make his own highlight reel. A talented perfectionist, his opposition often didn't know how to stop him from scoring. Backing up his own tremendous ability was a pretty capable rink that included his brother Glenn and two sets of front ends — Tim Belcourt and Kent Carstairs, and Wayne Middaugh and Peter Corner. Howard also won a lot of money, thanks to adopting a very aggressive style of play. He was able to think well ahead of his opposition and then deliver on just about any shot. After playing in Ontario for more than 20 years, Howard moved to Moncton, New Brunswick, and played for that province in two Briers.

Ron Northcott

Known as "The Owl" because the thick glasses he wore gave him an almost bookish appearance, Ron Northcott, along with Fred Storey and Bernie Sparkes at the front end, and three different thirds, won three Canadian men's championships.

Northcott was as smart on the ice as they come, rarely letting a team get an edge. If he managed to get a lead, it was not often that he would surrender it. With strong sweeping and shotmaking, the front end of Storey and Sparkes was among the best to ever play.

Ernie Richardson

Ernie Richardson skipped the only four-time winning team in the history of the Brier. The Regina rink was made up of Ernie, his cousin Arnold, at third, his brother Garnet (known as Sam), at second, and Wes (another cousin), playing lead. (In the last of their four wins, Mel Perry replaced Wes at lead.)

The rink also won four world championships and dominated every event in which it played. Since the rink won its fourth Brier in 1963 — the other three came in 1959, 1960, and 1962 — no other team has even come close to winning a fourth title. That's how remarkable their performance was. In baseball, there's Babe Ruth, in hockey there's Wayne Gretzky, in basketball there's Wilt Chamberlain, and in curling, there are the Richardsons.

Pat Ryan

Like Don Duguid, Pat Ryan has won a Brier while playing third (which came in 1995 for British Columbia's Rick Folk), but he will always be remembered for skipping Alberta rinks to consecutive Brier championships in 1988 and 1989. His team of Randy Ferbey, Don Walchuk, and Don McKenzie used a devastating hitting style to snuff out other rinks. They would often get two points early in the game and then hit every stone the other team put in play, until they won. Ryan may have been the smartest skip ever to step onto the ice.

Sandra Schmirler

Sandra Schmirler and her rink of Jan Betker, Joan McCusker, and Marcia Gudereit may have been the best women's team to date. Together, the four of them won three Canadian and world titles, as well as the first Olympic gold medal in curling, in 1998. Schmirler's rink was also dominant on the women's cashspiel circuit, earning more than any other women's team.

Not only did the team manage to win almost every time out, but they did it while holding down full-time jobs and raising families. After winning a game at the Olympic Trials in 1997, Schmirler had to delay a media interview so she could breast-feed her ten-week-old daughter.

Sandra Schmirler passed away on March 2, 2000, after a brief battle with cancer, at age 36. So well respected was Schmirler that her funeral was broadcast live on national television and a book about her life subsequently became a bestseller.

Ken Watson

Winnipeg's Ken Watson might have ended up with a better record than Ernie Richardson's rink if the Second World War hadn't interrupted play from 1943 to 1945. Watson won his first Brier in 1936 and another in 1942. But just as he was in his prime, the event was suspended for three years. He would win a third Brier in 1949. (Though he had a different front end for each team, his brother, Grant, was his third for all three victories.)

Watson helped curling in other ways, too. He would go on to help form the world championships and author the book *Ken Watson on Curling*, the first instructional volume for the sport. He was also one of the first curlers to use a sliding delivery.

Ed Werenich

A two-time winner of the Canadian and world championships, Ed Werenich really made his mark as a "for-money" player. Werenich skipped many teams during his career, which collectively earned more than $1 million (prize money is divided four ways among the players). Whenever and with whomever he played, he used an aggressive style of play that crowds loved.

Werenich was also very outspoken. He was once suspended from the Brier playdowns for making what the Canadian Curling Association called "disturbing remarks." In addition to being a great player and remarkable strategist, he may have been curling's first media superstar.

Chapter 22

Ten Memorable Curling Shots

There is a long list of great shots in curling, but some stand out more than others — not only for their level of difficulty, but also because they happened at critical moments in big games. With pressure building, a game or title on the line, and a large audience looking on, these players delivered shots that will be remembered for a long time to come.

Al Hackner's Double Takeout

What is perhaps the most memorable shot in all of curling happened at the 1985 Brier in Moncton, New Brunswick. Playing in the tenth end against Alberta's Pat Ryan, Northern Ontario skip Al Hackner needed to score two points in order to tie the game and force an extra end. His only chance was a very slim, high-risk, double takeout. The first stone that Hackner had to hit was almost totally covered by a guard in front of the rings, but he calmly threw his shot, hit the first stone, and watched as it spilled across the rings to make contact with the second stone. Hackner took two points, tied the contest, and won in the extra end.

Guy Hemmings's Draw to the Button

Québec's Guy Hemmings arrived at the 1998 Brier a relative unknown and made his way to the final before losing to Ontario's Wayne Middaugh. A year later, he was back, tied in an extra end in the semi-final against Gerald Shymko of Saskatchewan. With only his last rock left, Hemmings was looking at a Shymko rock behind a guard just biting the Button. Hemmings couldn't play a takeout; his only chance was to draw to the exact centre of the house — the Button. With Shymko's rock sitting so well, Hemmings had no margin for error.

Hemmings threw it perfectly. With good sweeping, the rock stopped exactly on the Button, giving Hemmings the coveted point and the victory.

Russ Howard's Combination Shot

At the 1992 McCain/TSN Skins Game, in Quebec City, John Bubbs of Manitoba appeared to have two-time world champion Russ Howard wired. Playing the final end, Bubbs had two rocks well guarded on the 4-foot. It looked like Howard had no chance to get at them. But Howard then called and played one of the most dramatic combinations in curling history: a triple raise, angle double takeout (try saying that three times fast!) to score two points and win the event. There were so many rocks in motion after that shot that it took a moment for everyone to realize Howard had actually made it.

Eugene Hritzuk's Last-Shot Hog

This shot was memorable for all the wrong reasons. In the final end of the 1988 Brier, Saskatchewan's Eugene Hritzuk led Pat Ryan of Alberta 7–5. Ryan had the final stone, but in these pre–free guard zone days, it was almost assumed that the game was over because Hritzuk could take out every Ryan stone and win. Hritzuk elected to try to play a freeze onto one of the Ryan rocks. His sweepers began brushing the rock furiously as soon as he let it go. But about halfway down the sheet, it was obvious that it wasn't going to make it. In fact, not only did the rock not make it, but Hritzuk hogged that final shot, and ended up handing the title to Ryan. It was one of the most dramatic flops in Brier history.

Hammy McMillan's Round-the-House Triple

Scotland, despite being the founding nation of curling, has not had much success at winning the world championships. But in 1999, Hammy McMillan, from Scotland, a likeable but somewhat rowdy character, set out to change that when he led his team to the world championships in Saint John, New Brunswick.

McMillan and his rink played well, and he pulled off one of the most remarkable triple takeouts ever seen. His shot, against Canada's Jeff Stoughton, was thrown with a tremendous amount of force. It hit a Canadian stone out in the 12-foot, then rolled — still with massive force — onto another Canadian stone at the back of the 12-foot. Then, thanks to the angle at which it hit that second stone, it ricocheted over to the other side of the rings and removed a third Canadian stone. McMillan's shot had started on one side of the sheet, removed three rocks, and finished all the way over on the other side of the house.

Orest Meleschuk's Hit and Roll

In the tenth end of the 1972 World Curling Championships, Canada's Orest Meleschuk, trailing by two, needed a nose hit on an American stone to force an extra end. He made the hit, but his stone rolled slightly to the outside, giving the Canadians one point instead of the two they needed to tie the game. Thinking they had won the title, American skip Bob Labonte jumped into the air in celebration. Then he slipped and fell, booting the Canadian stone closer to the centre. Canada was awarded two points, went into an extra end, and won.

Pat Ryan's Triple Raise, Double Takeout

Pat Ryan and his Edmonton team won back-to-back Briers on the strength of their hitting ability. They could throw hard and with accuracy. In the final of the 1988 world championships in Lausanne, Switzerland, the Ryan rink, which had eased through the Canadian championship, was struggling against Norway's Eigil Ramsfjell. One shot almost turned it around. Ramsfjell sat two rocks behind a wall of cover in the 4-foot and appeared to be ready to score two points. But Ryan played a triple raise, double takeout to remove the stones and score a point himself. The Canadian rink, unfortunately, went on to lose the game, and the world title, to Norway.

Sandra Schmirler's Hit and Roll

Sandra Schmirler and her rink were favoured to win the Canadian Olympic Trials in 1997 and go on to represent the country at the 1998 Winter Olympics. But in the deciding game, Schmirler found herself trailing against Shannon Kleibrink, of Alberta. In the seventh end, Kleibrink had a stone on the Button, protected by a slew of guards in front. The only way for Schmirler to get at the stone was to play off one of her own way out in the wings. She hit it perfectly and rolled her shooter into the centre of the house, removing Kleibrink's stone and scoring three points to take a 6–4 lead. She ended up winning the game, the Olympic spot, and, eventually, the gold medal.

Billy Walsh's Extra-End Winner

In the 1956 Brier, Manitoba's Billy Walsh and Ontario's Alf Phillips were deadlocked after the ten-game round robin with 8–2 records. There were no playoffs in the Brier at that time — the winner was decided by the round robin record. But with both these teams tied, it necessitated an extra game. After 12 ends of play in that extra game (this was the average length of games in those days), the contest was again all tied up. They would need to play a thirteenth end. In that extra end, Phillips had a rock 90 percent under cover on the 4-foot. Walsh had to throw a very light takeout that would just skim by the guard and push the Ontario stone to the back of the house, to score one. But the ice conditions were awful, even if Walsh threw the takeout perfectly, it might still get caught on frosty ice out at the side of the sheet. But it didn't. Walsh's shot was right on the money, slipping past the guard and pushing Phillips's stone to the back. Walsh scored one and won the Brier.

Ed Werenich's Triple Takeout

Ed Werenich was staring at a crowded house in the sixth end of a tight match in the 1983 Brier semi-final. There were a number of rocks in the house belonging to his opponent, Bernie Sparkes, of British Columbia, that were beginning to spell disaster. Werenich sized up the situation and decided to go big or go home. He called and made a triple takeout that allowed his Ontario rink to win. Werenich's rink defeated Alberta the next day, to win the Brier.

Chapter 23

Ten Tremendous Curling Games

In This Chapter

▶ Checking out ten palm-sweating, rip-roaring, edge-of-your-seat curling matchups

*O*f the hundreds of thousands of curling games that have been played over the years, a few can be called truly exceptional. Some because of great shots, others by reason of what was on the line. Whatever the case, the ten contests listed in this chapter are the ones I consider the most memorable.

I can say without a doubt that each and every one of these games had me glued to my seat (either in person or by reading and hearing about the accounts), enthralled with what unfolded on the ice. See if you agree with my picks.

Hackner–Ryan

Northern Ontario's Al Hackner met Alberta's Pat Ryan in the final of the 1985 Brier. The game was a relatively mundane affair for nine ends. But then it all changed. Trailing by two in the final end, Hackner executed perhaps the most memorable shot in curling history, making a very difficult double takeout to score two points and tie it up, forcing an extra end.

Shocked by the drama, the Alberta team wasn't able to regroup. Hackner stole one more point, for a 6–5 win and the championship.

Hemmings–Shymko

The most popular player at the 1999 Brier in Edmonton, Alberta, was Quebec skip Guy Hemmings, whose "bon vivant" attitude endeared him to the crowd. Another favourite was Gerald Shymko, of Saskatchewan, a massive farmer whose extra-large size was equalled by his smile.

These two teams met in a thrilling semi-final game, which will be specifically remembered for its conclusion. The two rinks were tied after ten ends and many memorable shots. But the best was yet to come. With one rock left to come from Hemmings, Shymko had one in the 4-foot protected by a guard. Hemmings's only chance was to draw to the absolute centre of the house. He did it, and the crowd erupted as it never had before at any Brier contest. Although he won that game, Hemmings went on to lose the final to Manitoba's Jeff Stoughton.

Howard–Sparkes

In 1986, veteran Bernie Sparkes, of British Columbia, and Ontario young gun Russ Howard, were battling in the semi-final of the Brier, with the winner set to go on the next day to play Alberta's Ed Lukowich for the crown. (A three-time Brier champion, Sparkes was appearing in his record eleventh contest.) With one end to play, the contest was close and a nail-biter for the large audience watching it on television. The game was tied after ten ends, making an extra end necessary. But the audience never got a chance to see that extra end. Why? The game had taken a long time to play and went over its allotted time. The network broadcasting the game, the Canadian Broadcasting Corporation, elected to go to the local news instead of showing the final few shots (Howard won 6–5). That's when the CBC learned just how important curling is in Canada. "We've never received so many complaints about anything," said Joan Mead, the producer. No televised curling game has been cut off since.

Howard–Sparkes Again

Howard and Sparkes met again a year later, this time in the Brier final, playing for Ontario and British Columbia, respectively. It was a close game, with three dramatic final ends. It was tied at 4 after the seventh end, but Ontario grabbed two in the eighth. Sparkes took three points in the ninth end to move in front 7–6. Then, with a dramatic last shot takeout that he has called "the toughest shot I've had to throw in my life," Howard scored five points and won 11–7.

Martin–Peters

Two of curling's heavyweights — Alberta's Kevin Martin and Manitoba's Vic Peters — met in the final of the 1998 Brier. Not only were the two playing for Canadian curling's top prize, they were doing so in front of a record crowd of close to 20,000. Peters took three points in the third end, but Martin came back with four points in the sixth end to take a 6–4 lead. Peters took two in the eighth to tie it and then stole two more in the ninth for an 8–6 lead. But Martin fought back and grabbed three points in the ninth end, setting up a dramatic final end.

Time played a big factor in that last end. Each team was nearing the end of its allotted 75 minutes (each rink is given 75 minutes to play its shots, recorded by a chess-style clock that starts running as the other team's shot finishes) and running out of time meant forfeiting the game. With only seconds remaining on the clock, Peters missed his last shot, allowing Martin to steal one point for a 10–8 win.

Richardson–Baird

Although I never actually saw this game, it has to rank up there with the others on my list just because of the significance. In 1964, after winning four Brier titles in five years, the Richardson family team of Ernie, Arnold (his cousin), Sam (his brother), and Wes (another cousin) found themselves playing against Ian Baird's Nova Scotia four in a final-round game. Although the Richardsons won the contest, they came up one victory shy of capturing a fifth Brier, which went to British Columbia's Lyall Dagg. Although they didn't know it at the time, it would be the Richardsons' last Brier game. What many would regard as the greatest team in the sport would never return to the event that they had helped make famous.

Ryan–Folk

Pat Ryan's Edmonton team, which won the 1988 Brier, was known as "The Ryan Express." That was largely because its members played a strong hitting game that saw them throw rocks like trains running down the track. A year later, in what may have been the most boring final in Brier history, Ryan led his rink to a 3–2 win over Rick Folk, of British Columbia. Fans almost fell asleep as six of the ten ends were blanked. Soon after, the free guard zone rule was brought into effect to help provide some offense to games.

Schmirler–Blach-Lavrsen

Playing against Denmark's Helena Blach-Lavrsen in the 1998 Olympics, Canada's Sandra Schmirler battled with the determined Danes for most of the game. Schmirler had at first planned to play conservatively, but when the Danes sailed their first shot of the game right through the rings, Schmirler switched into aggressive mode.

Although the game was close, the Canadian team kept control. In the final end, after a triple takeout by Canadian second Joan McCusker, the Schmirler rink hit everything the Danes put up, to secure a 7–5 victory. It was a significant win for Schmirler, as it solidified her team's position as the best women's rink in the game. It was a significant win for the game in general, as Schmirler's was the first Olympic gold medal handed out under curling's new status as a full-medal sport.

Walsh–Phillips

I never saw this game, but Alf Phillips, as great a sportsman as Canada has seen, recounted it to me in detail. Just listening to him made the hair on the back of my neck stand up. There was no playoff in the Brier prior to 1980. The team that ended up with the best round robin record won. But in 1956, Ontario's Phillips and Manitoba's Billy Walsh were tied after playing ten games; each had eight wins and two losses. A playoff was called — a rarity in Brier history — and even then, it almost wasn't enough. The game went to 13 ends before Manitoba, thanks to a stellar final shot by Walsh, secured the win.

Werenich–Darte

After she won the women's world championship in February 1986, Marilyn Darte (now Bodogh) claimed that her rink was talented enough to beat any man's team. She even issued a challenge to one of the game's top players at the time, Ed Werenich. Not one to shy away from a challenge, Werenich accepted. The game was scheduled after the semi-final of the men's world curling championships, held in Toronto in April 1986. As the date approached, Darte and Werenich — both of whom were never afraid of a microphone or television camera — lobbed insults back and forth through the media, which gobbled up the battle of the sexes. More than 7,000 people watched the game live (at the time, the largest live crowd the game had seen in Canada). Werenich beat Darte 10–2.

Chapter 24

Ten Terrific Curling Information Sources

In This Chapter

▶ Settling back with a couple of great curling newspapers

▶ Logging on to fun, informative curling Web sites

▶ Zeroing in on the best television network to watch curling on

▶ Using an unlikely but indispensable source of information: the rulebook

*A*fter reading through this book, you might be tempted to think you've learned all there is to know about curling. Actually, I'm hoping that this book just whets your appetite. I've put together a list of the ten best places you can turn to for more curling information.

Whether it's a newspaper you read, a Web site you visit, or a television station you watch, these information sources will help you keep up-to-date with what's happening on the competitive scene, with any amendments to the rules, or with new curling technology.

The Canadian Curling News

This is the oldest curling publication in the land, although it stopped publishing for a year or two. But this fine newspaper is back, covering curling across Canada. Its editor and publisher, Doug Maxwell, has more international contacts than just about anyone, and for that reason, the paper has a great amount of curling updates from around the world. It is published six times during the curling season (October through April).

Curling.com

A portal for all things curling, if you can't find what you're looking for on the www.curling.com Web site, then it probably doesn't exist. There are links to provincial associations, teams, technical help, and more. It's a great resource and a great place to start if you're looking for specific information about the game.

In the Hack.com

The No. 1 curling Web site www.inthehack.com is quickly becoming the best on-line spot to get caught up on fast-breaking news and gossip in the curling world. The immediacy of the medium has obviously helped it out, but it's fun and enlightening, too, thanks to the hard work of owner Mike Potter. The site has chat rooms, curling pools, and an on-line store where you can buy equipment and other curling-related items.

The Ontario Curling Report

I would have put the *Ontario Curling Report* first on my list because I'm the editor. But, according to my editor, I have to adhere to this silly convention of alphabetizing lists. You'll just have to pretend this came first. The *Ontario Curling Report* comes out six times during the curling season. Founded in 1973, it's the longest-running, continuously published curling newspaper in Canada. While most of the information inside is geared towards Ontario curlers, it has a fair share of national and international news, as well. It's broken many stories and lobbied successfully for changes in the game. I like to think it's influential as well as entertaining.

Ontcurl.com

This outstanding Web site is run by the Ontario Curling Association. It contains a wide variety of information, including competitive schedules and game results, a bonspiel search feature that helps you find the right event to play in, and even job postings. If only all associations had sites like this.

The Rulebook

You might wonder what this is doing in here, but there's a lot of information in the rulebook. Every curler should have one of these at the ready. There's plenty of good information in it that you should know. And if you're having trouble sleeping at night . . .

To get your hands on a copy in Canada, contact either the Canadian Curling Association (www.curling.ca) or the regional association in your jurisdiction.

Slam.ca

The curling page on the popular Canoe network of Web sites is at www.slam.ca/SlamCurling/home.html. This section of the site has reports and columns from all the Sun Media chain of newspapers. It's a great place to read about curling goings-on in such Canadian cities as Edmonton, Winnipeg, Toronto, and London.

Sweep

Curling's latest glossy magazine, *Sweep* has not been around that long, but has been accepted by Canadian curlers as a good read (if not all that good-looking). It has a wide variety of reports and columns, and seems to improve with every issue.

TSN (The Sports Network)

The biggest all-sports channel in Canada is one of the best places to get all the curling information you need. In addition to hundreds of hours of broadcasting live events, it has regular updates during its newscasts and treats curling like other major league sports. The network puts considerable resources behind curling, and it shows. If you need to know what's happening in the game, this is the place to turn.

Tsn.ca

The curling page on this Web site is at www.tsn.ca/curling. It has good resources for tracking championship events, some fun stuff, like a regular column from two-time world champion Marilyn Bodogh, and a chance to chat on-line with players right after the championship games broadcast on TSN.

Glossary

It's true. Curling has a lot of funny terms associated with it. All the funny ones I could think of (and some of the not-so-funny ones) are here in this glossary. Look them up.

Back line: The line on the playing surface that indicates the very end of the playing area.

Biter: A stone that is just barely touching the outside of the house.

Bonspiel: A tournament in which curlers compete.

Brier: The name of the Canadian men's curling championship. It is currently sponsored by Nokia.

Broom: Also known as a brush, an instrument used to sweep the ice surface so a stone will travel farther and bend less.

Button: The very centre of the target rings or house.

Cashspiel: A tournament in which curlers compete for money.

Corner guard: A stone in front of the rings and off to the side of the sheet that protects another stone or area of the ice.

Delivery: The action of throwing a stone to the other end of the playing surface.

Draw: A curling shot that stops in the house on its own, without coming into contact with other rocks.

End: One frame or inning in a game of curling. Games usually consist of eight or ten ends.

Free guard zone: The area between the Hog line and the Tee line, not including the front of the house.

Freeze: A curling shot where a stone stops in front of another one without moving the stationary rock.

Gripper: The sole of one of your curling shoes. It helps you keep your footing on the ice. See *slider*.

Hack: The foothold used to push out from, in the delivery. There are two at either end of the curling sheet.

Hammer: The last rock of the end.

Handle: The part of the curling stone that a player grips in order to deliver it.

Hit: A curling shot where the delivered stone removes a stationary stone from play.

Hit and roll: A curling shot where the delivered stone removes a stationary stone from play and then rolls to a different location.

Hog line: A line on the playing surface that indicates the point where a player must release a delivered stone. At the other end of the curling sheet, a delivered stone must cross the Hog line in order to be in play.

Hogged rock: A rock that fails to make it past the Hog line at the target end of the curling sheet.

House: Also known as the *rings,* this is the series of rings at either end of the curling sheet. It consists of a set of concentric circles, called the 12-foot, 8-foot, 4-foot, and the Button.

Hurry hard: A directive given to sweepers by the skip or third, to begin sweeping.

Ice technician: A person who prepares and cares for the ice on which the game is played.

In-turn: For a right-handed player, throwing the stone with a clockwise rotation.

Lead: A position on a curling team. The lead throws the first two stones of the end.

Mate: See *third.*

Measure: A process to determine: a) which of two stones is closer to the centre of the house; b) whether a stone is actually in the house. It is also the name of the instrument used to perform these measurements.

Negative ice: A condition of the playing surface where stones bend in the opposite direction than they normally would.

Nose hit: A curling shot where a stone removes a stationary rock from play and doesn't move after making contact.

Out-turn: For a right-handed player, throwing a stone with a counterclockwise rotation.

Pebble: Small bumps on the ice that the stone travels on, created deliberately by the ice technician.

Playdown: A competition that generally leads to a sanctioned championship.

Port: The opening between two stones that are in play.

Raise: A curling shot where a stationary stone is bumped forward by the delivered stone.

Rings: See *house.*

Rink: a) The name of a curling team; b) the name of a curling facility.

Rock: Also known as a stone (I use the terms interchangeably throughout this book), the granite playing utensil that a curler delivers. Regular-sized rocks weigh approximately 44 pounds.

Second: A position on a curling team. The second throws the third and fourth stones of the end.

Sheet: The frozen playing surface on which the game is played.

Skip: A position on a curling team. The skip throws the seventh and eighth stones of the end. He or she is the team leader (or quarterback), generally deciding what shots the team plays.

Slider: The sole of one of your curling shoes. It helps you move or slide along the ice. See *gripper.*

Split: A curling shot where a stationary stone is bumped into the house and the delivered stone also rolls into the house.

Splitting the house: A strategic play where two stones belonging to the same team are placed at opposite sides of the house.

Stone: See *rock*.

Takeout: A curling shot where a delivered stone removes a stationary stone from play.

Tankard: The trophy awarded to the winner of the Brier, the Canadian men's curling championship.

Tee: The hole in the centre of the house, where a measure is placed to measure stones. See *measure*.

Tee line: The line on the playing surface that runs through the middle of the house.

Third: A position on a curling team. The third throws the fifth and sixth stones of an end.

Vice: See *third*.

Weight: The amount of force used to deliver a stone.

Index